Yeats
An Annual of Critical and Textual Studies
Volume V, 1987

Studies in Modern Literature, No. 76

A. Walton Litz, General Series Editor
Professor of English
Princeton University

Consulting Editor:
Richard J. Finneran
Professor of English
Newcomb College, Tulane University

Other Titles in This Series

No. 6	*The Last Courtly Lover:* Yeats and the Idea of Woman	Gloria C. Kline
No. 57	*Love and Forgiveness in Yeats's Poetry*	Catherine Cavanaugh
No. 61	*Yeats: An Annual of Critical and Textual Studies, Vol. IV, 1986*	Richard J. Finneran, ed.
No. 64	*Poets, Poems, Movements*	Thomas Parkinson
No. 75	*Joyce's Use of Colors:* Finnegans Wake *and the Earlier Works*	J. Colm O'Sullivan

Yeats
An Annual of Critical and Textual Studies
Volume V, 1987

Edited by
Richard J. Finneran

Ann Arbor / London

Time and the Witch Vivien and *Vivien and Time* reprinted with the permission of A. P. Watt Ltd. on behalf of Anne Yeats and Michael B. Yeats.

Quotations from Yeats's "The Scholars," "No Second Troy," "When Helen lived," "When You are Old," "Oil and Blood," "Lapis Lazuli," "Crazy Jane on the Day of Judgement," "Sailing to Byzantium," "The White Birds," "Memory," "A Thought from Propertius," "Her Praise," "Broken Dreams," and "A Deep-sworn Vow" reprinted with permission of A. P. Watt Ltd. on behalf of Anne Yeats and Michael B. Yeats.

An unsigned review of Lady Gregory's *Poets and Dreamers* reprinted by permission of the Literary Executor of Arthur Symons and Henry W. and the Albert A. Berg Collection, The New York Public Library, Astor, Lenox and Tilden Foundations.

Quotations from Arthur Symons's letters reprinted with permission of The Board of Trinity College, Dublin.

Quotations reprinted with permission of Macmillan Publishing Company from *The Poems: A New Edition* by W. B. Yeats, edited by Richard J. Finneran. Copyright 1916, 1919, 1933 by Macmillan Publishing Company, renewed 1944, 1947, 1961 by Bertha Georgie Yeats. Copyright © Anne Yeats 1983.

Quotations reprinted with permission of Macmillan Publishing Company from *Essays and Introductions* by W. B. Yeats. Copyright © Mrs. W. B. Yeats 1961.

Quotations reprinted with permission of Macmillan Publishing Company from *The Variorum Edition of the Plays* by W. B. Yeats, edited by Russell K. Alspach. Copyright © Russell K. Alspach and Bertha Georgie Yeats 1966.

Copyright © 1987
Richard John Finneran
All rights reserved

Produced and distributed by
UMI Research Press
an imprint of
University Microfilms, Inc.
Ann Arbor, Michigan 48106

Library of Congress Cataloging in Publication Data
British Library CIP data is available
ISBN 0-8357-1819-0
LC No. 84-640978

Contents

Editorial Information   ix

Contributors   xi

Editor's Notes   xiii

Abbreviations   xv

Articles

Sailing from Avalon: Yeats's First Play, *Vivien and Time*   1
    David R. Clark and Rosalind E. Clark

The Three Deaths of Yeats   87
    Hugh Kenner

Sailing the Seas to Nowhere: Inversions of Yeats's Symbolism
    in "Sailing to Byzantium"   95
    Edward Lense

Reassessing Arthur Symons's Relationship with Lady Gregory   107
    Bruce D. Morris

Gaiety Transfiguring All That Dread: The Case of Yeats   117
    C. A. Patrides

Notes on the "Memory"-Sequence in Yeats's *The Wild Swans
    at Coole*   133
    M. L. Rosenthal

Dining with Landor   143
    R. H. Super

A Yeats Bibliography for 1985/1986   151
  K. P. S. Jochum

Dissertation Abstracts, 1986   199
  Compiled by Gwenn de Mauriac

Reviews

Joseph Adams, *Yeats and the Masks of Syntax*   209
  Reviewed by Edmund L. Epstein

Catherine Cavanaugh, *Love and Forgiveness in Yeats's Poetry*   220
  Reviewed by Thomas Parkinson

Paul de Man, *The Rhetoric of Romanticism*
C. K. Stead, *Pound, Yeats, Eliot and the Modernist Movement*   222
  Reviewed by George Bornstein

Joseph M. Hassett, *Yeats and the Poetics of Hate*   226
  Reviewed by Edward Engelberg

John Kelly and Eric Domville, eds., *The Collected Letters of
  W. B. Yeats: Volume 1, 1865–1895*   230
  Reviewed by Elizabeth Bergmann Loizeaux

Mary Lou Kohfeldt, *Lady Gregory: The Woman behind the Irish
  Renaissance*   235
  Reviewed by James F. Carens

Peter Kuch, *Yeats and A. E.: "The antagonism that unites dear
  friends"*   243
  Reviewed by James F. Carens

Elizabeth Bergmann Loizeaux, *Yeats and the Visual Arts*   246
  Reviewed by Terence Diggory

W. J. McCormack, *Ascendancy and Tradition in Anglo-Irish Literary
  History from 1789 to 1939*   253
  Reviewed by William H. O'Donnell

Steven Putzel, *Reconstructing Yeats:* The Secret Rose *and* The Wind
  Among the Reeds   255
  Reviewed by Carolyn Holdsworth

Passim: Brief Notices 265
  Mary FitzGerald

Editorial Information

Editor
Review Editor
Editorial Assistant

Richard J. Finneran
Mary FitzGerald
Gwenn de Mauriac

Editorial Board

George Bornstein ● David R. Clark ● George Mills Harper ●
K. P. S. Jochum ● Hugh Kenner ● William M. Murphy ●
Thomas Parkinson ● Stephen Parrish ● Jon Stallworthy

We welcome submissions of articles, notes, and editions. Unsolicited reviews are not accepted. Although we generally follow the *MLA Handbook for Writers of Research Papers*, 2nd ed. (New York: MLA, 1984), we do not include a bibliography of works cited; intending contributors are advised to request a style sheet from the editor at Department of English, Tulane University, New Orleans, Louisiana 70118, U.S.A. Submissions received by 15 May will be assured of consideration for publication in the following year.

The editor is grateful to the Graduate Council on Research, Tulane University, for a grant to aid in the preparation of this volume. All quotations from Yeats's writings, both published and unpublished, are made with the permission of the copyright holders. We are particularly indebted to Anne Yeats; Michael Yeats; A. P. Watt Ltd; Macmillan, London; and Macmillan Publishing Co., Inc.

This publication is affiliated with the Conference of Editors of Learned Journals and is indexed as *Yeats* in the *MLA International Bibliography*.

Contributors

George Bornstein, Professor of English, University of Michigan

James F. Carens, Professor of English, Bucknell University

David R. Clark, Professor of English, St. Mary's College, Notre Dame

Rosalind E. Clark, Assistant Professor of English, Texas A&M University

Gwenn de Mauriac, graduate student in English, Tulane University

Terence Diggory, Associate Professor of English, Skidmore College

Edward Engelberg, Professor of Romance and Comparative Literature, Brandeis University

Edmund L. Epstein, Professor of English, Queens College, City University of New York

Mary FitzGerald, Professor of English, University of New Orleans

Carolyn Holdsworth, Assistant Professor of English, Troy State University at Dothan

K. P. S. Jochum, Professor of English, Universität Bamberg

Hugh Kenner, Professor of English, Johns Hopkins University

Edward Lense, Associate Professor of English, Columbus College of Art and Design

Contributors

Elizabeth Bergmann Loizeaux, Associate Professor of English, University of Maryland

Bruce D. Morris, Senior Technical Writer, Verilink Corporation, San Diego, California

William H. O'Donnell, Professor of English, Memphis State University

Thomas Parkinson, Professor of English, University of California at Berkeley

C. A. Patrides, Professor of English (deceased), University of Michigan

M. L. Rosenthal, Professor of English, New York University

R. H. Super, Professor Emeritus of English, University of Michigan

Editor's Notes

Under the direction of Arthur Sniffin, the Yeats Archives at the State University of New York at Stony Brook are at last being properly catalogued. A new copy of the microfilms has been made, with frame numbers included; eventually these numbers will replace the present citation system ("SB0.00.000") used in this journal and elsewhere. Several visiting scholars have been brought to the collection to assist in the identification of the manuscripts. Individual or related items found at different places on the microfilms are being brought together. In the near future it is hoped that a finding aid will be available on computer to visitors to the collection. Although it will remain necessary to consult the original materials in the National Library of Ireland, especially for editorial projects, the completion of the cataloguing should make Stony Brook the primary location for Yeats manuscript research.

Conrad A. Balliet (Department of English, Wittenberg University, Springfield, Ohio 45501) continues to prepare a Census of Yeats Manuscripts. He would be grateful for any information on public or private holdings, especially those not cited in the standard sources. K. P. S. Jochum continues to collect material for a revised and expanded edition of his *W. B. Yeats: A Classified Bibliography of Yeats Criticism*. He would be grateful for additions and corrections to the first edition and also to his annual lists, which appear in this publication. He also welcomes offprints and review copies of current work, as well as notices of forthcoming publications. Address: Universität Bamberg, Postfach 1549, 8600 Bamberg, West Germany. Colin Smythe continues preparation of a new primary bibliography. Readers with corrections or additions to the third edition of the Wade/Alspach *Bibliography of the Writings of W. B. Yeats* are urged to contact him at P.O. Box 6, Gerrards Cross, Buckinghamshire SL9 8EF, England. Finally, the authorized biographies of Yeats and Mrs. Yeats continue in progress by, respectively, Roy Foster and Ann Saddlemyer.

George Bornstein's edition in the Cornell Yeats of the manuscripts of *Mosada* and *The Island of Statues* has just been published. It will be reviewed in our 1988 issue, along with Sandra Siegel's edition of the manuscripts of *Purgatory*. William H. O'Donnell's edition of *Prefaces and Introductions* in the new Collected Edition of the Works is now in press. Other volumes in both projects remain in active preparation.

Finally, we note with deep regret the death of C. A. Patrides in Ann Arbor, Michigan, on 17 September 1986. Best known as a major scholar of English Renaissance literature, on at least one occasion he directed his formidable talents towards the work of Yeats. It is a particular—if sad—privilege to be able to publish that essay in *Yeats*.

Abbreviations

The following abbreviations are used throughout the volume, on the model of "(Au 181)" to refer to page 181 of *Autobiographies*. In addition, some of the essays use special abbreviations, as indicated in notes. In order to distinguish them from the abbreviations listed below, they are italicized (unless an author's name).

Au	*Autobiographies*. London: Macmillan, 1955.
AV-A	*A Critical Edition of Yeats's* A Vision *(1925)*. Ed. George Mills Harper and Walter Kelly Hood. London: Macmillan, 1978. [Notes and Bibliography cited in italic numerals.]
AV-B	*A Vision*. London: Macmillan, 1962.
B	Allan Wade, *A Bibliography of the Writings of W. B. Yeats*. 3rd ed. Rev. Russell K. Alspach. London: Rupert Hart-Davis, 1968.
CL1	*The Collected Letters of W. B. Yeats: Volume One, 1865–1895*. Ed. John Kelly and Eric Domville. London & New York: Oxford University Press, 1986.
E&I	*Essays and Introductions*. London & New York: Macmillan, 1961.
Ex	*Explorations*. Sel. Mrs. W. B. Yeats. London: Macmillan, 1962; New York: Macmillan, 1963.
JSD	*John Sherman and Dhoya*. Ed. Richard J. Finneran. Detroit: Wayne State University Press, 1969.
L	*The Letters of W. B. Yeats*. Ed. Allan Wade. London: Rupert Hart-Davis, 1954; New York: Macmillan, 1955.
LDW	*Letters on Poetry from W. B. Yeats to Dorothy Wellesley*. Intro. Kathleen Raine. London & New York: Oxford University Press, 1964.
LMR	*Ah, Sweet Dancer: W. B. Yeats Margot Ruddock, A Correspondence*. Ed. Roger McHugh. London & New York: Macmillan, 1970.

LNI	*Letters to the New Island.* Ed. Horace Reynolds. Cambridge: Harvard University Press, 1934.
LRB	*The Correspondence of Robert Bridges and W. B. Yeats.* Ed. Richard J. Finneran. London: Macmillan, 1977.
LTSM	*W. B. Yeats and T. Sturge Moore: Their Correspondence, 1901–1937.* Ed. Ursula Bridge. London: Routledge & Kegan Paul; New York: Oxford University Press, 1953.
LTWBY	*Letters to W. B. Yeats.* Ed. Richard J. Finneran, George Mills Harper, and William M. Murphy. London: Macmillan; New York: Columbia University Press, 1977.
Mem	*Memoirs.* Ed. Denis Donoghue. London: Macmillan, 1972; New York: Macmillan, 1973.
Myth	*Mythologies.* London & New York: Macmillan, 1959.
OBMV	*The Oxford Book of Modern Verse, 1892–1935.* Chosen by W. B. Yeats. Oxford: Clarendon Press, 1936.
P	*The Poems: A New Edition.* Ed. Richard J. Finneran. New York: Macmillan, 1983; London: Macmillan, 1984. [Cited from corrected second printing (1984) or later printings.]
SB	*The Speckled Bird, with Variant Versions.* Ed. William H. O'Donnell. Toronto: McClelland and Stewart, 1976 [1977].
SR	*The Secret Rose, Stories by W. B. Yeats: A Variorum Edition.* Ed. Phillip L. Marcus, Warwick Gould, and Michael J. Sidnell. Ithaca & London: Cornell University Press, 1981.
SS	*The Senate Speeches of W. B. Yeats.* Ed. Donald R. Pearce. Bloomington: Indiana University Press, 1960.
TB	*Theatre Business: The Correspondence of the First Abbey Theatre Directors: William Butler Yeats, Lady Gregory, and J. M. Synge.* Ed. Ann Saddlemyer. Gerrards Cross: Colin Smythe; University Park: Pennsylvania State University Press, 1982.
UP1	*Uncollected Prose by W. B. Yeats.* Vol. 1. Ed. John P. Frayne. London: Macmillan; New York: Columbia University Press, 1970.
UP2	*Uncollected Prose by W. B. Yeats.* Vol. 2. Ed. John P. Frayne and Colton Johnson. London: Macmillan, 1975; New York: Columbia University Press, 1976.
VP	*The Variorum Edition of the Poems of W. B. Yeats.* Ed. Peter Allt and Russell K. Alspach. New York: Macmillan, 1957. [Cited from the corrected third printing (1966) or later printings.]
VPl	*The Variorum Edition of the Plays of W. B. Yeats.* Ed. Russell K. Alspach. London & New York: Macmillan, 1966. [Cited from the corrected second printing (1966) or later printings.]

Sailing from Avalon:
Yeats's First Play, *Vivien and Time*

David R. Clark and Rosalind E. Clark

Yeats's First Play

Yeats was a dramatist first.[1] "I had begun to write poetry in imitation of Shelley and of Edmund Spenser, play after play—for my father exalted dramatic poetry above all other kinds—and I invented fantastic and incoherent plots" (Au 66–67). The oddness of imitating a great nondramatic poet in "play after play" escapes Yeats, possibly because Shelley too had imitated Spenser in dramatic poems; but Spenser, if listening in from his poetic immortality, may have been startled by Yeats's statement. Only one who indeed felt himself to be a dramatist could have written with such unconscious contradiction. "Sailing from Avalon" presents *Vivien and Time,* the earliest of the works to which Yeats refers, one which antedates any of his published poems or plays.

Readers in 1889 of Yeats's brief dramatic sketch "Time and the Witch Vivien," published in *The Wanderings of Oisin and Other Poems,*[2] were unaware, as are readers of it today in *The Variorum Edition of the Poems of W. B. Yeats* (VP 720–22) or *The Poems: A New Edition* (P 514–17), that this playlet was salvaged from a play of two acts, *Vivien and Time,* which Yeats wrote some time between the autumn of 1882 and the very beginning of 1884.[3] Although it survived in the 1892 reissue of the volume in which it appeared, the playlet was not reprinted in *Poems* (1895), which contained "all the writer cares to preserve out of his previous volumes of verse."[4] Nor was it included in any other collection during Yeats's lifetime. In "Sailing from Avalon" we see the published "Time and the Witch Vivien" as part of the unpublished *Vivien and Time,* which Yeats himself identifies as "my first play" (CL1 155).

Vivien and Time is Yeats's starting point. Here begins the great evolution of his total work, of which no step is irrelevant or unconnected. Not just the isolated greatness of particular works but the unity of all has pushed Yeats's reputation steadily upwards during this century. By the 1960s Yeats was recognized as "one of the established writers in the history of English poetry," "the greatest modern poet." Today he has risen "From Great Modern Poet to Canonical Classic."[5] To see Yeats's work as a whole, to distinguish his essential development, we perhaps need to return to the very beginning.

Yeats's reputation is secure. It will not suffer from the publication here of his first hesitant attempt at drama. The full play will illuminate the fragment "Time and the Witch Vivien." It will also illuminate later works by showing that certain themes and images were perennial with Yeats—and certain forms, as well. It is interesting that his first play, like his middle-period dance plays, was in form a drawing-room drama of which the high point is the manifestation of a spirit, in this case the figure of Time.

Principally this play is of value in showing us the Yeats who had not yet found his ostensible "subject matter," his "theme." In it Yeats's constant preoccupations appear in their pre-Irish form. Under the heading "Subject-matter" Yeats wrote in 1937 that "It was through the old Fenian leader John O'Leary I found my theme" (E&I 510). O'Leary did not return to Ireland from exile until late in 1884.[6] *Vivien and Time* was completed by 7 January 1884, on which date Yeats's proud father, who had lent a manuscript of the play to Professor Edward Dowden of Trinity College, Dublin, wrote asking for its return.[7] The copy published here has the date "January the 8th / 1884" both on its cover and after the "Dedication" poem.

Dowden's influence was strong on Yeats at this time, and Dowden thought Irish subject matter confining (*MM* 48). At least a year would go by before Yeats could come under the influence of O'Leary, be sent to Eugene O'Curry, discover Standish O'Grady, and perceive the "great tapestry" hanging behind all Irish history: "Nobody looking at its dim folds can say where Christianity begins and Druidism ends" (E&I 513–14). When Yeats wrote *Vivien and Time* he had not yet been persuaded by O'Leary to admire the Young Ireland poets who, however bad their poetry, "spoke or tried to speak out of a people to a people." Yet he already longed "to get back to Homer, to those that fed at his table," "to cry as all men cried, to laugh as all men laughed" (E&I 510–11). He "read nothing but romantic literature," knew himself "vague and incoherent" (E&I 510). Although he had learned Irish folk tales at his mother's knee, the folklore behind *Vivien and Time* comes from the brothers Grimm (Au 47). Yeats's witch Vivien, though in some ways a recognizable sister of later enchantresses like Niamh in "The Wanderings of Oisin" or the Woman of the Sidhe in *The Only Jealousy of Emer*, is not Irish. She comes from the Arthurian literature as treated by Tennyson.

Nor had Yeats's interest in the occult well begun. He was not to meet his "mystical friend"[8] George W. Russell (AE), who probably introduced him to Eastern and Theosophical literature,[9] until he entered the Metropolitan School of Art in May 1884. Meeting Russell gave Yeats confidence that, as Ellmann puts it, "the dream of the magician was no longer an absurdity" (*MM* 33). Up to that point Yeats's interest in magic was little more than a literary pose out of Scott (Au 46), Byron, and Shelley (Au 64). *Vivien and Time* shows us Yeats as he was before Ireland and the occult possessed him.

Nor had love possessed him, although his feeling for the prototype of "Vivien" indicated the kind of relationship which would dominate much of his later life. But it was not until January 1889 that Maud Gonne, a "classical impersonation of the Spring" (Au 123), would walk like a goddess into the Yeats house.

Yeats begins *Vivien and Time* with a dedicatory poem to the girl who suggested the character of Vivien. Among the "many statues fair" standing in the "dreaming palace" of Yeats's imagination—statues of the heroines of Elizabethan tragedy—is one before which he casts "a wayward play." The figure which receives his "Dedication"

> ... is a pale elf statue
> With sweet Titania's grace
> But black's the hair, as though it were
> The peeping pansy's face.
>
> The eyes as the wine are bright
> In Circe's charmèd cup:
> O dark are the eyes as the morning skies
> When scarce the day is up.
>
> [SB23.3.163][10]

The description is like that of Naschina in "The Island of Statues":

> Oh, more dark thy gleaming hair is
> Than the peeping pansy's face,
> And thine eyes more bright than faery's,
> Dancing in some moony place. . . .
>
> [P 455]

In *Reveries Over Childhood and Youth* (1916) Yeats tells how he first met Laura Armstrong, a distant cousin related to him through the Corbet family (CL1 155n2):

> I was climbing up a hill at Howth when I heard wheels behind me and a pony-carriage drew up beside me. A pretty girl was driving alone and without a hat. She

told me her name and said we had friends in common and asked me to ride beside her. After that I saw a great deal of her and was soon in love. I did not tell her I was in love, however, because she was engaged. She had chosen me for her confidant and I learned all about her quarrels with her lover. Several times he broke the engagement off, and she fell ill, and friends had to make peace. Sometimes she would write to him three times a day, but she could not do so without a confidant. She was a wild creature, a fine mimic, and given to bursts of religion. I had known her to weep at a sermon, call herself a sinful woman, and mimic it after. I wrote her some bad poems and had more than one sleepless night through anger with her betrothed. [Au 76]

It was for this creature, a combined Titania and Circe, that Yeats wrote *Vivien and Time*. Apparently the play was performed, with Laura in the title role. J. B. Yeats's 7 January 1884 letter to Dowden, asking for the return of the manuscript, says that his son "wants it for a rehearsal which is to come off immediately."[11] Based on a letter from Laura to Yeats (probably but not necessarily the one quoted below) and on a conversation with John Eglinton (a schoolfellow of Yeats), Ellmann states that *"Vivien and Time* was rehearsed and possibly presented by Yeats and a group of his friends at the home of a Judge Wright on Howth. The girl who played Vivien, Laura Armstrong, appears to have been the boy's first love" (MM 36). Laura herself was a judge's child, "the youngest and prettiest of the daughters of Sergeant Richard Armstrong, a distinguished Dublin barrister who had gone mad years before," as Murphy puts it.[12]

That this "Vivien" was indeed a tantalizing witch is shown by her one surviving letter to Yeats, dated from Dublin several months after the rehearsals for the play:

60 Stephen's Green
Dublin
10.8.84

My dear Clarin,

What can I say to you for having been so rude to you—in not being at home when you called and I had asked you? I am really very sorry about it. I hope you will forgive me. It so happened that I was positively obliged to go out at the hour I had appointed for you to come but it was only to a house quite close here—and I told our maid to send me over word when you *came*—she did so— (but I find since it was just before you *went*!) and I was rising to leave the room. I looked out of the window and to my great disappointment—saw my Clarin leaving No. 60. It was too bad—and I am indeed sorry I missed you.—I like yr poems more than I can say—but I should like to hear you read them—I have not nearly finished them. Could you come some aft:—and read a little to me, I shall be in all Tuesday afternoon. *I promise*! so can you come? I should have written to you sooner but I have been away from home. Pray excuse my silence. Trusting to see "the poet"—! and with kind regards—Believe me

> Ever yrs
> "Vivien"
> [CL1 155n2]

She liked the poems more than she could say, but had not nearly finished reading them. . . . Obviously the poetry held little interest except as a means of dangling the poet! Wade prints an unpublished poem from this period which seems a response to further dangling:

> A double moon or more ago
>   I writ you a long letter, lady,
>   It went astray or vexed you, maybe.
> And I would know now yes or no.
>
> Then dying summer on his throne
>   Faded in hushed and quiet singing;
>   Now winter's arrow's winging, winging,
> And autumn's yellow leaves are flown.
>
> Ah we poor poets in our pride
>   Tread the bare song road all our summer,
>   To wake on lips of some newcomer
> "A poor man lived here once and died."
>
> How could we trudge on mile by mile
>   If from red lips like quicken berry,
>   At some odd times to make us merry,
> Came nowise half of half a smile?
>
> And surely therefore I would know
>   What manner fared my letter, lady,
>   It went astray or vexed you, maybe,
> A double moon or more ago.
>   [L 117n]

    Little more than a month after writing her dangling letter to Yeats, Edith Laura Armstrong married Henry Morgan Byrne in St. Peter's Church, Dublin, 17 September 1884.[13] Later in life she married a Welsh gardener, "a very decent and intelligent man," whom she nagged until he left her. She "was taken by whims which she insisted on exercising, such as suddenly altering all the furniture on the spot."[14]

    In Yeats's semi-autobiographical novel *John Sherman*, written in 1888 but not published until 1891, Laura appears as Margaret Leland, "the flighty and inconsiderate heroine,"[15] who "wore the most fascinating hats," read Bulwer-Lytton, and hated frogs (JSD 62). Like Laura, Margaret had difficult engagements. She "had been jilted and was in despair, had taken to her bed with every resolution to die, and was growing paler and paler." Her fiancé's sister, however, thought it "was temper that ailed Margaret, and she was a little vixen, and that if she had not flirted with everybody the engagement would never have been broken off" (JSD 63).

Margaret's lively spirit, not her mere face, attracts John Sherman, as Laura's "wild dash of half insane genius" attracted Yeats (CL1 155). "She was a pretty girl with quite irregular features, who though not really more than pretty, had so much manner, so much of an air, that every one called her a beauty: a trefoil with the fragrance of a rose" (JSD 64). "As Margaret darted about at the tennis, a red feather in her cap seemed to rejoice with its wearer. Everything was at once gay and tranquil. The whole world had that unreal air it assumes at beautiful moments, as though it might vanish at a touch like an iridescent soap-bubble" (JSD 65).

The Reverend William Howard also finds a contrast between Margaret's features and the spirit that animates them. "As he was shown in he noticed, with a momentary shock, that her features were quite commonplace. Then she saw him, and at once seemed to vanish wrapped in an exulting flame of life" (JSD 97). If Laura, as in Yeats's "Dedication" to *Vivien and Time,* mixed the qualities of Titania and Circe, it was her Circe-like qualities that Yeats allowed Howard to see in Margaret Leland. Or perhaps her Lilith-like qualities. "As she spoke her face quivered with excitement. The exulting flame of life seemed spreading from her to the other things in the room. To Howard's eyes it seemed as though the bright pots and stuffed birds and plush curtains began to glow with a light not of this world—to glimmer like the strange and chaotic colours the mystic Blake imagined upon the scaled serpent of Eden" (JSD 97). Margaret Leland is a fairy for Sherman and a witch for Howard!

Like Vivien, Margaret is vain and jealous. Before discovering her limitations, Sherman proposes marriage and is accepted. But he cannot understand his difficulty in writing the news of his engagement to a friend back home, Mary Carton. Margaret insists that he write and exults when he promises to do so. "'If I were in her place I know what I would like to do when I got the letter. I know who I would like to kill!'—this with a laugh as she went over and looked at herself in the mirror on the mantlepiece" (JSD 75–76). Vivien's jealousy, too, evokes murderous thoughts, and she attempts to kill her rival, Asphodel, because of her beauty.

Murder and mirrors! Vivien repeatedly consults a magic mirror in *Vivien and Time* and watches her image in the pool of a fountain in "Time and the Witch Vivien." One wonders if Laura, prototype of both heroines, was noticeably fascinated by her own reflection. But this subjective, self-dramatizing quality is not presented as entirely negative in *John Sherman*. Here, as in Yeats's characterizations of Richard II and Henry IV in his 1901 essay "At Stratford-on-Avon" (E&I 96–110), we have an early example of his sympathetic analysis of the subjective type of person versus the objective type:

> After a little Margaret said she was tired, and, sitting on a garden-seat among the bushes, began telling him the plots of novels lately read by her. Suddenly she cried: "The novel-writers were all serious people like you. They are so hard on people like me. They always make us come to a bad end. They *say* we are always acting, acting, acting; and what else do you serious people do? You act before the world. I think, do you know, *we* act before ourselves. All the old foolish kings and queens in history were like us. They laughed and beckoned and went to the block for no very good purpose. I daresay the headsmen were like you."
> "We would never cut off so pretty a head."
> "Oh, yes, you would—you would cut off mine to-morrow." All this she said vehemently, piercing him with her bright eyes. "You would cut off my head to-morrow," she repeated, almost fiercely; "I tell you you would." [JSD 65–66]

Sherman is the objective man of Yeats's view of personality (later explained in the "system" of *A Vision*) as Margaret and William Howard are subjective.[16]

Margaret's piercingly bright eyes are another feature deriving from Laura/Vivien, whose eyes in the "Dedication" to the play are bright as the wine in "Circe's charmèd cup" and yet dark "as the morning skies / When scarce the day is up" (SB23.3.165). Both Margaret's lovers are affected by her eyes. "Several times she gazed at [William Howard] with those large dark eyes of hers, of which the pupils to-day seemed larger than usual. They made him feel dizzy and clutch tightly the arm of his chair" (JSD 97). John Sherman, too, before his disillusionment, was subject to those eyes: "The next day and the day after, Sherman was followed by those bright eyes. When he opened a letter at his desk they seemed to gaze at him from the open paper . . . " (JSD 66). However, like his author, the dangled poet, Sherman has his awakening:

> One evening he said to his mother, "Miss Leland has beautiful eyes."
> "My dear, she puts belladonna in them." [JSD 66]

Ultimately, John Sherman turns away from Margaret towards Mary Carton, as in *Vivien and Time* Clarin turns away from Vivien towards Asphodel. John explains to Mary, "Margaret glitters and glitters and glitters, but she is not of my kind" (JSD 106). Yeats's 21 March [1889] letter to Katharine Tynan (whom William M. Murphy believes to be the model for Mary Carton) takes a similar apologetic tone, not only about Laura, but also about Maud Gonne:

> Who told you that I am "taken up with Miss Gonne". I think she is, "very good looking" and that is all I think about her. What you say of her fondness for sensation is probably true. I sympathize with her love of the national idia rather than any secondary land movement but care not much for the kind of red Indian feathers in which she has trapped out that idea. We had some talk as to the possibility of getting my "Countess O'Shea" acted by amateurs in Dublin and she felt inclined to help, indeed suggested the attempt herself if I remember rightly. I hardly expect it will ever get outside the world of plans. As for the rest she had a borrowed interest, reminding me of Laura Armstrong without Laura's wild dash of half insane genius. Laura is to me always a pleasant memory she woke me from the metallic sleep of science and set me writing my first play. Do not mistake me she is only as myth and a symbol. Will you forgive me having talked of her—She interests me far more than Miss Gonne does and yet is only as a myth and a symbol. I heard from her about two years ago and am trying to find out where she is now in order to send her "Oisin". "Time and the Witch Vivien" was written for her to act. "The Island of Statues" was begun with the same notion though it soon grew beyond the scope of drawing room acting. The part of the enchantress in both poems was written for her. She used to sign her letters Vivien. [CL1 154–55]

Clearly the fate of being supplanted, which had overtaken the enchantress of *Vivien and Time*, of *The Island of Statues*, and of *John Sherman*, had caught up with Laura Armstrong. Certain future poetic dramas would model their heroines after a new enchantress, or be dedicated to her, or even be written for her to act. Time's skill proved powerless to defeat Maud Gonne's reign in Yeats's poetry. She stands there without a shadow.

Yeats almost certainly got the name "Vivien" from Tennyson's "Merlin and Vivien," though Arnold in his "Tristram and Iseult" uses "Vivian." She was "Nimuë" in Tennyson's 1857 version, but in 1858 Burne-Jones suggested the change to "Vivien" when "he found that the poet in his Idyll had modernised and altered the character while preserving the ancient name."[17] According to Lucy Alan Paton, "Niniane" is probably the original name of the Lady of the Lake in romances, but there are many variants, and "Viviane" is found in *Merlin* (1528), II.cxxvi, cxxvii; *Vulgate Merlin*, throughout; and Paris, *Les Romans de la Table Ronde*, throughout.[18]

The name "Sir Clarin of Tadmor" may be Yeats's own invention, but "Clarin" is indeed listed in G. D. West's *Index of Proper Names in French Arthurian Prose Romances*.[19] A "Clarin" is "Mordrain's godson" and "Castellan d'Evalachin" in the *Histoire de Grimaud*.[20] Another Clarin is a knight entitled Le Noir whose castle is besieged by Karados in *Guiron le Courtois* and in *Les Prophecies de Merlin*.[21] Clarin is listed in Langlois, *Table des noms propres de toute nature compris dans les Chansons de Geste*, as appearing in *Rolant* and in *Anseis de Cartage*.[22] Yeats may have found the name in some contemporary retelling of a romance or chanson de geste.

"Tadmor" is the old name for Palmyra, 150 miles northeast of Damascus, an ancient city, very powerful until reduced by Aurelian in A.D. 272 after Zenobia's revolt against Rome. It remained wealthy through the period of the Crusades and into the fourteenth century. The ruins were known to the West in the eighteenth century and the inscriptions in the nineteenth. A great fiscal inscription was discovered by Prince Abamalek Lazarew in 1882, less than two years before the date given on the manuscript of *Vivien and Time*.[23]

"Asphodel" has, of course, been the immortal pale flower of the other world ever since Homer showed the shade of Achilles striding proudly along the meadows of Erebus.[24] Sabrina, in Milton's *Comus*, was, as part of her "quick immortal change" into "Goddess of the River" Severn, bathed "In nectar'd lavers strew'd with Asphodel." Pope, in his "Ode on St. Cecilia's Day," has Orpheus intercede with Proserpine "By those happy souls, who dwell / In yellow meads of Asphodel." Shelley's "Arethusa," in her new life after union with Alpheus, flows with him through "meadows of Asphodel." Tennyson's "Lotos Eaters" enjoy in advance the rewards of the dead who "in Elysian valleys dwell, / Resting weary limbs at last on beds of Asphodel." It is hard, however, to think of a work prior to Yeats's *Vivien and Time* in which "Asphodel" is used as the name of a character.

The connection between the play *Vivien and Time* and the published playlet "Time and the Witch Vivien" is obvious; and not only from the close correspondence between their titles, characters, and themes. Several pages are separated from the manuscript of the play in act II, scene 2. These torn out pages contain one of the most important episodes of the plot, the death of Vivien.[25] Her death is the subject of the published playlet. "Time and the Witch Vivien" is a revision of the pages torn from *Vivien and Time*. But before we note the extent and nature of that revision we should take a look at the whole play.

Here is the plot into which act II, scene 2, and "Time and the Witch Vivien" both fit. Queen Vivien loves Clarin the poet, but her love changes to hatred when she realises he is indifferent to her and loves Countess Asphodel. Vivien asks her magic mirror if she is the fairest (Yeats borrows heavily from the story of Snow White), but the mirror replies that Asphodel is fairer. Vivien orders her soldiers to slay Asphodel. She then puts a spell on Clarin so that he will wander a prey to spirits of unrest until he dies. Then she learns that the soldiers had pity on Asphodel and that she is not dead but is hiding in a cottage in the desert. Vivien disguises herself as a gypsy (again like the queen in "Snow White") and goes to the cottage. She tricks Asphodel into smelling a magic flower. Asphodel falls to the ground. She is not dead, however, but will lie in a trance as long as Clarin lives, then rise and be driven by the same spirits of unrest until she dies.

Clarin learns of Asphodel's enchantment and gathers a fairy army to avenge himself on Vivien. Next comes the crucial scene, in which Time kills Vivien. Then Clarin comes in, too late to take his own vengeance. When he discovers Vivien lying apparently dead on stage, he says "That mighty shade [i.e., Time] has been before." He then remembers that the grey pedlar foretold that he (Clarin) would kill the queen and die soon afterward: he "would meet / A great queen whom I'd slay with mine own hand / O scarce survive her for a minute's space" (SB23.3.190-91). As it is Time, not Clarin, who kills Vivien in both the published and the unpublished scene, the prophecy does not exactly correspond to the plot. Either this is an oversight of the author, which seems unlikely, or there is a mistake in the manuscript. Perhaps "O" was meant to be "Or"—Clarin would slay Vivien "O[r] scarce survive her. . . . " The prophecy would then be accurate, as Clarin dies at the end of the scene. Asphodel returns to consciousness in the desert and begins her restless wanderings.

Though revised to stand by itself, "Time and the Witch Vivien" retains most of the links with the total play which the original scene had. In the published version, Vivien first looks at her reflection in the fountain, admiring both her own beauty and her skill as an enchantress. Time, an old pedlar with a bag, scythe, and hour-glass, enters. Vivien plays at dice with him, trying to win his hour-glass. She loses, and then plays chess for triumph in her many plots. She loses again; defeat is death, and as the scene ends, she dies. In the unpublished play, Vivien is found before, not a fountain, but a magic mirror which is lit by a taper. Some of the imagery is different, many of the lines are less polished than in the published playlet, and Vivien's death is less climactic (since it is not the end). Otherwise the action is the same, and the linkages with the rest of *Vivien and Time* are the same. Time is a central character in both plays.

In *Vivien and Time*, although Time appears only in act II, scene 2, he has an importance out of all proportion to the brevity of his appearance. Time is listed fourth in the "Dramatis Personae." He is mentioned often as the grey pedlar, and every reference to him is an ominous foreshadowing of Vivien's fate. The "Dedication" poem tells the subject matter of the play: "a goblin queen, and a goblin dream / And a pedlar grey" (SB23.3.163).

In act I, scene 1, Clarin reads a ballad "Bought from a pedlar with a bag and scythe" (SB23.3.167). The ballad is about Time—a hoary old man who holds an hour-glass. The ballad echoes the plot:

> In life love hath ended
> Old Time hath descended. . . .
>
> [SB23.3.168]

Asphodel rebukes Clarin for his choice of a ballad, for she says "Our only enemy is withered time" (SB23.3.168). Vivien, in love with Clarin, ceases to love him and plots against him. Figuratively speaking, she is "playing against Time" to succeed in her many plots before Time catches up with her. At her birth the augurs foretold that "lame-footed fate would o'ertake me / When the tide of my strength was full." She is always trying to keep one step ahead of the prophecy and hopes to "mock the dread presage that came / From the hollow cave of the gray dreamers" (SB23.3.177). Time, the pedlar, is mentioned again—the Page sees him pursuing Clarin on his restless wanderings, a sign that Clarin's death is near. Thus the scene is set for Time's actual appearance as a character in act II, scene 2.

Not only the theme of Time but also allusions to Merlin connect the published scene with the full-length play. In the latter, the magic mirror swears by "dread Merlin's self" that Asphodel is fairest (SB23.3.170). Vivien finds the spell of unrest in Merlin's book, a huge magic book which grows fiery hot when the spell is read aloud. Although she uses his magic, Vivien is scornful of Merlin. When the Page asks about the spell, Vivien calls it "the wild poem of a wild old man" (SB23.3.175; a strange foreshadowing of the "wild old wicked man" [P 310] who is a persona in Yeats's late poetry). Although Vivien intends to deceive the Page by convincing him that the spell is harmless, she deceives herself also. She believes that she herself is greater than Merlin. The allusions to Merlin in the complete play form a context for Vivien's dialogue with Time. In both the published scene and the manuscript she compares Time to Merlin: "Yet whiter beard have you than Merlin had" (P 515). She reminds him of the story of Merlin and Nimuë: "young girls' wits are better / Than old men's any day, as Merlin found" (P 516). Vivien must be first in everything. Looking into the fountain, she says "Where moves there any beautiful as I, / Save . . . / My image yonder? . . . / . . . / No; nor is there one / Of equal power in spells and secret rites" (P 514). She, like Circe, is an enchantress; like

Circe, she is finally overcome by a wily old man. In act II, scene 2, Vivien claims that she is greater than Circe:

> Vivien. Great Circe, Circe, now thy fame is fled
>   Since mine was born that shall have wing until . . .
> Mirror. Until the fountains on the steeps have rest
>   And 'fore the sun the flowers' lips are closed.
> Vivien. And that is forever.
>
> [SB23.3.175]

She believes that the mirror foretells her triumph, but in the end a bitter frost in fairyland freezes the fountains and flowers, and the mirror's prophecy is fulfilled as she dies.

In act II, scene 2, the two main themes of the play, the pride and power of the enchantress and the idea of Time, are brought forward in a dramatic confrontation between the two great antagonists. The main point of the play is that power, both temporal and magical, must yield to Time, and this is the scene in which that happens.

The theme of peace is an important link between "Time and the Witch Vivien" and *Vivien and Time*. In the published scene peace is mentioned twice. In Time's bag are "mellow thoughts / Where dwell the minds of old men having peace. . . . " Vivien says to Time "I do not need your scythe. May that bring peace / To those your 'mellow' wares have wearied out" (P 515). Vivien equates peace with the scythe, or death. In the unpublished play, act I, scene 4, Vivien, disguised as the gypsy, tells Asphodel's fortune. She looks at her palm and says "The line of peace is wondrous deep and long: / . . . / Most instant and most deep the peace shall be" (SB23.3.185). Asphodel falls into a peaceful magic sleep. But it is not Vivien's wish to give her peace forever. Peaceful sleep or death is not her idea of revenge: "Die not, for that were but a weak revenge" (SB23.3.185). Vivien's spells make the lovers wander until death, drawn on by spirits of unrest:

> Him whom I name
> Wrap him like flame
> Ye souls of unrest
> . . . .
> Arise, arise
>   Rest on his eyes
>   See that they weep
>   See they ne'er sleep
> Till he dies, dies. . . .
>
> [SB23.3.173–74]

So runs the spell in Merlin's book. At Clarin's death Asphodel wakes, her "whole soul bitterly athirst for peace" (SB23.3.192), but she is now doomed to wander in her turn. As the play ends, two voices lead her on, promising peace:

> *First voice.* Peace in the end you shall have
> And your o'erworn heart shall have rest
> *Second voice.* When the yew and the cypress wave
> In the cold earth over your breast.
>
> [SB23.3.194]

Having pointed to the linkages between the published "Time and the Witch Vivien" and other scenes of the unpublished parent play, we now mention, though briefly because they will be evident to the reader's eyes, the revisions, their nature and extent. The scene torn from the manuscript was altered to make it suitable for publication on its own. References to specific settings, characters, or incidents which would have been unintelligible to readers of only the single scene were removed. In the original scene, for example, Vivien's opening speech contains a reference to the earlier prophecy by the magic mirror that Vivien cannot die until the fountains cease to flow as well as a reference to Asphodel meant to show the passage of time between acts I and II: "The lily-wristed Asphodel has slept / These summers three" (SB22.3.65). These references are removed and a new opening speech written which concentrates on Vivien's pride in her beauty and skill rather than on her lust for power.

However, the end to Vivien's soliloquy is almost the same in the two versions. In *Vivien and Time*

> Some great spirit passes in the desert.
> Turning it enters by the city gate.
> . . . .
> Now 't'as passed the sentries; 'tis at the door;
> It is here.
>
> [SB22.3.66]

In "Time and the Witch Vivien"

> Some fierce magician flies or walks
> Beyond the gateway—by the sentries now. . . .
>
> [P 514]

In "Time and the Witch Vivien" the scene takes place in Vivien's magic room. The description of the room, "*A marble-flagged, pillared room. Magical instruments in one corner. A fountain in the center*" (P 514), is different from that in the unpublished play. There, in act II, scene 2, the setting is described as "*Room in the castle as in Scenes 2 and 3 of Act*

I. *Time night, a pale taper burning before the Magic Mirror*" (SB22.3.65). The description of Vivien's room in act I, scene 2, is "*A room in the castle. Magic mirror to R. surmounted by a skull in the background. A subdued light over everything*" (SB23.3.170). In the published version Yeats has substituted the fountain for the magic mirror. Vivien admires her reflection in the water just as she looks at herself in the mirror in act I, scene 2. Undoubtedly Yeats changed one for the other because he felt the mirror was too obviously borrowed from "Snow White," though Vivien uses the fountain for almost the same purpose: "Where moves there any beautiful as I . . . ?" (P 514) she asks the fountain. In the unpublished version the mirror laughs at the deaths of Vivien and Clarin successively as the scene closes.

The published scene ends abruptly. Time wins the chess game and says

>   *Time.*   Mate thus.
>   *Vivien.*   Already?
>   Chance hath a skill!   [*She dies.*]
>
>   [P 517]

In the manuscript the end of the game is marked by Time's laugh and the fall of the curtain. When the curtain rises, Vivien is left alone to die at her leisure, a less effective end, but, after all, the unpublished play does not end there.

And not all is gain in Yeats's revisions. The swan image, for instance, which is so important elsewhere in *Vivien and Time* and was to become one of the most striking images in Yeats's later work, appears only in the manuscript:

>   *Queen.* The wild swan has sunk from the blinding blue.
>   No more I trouble with my wayward life.
>   Old dreaming night, O hungry oblivion,
>   O sister death, I take thy hand, I come. (*She dies.*)
>
>   [SB22.3.70]

In the following pages *Vivien and Time* is printed entire, with the six separated pages containing most of act II, scene 2, restored. Those restored pages are printed together with "Time and the Witch Vivien" so that the reader may make comparisons.

A Note on the Transcription of *Vivien and Time*

See "A Description of the Manuscript of *Vivien and Time*" for National Library of Ireland Ms. 30,357, a maroon notebook bearing the inscription "Viven [sic] and Time / a dramatic poem / January the 8th / 1884," and for Ms. 30,460, the six pages which have been restored.

What follows here is not a diplomatic transcription but a reading text. Styling of act, scene, and speaker indications as well as of stage directions has been silently normalized. Cancelled words and letters are not reproduced. Yeats's revisions and additions are silently inserted. Compound or hyphenated words which Yeats gives as two separate words have been silently joined. Spelling and capitalization are normalized. Punctuation has not usually been supplied to the lyrics, except for end stops. Elsewhere the editors have made a more liberal use than did Yeats of punctuation, including dashes, semicolons, and colons. An attempt has been made to preserve both possible meanings of ambiguous expressions. Where an ambiguous passage is difficult to read, clarifying punctuation and spelling have been supplied, but the original text is given in the notes, sometimes with an alternative interpretation. Where an ambiguous passage is readily readable, however, Yeats's punctuation (as well as his ambiguity) is preserved.

Material in square brackets has been added by the editors. Quotations from Yeats's text are italicized in the Textual Notes. Each page of Yeats's manuscript is identified by its Stony Brook number. The citation is placed at the start of each page.

Vivien and Time [SB23.3.162]

Dramatis Personae

Vivien, *The Goblin Queen*
Asphodel
Clarin
Time
Page

Dedication [SB23.3.163]

I've built a dreaming palace
    With stones from out the old
And singing days, within their graves
    Now lying calm and cold.

Of the dreamland marble
    Are all the silent walls
That grimly stand, a phantom band,
    About the phantom halls.

There among the pillars
    Are many statues fair
Made of the dreamland marble
    Cut by the dreamer's[1] care,

And there I see a statue
    Among the maids of old
On either hand, a goodly band,
    So calmly wise and cold.

On one side is Miranda [SB23.3.164]
    For virgin beauty famed
Nearby is Penthea
    As she was fitly named—

O most fair and sad was she
    Of the fairest saddest pages
Of all the burning dramas
    Of the great Eliza's sages.

But there this image is
    Mid fair and pearly light
From the dreamland marble
    Like unto hawthorn white.

It is a pale elf statue
    With sweet Titania's grace
But black's the hair, as though it were
    The peeping pansy's face.

The eyes as the wine are bright [SB23.3.165]
    In Circe's charmèd[2] cup:
O dark are the eyes as the morning skies[3]
    When scarce the day is up.

And here I down before it
    Cast a wayward play
Of a goblin queen, and a goblin dream
    And a pedlar grey,

Of a speaking magic mirror
    Of a sad and heartless queen
Of young Asphodel and Clarin
    With his harp of lyric teen.

W. B. Yeats
January the 8th
1884

Act I [SB23.3.166]

Scene 1

A laurel grove. Time night. Clarin, zittar in hand, sitting on a large oak chair over the back of which hangs a leopard skin.

Clarin. I find no solitude by wood or stream
    For a radiant shadow haunting me.
    Hear you the southwest wind in the branches?
    It is calling, 'Asphodel, O Asphodel!'

(Enter to R. Vivien and Asphodel, behind, arm-in-arm, the first with a mask in her hand, the second masked.)

    The enamoured nightingale hath stolen
    For a chorus thy name, my disturber,[4]
    And the laurel fondles the sound in joy.
    What other note hath the sounding zittar?
Vivien. A most wondrous! Say, Sir Melancholy,
    Of the immortals who is favoured so?
    No lower than great Dian' Clarin looks:
    Surely it is the moon, no lower thing.
Clarin. Being supremely wise you've rightly guessed:
    I spoke but of the moon personified,   [SB23.3.167]
    As was the fashion in those ancient days
    When sea-built Troy the duchess Helen knew.
    But thou, being learned 'fore all ladies,
    Know all this.
Vivien.   I am weary with the dance.
    Have you any pleasant tale to tell
    Of pale Helen or of Menelaus,
    The stern old duke, or Paris, for I'm tired.
Clarin. Why, what wonder of the song-worn dead
    Have not the phantoms taught thee, goblin queen?
    But here's a ballad bought this very hour
    From a lean pedlar with a bag and scythe.
Vivien (troubled). Bought from a pedlar with a bag and scythe?[5]
Clarin (reads).
    Two shining drops of gracious dew
    Two sprigs of rosemary and rue
       Two loving friends there are
       None fairer in story   [SB23.3.168]
    But yonder is hoary

>   Time on a whirling star
>   Falling are the golden sands
>   In the glass in his old, old hands.
>
>   The rosemary dead and the rue
>   In the monsoon burnt and the dew
>   Faints 'mid sunbeams that ban it
>   In life love hath ended
>   Old Time hath descended
>   From his far-circling planet.[6]
>   Falling are the silent sands
>   In the glass in his old old hands—

Asphodel. A most uncourtier song, for know you not
    Our only enemy is withered time
    Here in the Castle Joyeuse, Sir Clarin?
Clarin. If mirth you need, why sought you the laurel?
    The flood tide of joy is full in the hall.
Vivien. If sang you of us, well say who's fairer
    Of us who care not for the shadow'd[7] dead   [SB23.3.169]
    Of empty story—so between us judge.
      (*Asphodel unmasks.*)
Asphodel. Gladly from such a contest I'd withdraw.
Clarin. Always the queen in her own right hath claim
    Of victory (*He recognises Asphodel.*) Yet troubadours always
    Are free to judge in wilful wise, so then
    My verdict is for Countess Asphodel.
Asphodel. O Sir Clarin—
Clarin.   Hear you! Again they dance!
    So, Countess Asphodel, a measure, pray!
Vivien. The sad moon, Sir Clarin hath deserted.
    That wan mistress shall die of jealousy.
      (*Exeunt to R. Clarin and Asphodel.*)
    Slighted (*she sits in Clarin's chair*) in person and in royalty!
    The woman and the queen both are slighted,
    Doubly dangerous to those who slight them.   [SB23.3.170]

Scene 2

A room in the castle. Magic mirror to R. surmounted by a skull in the background. A subdued light over everything. Enter to R. Vivien, the mask being still in her hand. She stands before the glass.

Vivien. O glass, glass, glass, I come to ask of thee
    If I am not the fairest in the land,
    For, glass, I have been most sadly slighted.
Mirror.
    In each house I've an eye
    To be damned and die
    A thousand shapes have I,
    But by dread Merlin's self I swear
    Never have I aught as fair
    As Asphodel the Countess seen.
    O no not Dido that sad queen
    Had so majestical a mien.
Vivien. O glass, you are a sorry comforter;   [SB23.3.171]
    But ne'er to brook a rival I have sworn.
      (*Writes on her tablets.*)
    And now I sign her death warrant.
    When the rosemary's dead the rue shall live
    So much more in the sun. O Asphodel,
    It is not well to be so fair! Clarin's so loved
    By all the nobles that[8] him I cannot touch,
    Unless with owlish wisdom in the dark.
      (*A Page appears at the door to R., carefully enclosing something in both his hands.*)
Page. Look, look you here!
Vivien.   What have you there, my child?
      (*The Page shows a large tropical butterfly. The Queen lays it on the table.*)
    'Tis dead—you should not slay these sunny things;
    They say they're souls of long dead fairies.
      (*The Page begins to cry.*)
    Do not cry, my child, they're dying always—
    The cold nights slay and all birds slay them.
    What matter if you or I slay also?
      (*Puts the child sitting on the table, close by Merlin's book.*)
Page. Why is that book so large?   [SB23.3.172]
      (*Tries to open it.*)
Vivien.   Can you read, child?
Page. Yes, quite fast, for Asphodel has taught me.
      (*The Queen opens the book.*)
Vivien. Read then.
Page (*reads with difficulty*).
    Him whom I name
    Wrap him like flame
    Souls of unrest

Vivien. Stay, stay—(*aside*) these charms of Merlin's have most might
   When said by sinless children's lips;
   But I must make him repeat Clarin's name.
   (*Aloud.*) My most dear child, whom love you best in the world?
Page. Why, Asphodel, of course. Don't you?
Vivien.   Whom next?
Page. Clarin, for he showed me a squirrel's[9] dray.
Vivien. What's his full name—Clarin's full name? Speak loud!

[SB23.3.173]

Page. Sir Clarin of Tadmor, as all men know.
Vivien. Now read.
Page (*reads. As he reads the Queen grows more and more excited*).
   Him whom I name
   Wrap him like flame
   Ye souls of unrest
   Who dwell on the crest
      Of the wind-worn waves—
      —In emerald caves
   Where the salt foam raves
   O cease ye to rest—
      See, a blue flame played on the book just then! O let me stop!
Vivien. No, you but dream. Read, read!
Page (*reads*).
   Him whom I name
   Wrap him like flame
   Arise, arise   [SB23.3.174]
      Rest on his eyes
      See that they weep
      See they ne'er sleep
   Till he dies, dies
      Let his body burn
   Till his ash lies
      In his mural urn
   Let his whole brain melt
   As a cloudy belt
   Till he dies, dies—
      The book is fiery hot.
Vivien.   Read, read!
Page (*reads in fear*).
   Him whom I name   [SB.23.3.175]
   Wrap him like flame
   Things that were fair
   As Eve's bright hair

                    To Adam of old
                        Grow formless and cold
                    To his weary stare.
                That is all. O what is it, your Majesty?
Vivien. 'Tis the wild poem of a wild old man.
                Here, bear these tablets to the seneschal.
                Begone, I'd be alone.
                    (*Exit Page to R. She takes the butterflies and says excitedly*)
                O butterflies, butterflies ruined by a child,
                What did the laughter of thy wings for thee?
                What did the people's favour do for thee,
                Or all the fancies of thine idle harp?
                Beneath some evil star ye twain were born.
                Great Circe, Circe, now thy fame is fled
                Since mine was born that shall have wing until . . .
Mirror. Until the fountains on the steeps have rest
                And 'fore the sun the flowers' lips are closed.
Vivien. And that is forever. [SB23.3.176]

Scene 3

A room in the castle. The queen Vivien, arranging flowers in a large antique vase, thus begins to speak:

[*Vivien.*] I triumph, for Asphodel is slain
                Where the shadowy pool in the desert
                Leers upon heaven like a demon's[10] eye,
                Where again the echoes by this are still
                So little of noise does a murder make.
                I think she now wanders a whimp'ring ghost.

                            *   *   *

                Men saw in the heaven when I was born
                When a wild swan passed in the blinding blue
                Great was the might and the mirth of his wings
                Down 'fore their feet fell he dead in the way.
                Then wan-faced augured the gray sign-tellers
                That my life should have might like that wild wing [SB23.3.177]
                That had for a soul the powers of night
                For 'twas no common bird, those old men said,
                But that lame-footed fate would o'ertake me
                When the tide of my strength was full.
                So evil augured the grey sign-tellers;

> But Clarin whom alone I feared of men
> Has journeyed forth to find new lands of woe,
> Lands which the wild soul of his zittar e'en
> That was 'fore all sage things in sorrow versed
> Knew not even in its tuneful heart.
> Sir Clarin the wild singer of wild songs
> I had a fancy for him once of old
> Till his indifference—(*to a flower*) lie there
> Among thy sister mummers of the year
> O pale Narcissus—till his indifference
> Roused hate. So now he's gone and I grown bold
> May mock the dread presage that came
> From the hollow cave of the gray dreamers.
> (*Enter Page, who carefully avoids the great book of Merlin that lies on a side table. In one hand he has a letter, in the other a mourning wreath.*)

Page.   A letter, your Majesty.
Vivien.   Ho, killer   [SB23.3.179]
> Of butterflies! (*Takes the letter.*) What news have you today?
> (*She takes flowers from the vase and begins arranging them in his dress.*)

Page.   Last week when I was walking down the path
> Having just been here I met Sir Clarin.
> His eyes were wild and he grasped at the air
> As though he too were chasing butterflies.
> He muttered to himself and saw me not
> Though I called and threw my cap at him.
> A world-worn pedlar with a bag and scythe
> Trod close behind. (*The queen shivers.*) Poor Clarin also dies.

Vivien.   He is a strange man and has strange fancies.
> (*Sees wreath.*)
> That wreath—

Page.   'Tis of some snowy blossoms made
> That for tears stand or for some tearful thing.
> So read my sister from a little book,
> Weaving this wreath that I go now to hang
> Upon the column by the river's marge
> That is for memory of Asphodel.
> 'Twas very kind of you to build it there—   [SB23.3.178]
> Bright are the waters and golden their tongue
> And there the tufted sedge is pendulous.

Vivien.   Pay honour to the dead always, my child.
> (*Opens the letter, starts, and mutters excitedly.*)

Not dead! What! has the deep and hungry pool
Ungorged its prey? What! Are the dead uncharneled?
   (*She continues to read. Starts and drops it.*)
As the law is, O traitors, shall ye die,
False soldiers and still falser seneschal!
She lives and through the desert wanders safe.
To one, she resembled his own dead child,
To one old man, one whom in youth he knew
And danced with on some old world village green,
That growing weak they could not slay this child.
Am I not queen? And live they not but by my breath?
Page.   Do not so grieve for Asphodel that's dead;
   My mother says she's better off above
Amongst the merry saints than here on earth.
Vivien.   'Twas not for her I grieve. What, do you think
   The whole world pivots round dead Asphodel?   [SB23.3.181]
   (*Turns to him.*)
Some of my subjects must die by the law
And like Rachel I weep for my children.
—Ha, ha, I have a thought: she shall not live!
The wild swan soars!

Scene 4

Before a cottage in the desert. Enter to R. Clarin. Through the cottage door Asphodel is seen sitting spinning, her back turned.

Clarin.   By day and night crying aloud her name
   On hills and in the sombre forest
   Where shuddereth eternal night I seek
   Where pensive streamlets muse forever
   Like children in a dream so still they are
   Ever I follow the flying shadow
   But yet it flies and I must seek, still seek.
   Yonder it is on the hillside glowing
   While I live I follow without ceasing.
   I come, I come, shadow of Asphodel!
      (*Exit to L. Asphodel turns round and says*)   [SB23.3.180]
[*Asphodel.*]   Did someone cry my name? No, I had dozed.
      (*Turns back to her wheel. Enter Gypsy.*)   [SB23.3.181]
Gypsy (*singing on a guitar*).   [SB23.3.182]
   O an evil thing
      I suffered of you

Has withered my heart
    Right unto the core

Spirits of doom
    Plagues of a feather
Trooping as one
    Gather together

My voice sinks down
    To the country lone
Where each one sits
    On a blood-red throne

My voice sank down
    And each one started
Up on his throne
    And earthward darted.

[SB23.3.175]

(*Asphodel comes slowly to the door while she is singing.*)
Asphodel. Have you any news of the world, gypsy?
Gypsy (*not seeing her*).   What! Claim I not most strict obedience
    From noble and from beggar all alike?
    Yet these dead dogs in impudence[11]
    Waked proud and spoke of mercy to the queen!
    But now their wrinkled heads can beg it from
    The sombre crows upon the castle gate.
Asphodel. My poor woman, some grief is burning thee.
    I caught not thy words but they seem troubled.
Gypsy. Once in dead of night two genii fought,
    A good one and an evil, for my soul.
    The genie of evil slew the other,
    And therefore I mutter, being possessed.
Asphodel. O pray to the good saints! Their love is great.
    (*She sits beside her.*)   [SB23.3.184]
Gypsy. No, the angel of evil would kill me.
    He's by me now, standing invisible.
Asphodel. To holy Mary I will pray for thee.
    But come within, you're weary of travel,
    And we'll exchange stories with each other.
    I'm hiding from a queen who seeks my life.
    Yes, I too have known sorrow, so come in.
        (*The gypsy stands up.*)
Gypsy (*seeing a horseshoe that* [*hangs*] *over the door*).
    I may not go in; I may not linger.

Close in the desert my tribe is waiting.
I sat but by your door to rest this form
That is a weary weed of womanhood,
A frail wreck of its beauty and old strength.
But 'fore I go, of me take this flower
I give in gratitude for gracious words.
Asphodel. O one of autumn's passionate children,
    When scarcely tuned is the wild harp of spring!   [SB23.3.185]
    Stand back, stand back—I fear thee!
    (She steps back. The Gypsy advances.)
Gypsy.   We gypsies,
    As you know, do deal with things above mankind.
    But let me tell thy fortune, holy maid.
    (She takes her hand. Asphodel tries to draw it away.)
    The line of peace is wondrous deep and long:
    Ne'er saw I such a line on mortal hand.
    Most instant and most deep the peace shall be.
    Smell the flower.
Asphodel.   I seem to know your voice.
    (She smells the flower and falls back in a trance.)
Gypsy. Die not, for that were but a weak revenge,
    But till thy lover Clarin dies, sleep, sleep;
    And when he breathes his last live breath on earth—
    Be it today, tomorrow, or the next,
    Next year or in a thousand thousand years,
    At morning or at noontide or at night—
    Awake and let thy soul see only then
    (Born of the o'erworn embers of thy sleep)   [SB23.3.186]
    A deadly phantom that shall lead thee on
    From land to land as Clarin wanders now,
    Haggard-eyed with his dear phantom flying.
    But tender it is as the winged dew
    Or as the lady Hope herself, by thine.
    So doth the fever pass like racket ball
    From you to him, from him to you.
                    Poor fools!
    Poor racket ball in Vivien's driving bat!
    (Throws off her disguise and stands revealed the Queen.)
Vivien. Shine, sun, and blow, ye summer winds,
    Sweet vagrants, for I'm glad with triumphing.

(*Sings*)
> Every flower bows his head
> Passion worn and passion fed
> Green and gold and lustrous yellow
> Glutted with excess of sun
> All the flowers quire as one
> Now where is the wild swan's fellow?

(*Exit.*)

Act II [SB23.3.188]

Scene 1

Clarin comes in supporting his failing steps on a boar[12] spear, his hair gray before its time with grief.

Clarin. Conscience, a little longer be thou still!
  Write not upon thy books O yet, recorder;
  O write not yet Clarin hath slain his queen!
  My oath of fealty is spotless still.
  Planets, you pale mariners of night,
  Have pity on a fellow wanderer!
  Look all as ye were wont of old to look
  When oft I wooed you in this laurel copse.
  O disturb me not with your wan faces!
  Why seem ye all, pale ones, so lustreless?
  I kiss my hand to you as heretofore:
  Be fair to me as once ye were of old.
  Wanderers, I tell you I am guiltless
  Of great Vivien's blood!
              My meddling harp,
  Why won[13] thou from the fairy king his forces
  That shall in viewless combat on this night
  O'erthrow the goblin servants of the queen   [SB23.3.189]
  That I may slay her and my fame in one
  And be a knight for endless time disgraced
  For a broken oath? No more shall bards
  Sing of the deeds of Clarin, for a crime
  Shall quench his fame tonight, rather my soul.
  Fairies, I cannot slay her now. A voice!
  I think a voice said 'Asphodel!' just then.
    (*He listens.*)
  Young Asphodel in thy magic trance
  Hid in a secret cavern by the sea,
  For her, for her—Oh hear, ye fairy things—
  We storm the castle at the dawn of day.
    (*Exit.*)

Sailing from Avalon 29

[Here follow the six pages restored to manuscript NLI 30,357 from manuscript NLI 30,460. They are printed together with "Time and the Witch Vivien" for comparison.]

[Manuscript NLI 30,460, from *Vivien and Time*]

Act II [SB22.3.65]

Scene 2

Room in the castle as in Scenes 2 and 3 of Act I. Time night, a pale taper burning before the Magic Mirror. Queen alone.

Queen. The lily wristed Asphodel has slept
    These summers three, and I have quaffed full deep
    The glorious cup of magic, till in drinking
    That dread forbidden wine that once I dreamt
    And read of only my soul grows
    The image of the mighty viewless ones.
    No 'tis changed, sweet metamorphosis,
    To one great throbbing string that throbbing calls
    Only one wild word, one wild word,
    Power, power, outspeeding envy self,
    The only drink for my unceasing thirst.
    O word, as the song of the sea to streams
    Art thou to me; in thee I'd lose myself,

["Time and the Witch Vivien" from *The Wanderings of Oisin and Other Poems*, 1889 (P 514–17)]

Time and the Witch Vivien [P 514]

A marble-flagged, pillared room. Magical instruments in one corner. A fountain in the centre.

Vivien (*looking down into the fountain*). Where moves there any
    beautiful as I,
  Save, with the little golden greedy carp,
  Gold unto gold, a gleam in its long hair,
  My image yonder? (*Spreading her hand over the water.*) Ah, my
    beautiful,

Vivien and Time

Outgrowing human sense and human thought.
As I have pity for the fleeting race
Of men who bend to every sudden blast
Of joy or grief or scorn, and as they bend
Say it is human thus to bend, well then [SB22.3.66]
So much less human I who shall not bend
Until upon the steeps the fountains rest
And 'fore the sun the flowers' lips are closed.
  (*She starts and trembles.*)
Some great spirit passes in the desert.
Turning it enters by the city gate.
I felt its influence through all my veins.
'Tis swifter far than swiftest dream.
Now 't'as passed the sentries; 'tis at the door;
It is here.
  (*Enter an old pedlar with a black bag, a scythe, and an hour-glass.*)
          No check are bolted doors for thee,
Thou wrinkled squanderer of human gold.

Time and the Witch Vivien

What roseate fingers! (*Turning away.*) No; nor is there one
Of equal power in spells and secret rites.
The proudest or most coy of spirit things,
Hide where he will, in wave or wrinkled moon,
Obeys.
          Some fierce magician flies or walks
Beyond the gateway—by the sentries now—
Close and more close—I feel him in my heart—
Some great one. No; I hear the wavering steps
Without there of a little, light old man;
I dreamt some great one. (*Catching sight of her image, and
  spreading her hand over the water.*)
                    Ah, my beautiful,
What roseate fingers!

  (*Enter Time as an old pedlar, with a scythe, an hour-glass, and a
  black bag.*)

          Ha, ha! ha, ha, ha! [P 515]
The wrinkled squanderer of human wealth.

Sailing from Avalon   31

Vivien and Time

(*She laughs.*)
But come, come sit thee down. I'd buy of thee.
Come, father.
Father Time. No, I never sit nor rest.
Queen. Well then, to business. What is in thy bag?
  (*Putting the bag and hour-glass on the table. Time rests on his scythe.*)
Father Time. Gray hairs and crutches for old age hath Time   [SB22.3.67]
  And stately mansions of mild mellow thoughts
  Where dwell the souls of old men having peace.
  Such are the ripe fruits Time hath in his bag.
Queen (*with a motion of disgust*).
  No. None of these for me, old father wrinkles.
Time. Someday mayhap you'll buy.
Queen.   Never.
Time.   Never? (*Laughs.*)
Queen. You laugh. Why?
Time.   Best laugh is last. I laugh last always.
Queen (*lays the glass on one side. Time puts it up again*).
  Your scythe I do not need. Let that bring peace

Time and the Witch Vivien

Come here. Be seated now; I'd buy of you.
Come, father.
Time.   Lady, I nor rest nor sit.
Vivien. Well then, to business; what is in your bag?
Time (*putting the bag and hour-glass on the table and resting on his scythe*). Grey hairs and crutches, crutches and grey hairs,
  Mansions of memories and mellow thoughts
  Where dwell the minds of old men having peace,
  And—
Vivien. No; I'll none of these, old Father Wrinkles.
Time. Some day you'll buy them, maybe.
Vivien.   Never!
Time (*laughing*).   Never?
Vivien. Why do you laugh?
Time.   I laugh the last always.
  (*She lays the hour-glass on one side. Time rights it again.*)
Vivien. I do not need your scythe. May that bring peace

Vivien and Time

  Unto those men your "mellow" gifts have wearied.
   I'd buy your glass.   [SB22.3.68]
Time.   And that I will not sell.
  Without my glass I'd be a sorry clown.
Queen. Yet whiter beard have you than Merlin had.
Time. For slumber 'neath an oak I have no taste.
Queen. How old are you?
   (*She lays the glass down.*)
Time.   Before thy granddame Eve I was.
   (*Puts standing upright again.*)
Queen. Oh I am weary of that foolish tale.
  'Tis said 'mong men you are a gambler, Time.
  So come, I'd play thee for thine hour-glass.
  I like such things about me; they are food
  For antiquarian meditation (*fetches the dice*).
Time. The best of three shall win the glass.
Queen (*throws*). Three-six.
Time (*throws*). Four-six.   [SB22.3.69]
Queen. By one point thou art first (*throws*). Five-six. Ha.

Time and the Witch Vivien

  To those your 'mellow' wares have wearied out.
   I'd buy your glass.
Time.   My glass I will not sell.
  Without my glass I'd be a sorry clown.
Vivien. Yet whiter beard have you than Merlin had.
Time. No taste have I for slumber 'neath an oak.
Vivien. When were you born?
Time.   Before your grandam Eve.
Vivien. Oh, I am weary of that foolish tale.
  They say you are a gambler and a player
  At chances and at moments with mankind.
  I'll play you for your old hour-glass. (*Pointing*   [P 516]
   to *the instruments of magic.*)   You see
  I keep such things about me; they are food
  For antiquarian meditation.   (*Brings dice.*)
Time.   Ay,
  We throw three times.
Vivien. Three-six.
Time. Four-six.
Vivien. Five-six. Ha, Time!

Sailing from Avalon 33

<u>Vivien and Time</u>

Time (*throws*).   Six-six.
Queen.   O I have lost. They're loaded dice as always
   Are the dice time playeth with, but father,
   Another chance. I'd play thee at the chess;
   For a young girl's wits against a bent old man's
   Are mated any day as Merlin found.
      (*Wheels over the chess men.*)
   The passing of those little grains is snow
   Upon my soul, old Time.
      (*She lays the hour-glass upon its side.*)
Time.   No, thus it stands.
      (*Puts it up again.*)
      (*The Queen sits at the chess-board.*)
Time.   You've lost the glass. For other stakes we play.
Queen.   Well then, for triumph in my many plots.
Time.   Defeat is death. (*They play.*)
Queen.   To fail in plotting is to die.   [SB22.3.70]
   Thus play we first with pawns, small things and weak,
   And then the great ones come, and last the king.
   So men in life and I in magic play,

<u>Time and the Witch Vivien</u>

Time.   Double sixes!
Vivien.   I lose! They're loaded dice. Time always plays
   With loaded dice. Another chance! Come, father;
   Come to the chess, for young girls' wits are better
   Than old men's any day, as Merlin found.
      (*Places the chess-board on her knees.*)
   The passing of those little grains is snow
   Upon my soul, old Time.
      (*She lays the hour-glass on its side.*)
Time.   No; thus it stands. (*Rights it again.*)
   For other stakes we play. You lost the glass.
Vivien.   Then give me triumph in my many plots.
Time.   Defeat is death.
Vivien.   Should my plots fail I'd die.   (*They play.*)
   Thus play we first with pawns, poor things and weak;
   And then the great ones come, and last the king.
   So men in life and I in magic play;

Vivien and Time

    First dreams and goblins and the lesser sprites,
    But now with Father Time I'm face to face.
Time (*laughs*).
      (*The curtain falls for a moment. The curtain rises. The Queen alone, her head on her hands, gazing at the chess-board.*)
A Voice.   Lost.
The Mirror.   Lost.
Queen.   The wild swan has sunk from the blinding blue.
    No more I trouble with my wayward life.
    Old dreaming night, O hungry oblivion,
    O sister death, I take thy hand, I come.

                                      (*She dies.*)

Time and the Witch Vivien

    First dreams, and goblins, and the lesser sprites,
    And now with Father Time I'm face to face.

                                      (*They play.*)

    I trap you.
Time.   Check.
Vivien.   I do miscalculate.
    I am dull to-day, or you were now all lost.   [P 517]
    Chance, and not skill, has favoured you, old father!

                                      (*She plays.*)

Time.   Check.
Vivien.   Ah! how bright your eyes. How swift your moves.
    How still it is! I hear the carp go splash,
    And now and then a bubble rise. I hear
    A bird walk on the doorstep.   (*She plays.*)
Time.   Check once more.
Vivien.   I must be careful now. I have such plots—
    Such war plots, peace plots, love plots—every side;
    I cannot go into the bloodless land
    Among the whimpering ghosts.
Time.   Mate thus.
Vivien.   Already?
    Chance hath a skill!   (*She dies.*)

Sailing from Avalon　35

[Manuscript NLI 30,357 of *Vivien and Time,* continued]

Both Voices (laugh). [SB23.3.190]
The Page (speaking without).
　　Keep back, strange pale man! This is the Queen's room.
　　　(*A struggle; a cry.*)
Clarin (rushing in with a drawn sword).
　　Now vengeance on the Queen, and then to seek
　　A potent spell in Merlin's stolen book
　　To rouse young Asphodel from magic trance.
　　　(*He sees the Queen lying dead; goes over and touches her.*)
　　Dead. Dead. That mighty shade has been before.
　　　(*Turns to the door.*)
　　O my good goblins, we are late, all late!
　　O now who wonders that the night had signs,
　　That there was bitter frost in fairy land
　　Which never happened in all time before
　　And fairy souls from streams and flowers fled
　　Wherefore upon the steeps the fountains rest
　　And 'fore the sun the flowers' lips are closed?
　　I now remember how an old grey man
　　A world-worn pedlar with a bag and scythe
　　Told me how I in after life would meet
　　A great queen whom I'd slay with mine own hand
　　O[r] scarce survive her for a minute's space.[14]　　[SB23.3.191]
　　The streams shall never hear my harp again.
　　O woe! There is a frost in fairy land
　　And on the steeps the fountains rest.
　　　　　　　　Oh Asphodel!
　　　(*Dies.*)
Mirror (laughs).

Scene 3

A dark grove. Enter Asphodel. No light on the stage or audience. Light only on Asphodel.

Asphodel.　O what a strange long sleep I've had! How long?[15]
　　And stranger dreams I've dreamt in sleep,
　　Of how a queen once loved me—loved—yes, loved!
　　And hated then more than she loved at first.
　　All vivid was as though it had been life:

How in those strange dark quiet days that flowed
In the short compass of one dream I found   [SB23.3.192]
Young Clarin whom I seemed to love.
Now all is fading and I feel[16] alone,
My whole soul bitterly athirst for peace.

First Voice.
    Soon like us you'll find her
      And dwell with her above
    All mortal things and bind her
      If you neither hate or love.

Second Voice.
    But quench, O thing of dust,
      Those awful flames that dart
    And gleam beneath the crust
      Of thy all-throbbing heart.

Asphodel.   When shall I find peace, oh fairy voices?
First Voice.
    When tall trees are crashing
    And lightning is flashing
    When thunder doth toll   [SB23.3.193]
    And wild waters roll

Both Voices.
    Still peace dwells alone
    On her judgement throne

Second Voice.
    When the bolts of death rattle
    'Mong the dying in battle
    O broods silence profound
    On the lone desert ground

Both Voices.
    Still peace dwells alone
    On her judgement throne.

Asphodel.   And Clarin—
First Voice.   Sister!
Second Voice.   Sister!
First Voice.   [SB23.3.194]
    Peace in the end you shall have
    And your o'erworn heart shall have rest

Second Voice.
    When the yew and the cypress wave
    In the cold earth over your breast.
    (*Exit Asphodel upon her wanderings.*)

End

Themes, Images, and Form

Vivien and Time is significant not only because, as Yeats asserts, it is his "first play" (CL1 155), but also because it informs us about his early reading, and because it contains important themes and symbols used in his later writings. We learn from the play that in this very early period he was exploiting Indo-European folk tales such as "Snow White" and folk beliefs such as that a horseshoe over the door keeps evil beings from entering. He already finds references to Homer and Troy strongly evocative, though he gives them a medieval flavor with "Duchess" Helen. Circe and Diana are other figures from classical myth that he makes use of. We learn further that Provence was a magical place to Yeats long before his interest in "Speaking to the Psaltery" and the still later influence of Ezra Pound. Clarin is a troubadour, and the courtly love ideal controls his actions. The Arthurian cycle, a frequent referent in the later work, is the background to this early work. The Judeo-Christian myth of Eden attracts Yeats here long before that myth has an occult significance to him,[26] and "Things that were fair / As Eve's bright hair / To Adam of old" (SB23.3.175) has all the nostalgia of "John Kinsella's Lament for Mrs. Mary Moore" (P 342–43), published less than two months before his death.

We learn that he read and honored "the great Eliza's sages," particularly Shakespeare, and more particularly *The Tempest*. In the "Dedication" (SB23.3.163–65) the figure of Laura Armstrong is seen "Among the maids of old," of whom Yeats mentions only two. One is "Miranda / For virgin beauty famed." We are not surprised that Yeats singles out a Shakespearean heroine and specifically the magician's daughter. But his allusion to the other maid, "Penthea," is startlingly informative.

Nowhere in Yeats's published utterances does he mention John Ford or his play *The Broken Heart*, in which Penthea, betrothed to one man but then forced to marry another, goes mad and dies and is avenged by her betrothed. On 8 January 1884 Yeats writes a passionate tribute to Ford's heroine (whose name means "complaint"):

> Nearby is Penthea
> As she was fitly named—
>
> O most fair and sad was she
> Of the fairest saddest pages
> Of all the burning dramas
> Of the great Eliza's sages.
>
> [SB23.3.164]

Penthea's tragedy results from her loyalty to what Yeats later called "the old high way of love" (P 81). Penthea is forced to be untrue to her conception of herself, forced to violate the "high courtesy" (P 81) of the conventions of courtly love. As M. L. Wine comments, "Ford does not ask 'Why does one act?' but rather 'How will one act?'"[27] Ford's heroines "self-consciously seek identity; and they succeed by gracefully adhering to a code of noble gestures that in effect becomes a principle enabling them to assert continually their personal reality. Where nothing is certain, the assertion of the ego's image in conscious poses is at least something to believe in. . . . The individual ego takes an absolute stand in a socially relative world."[28] How Yeatsian this sounds! One is reminded of Yeats's wish to prepare his daughter to meet the storm of future years: "So let her think opinions are accursed" and learn that "all hatred driven hence, / The soul recovers radical innocence / And learns at last that it is self-delighting, / Self-appeasing, self-affrighting . . ." (P 189). Or of his tribute to the declining Lady Gregory:

> Why should I be dismayed
> Though flame had burned the whole
> World, as it were a coal,
> Now I have seen it weighed
> Against a soul?
>
> [P 97]

For "the old high way of love" Yeats strove until "weary-hearted" (P 81). The song for Penthea's death ends "Love's martyrs must be ever, ever dying."[29]

The fascination with magic and medievalism which Yeats shared with the Romantics and Pre-Raphaelites is shown in *Vivien and Time* not just on the surface—Vivien with her Gothic room of magic and Merlin's book—but also in the profoundly serious themes of unappeasable longing and possession by supernatural beings and the imagery which carries these themes. In *Vivien and Time* people who are possessed become haggard and pale. The images are reminiscent of Keats's "La Belle Dame Sans Merci." As Keats's "palely loitering" knight who has lost his fairy vision is "haggard and woebegone" like other "death-pale" warriors who have been bewitched by the enchantress, so Clarin is "Haggard-eyed with his dear phantom flying" (SB23.3.186) and the Page calls him a "strange pale man" (SB23.3.190). This use of paleness predates by many years its appearance in *The Wind Among the Reeds* as a sign for longing for the supernatural or possession by it. There, as Ellmann has noted, the beloved is always pale—with "cloud-pale eyelids," "pale brows," and a "pearl-pale hand";[30] and in "The Hosting of the Sidhe" Niamh cries out "Our cheeks are pale" (P 55). In *On Baile's Strand* (1903) Aoife and her son have "a stone-pale cheek" (VPl 504).

The figure of the wandering poet or singer is an important one in almost every period of Yeats's work. Clarin, "the wild singer of wild songs" (SB23.3.177) "with his harp of lyric teen" (SB23.3.165) is the earliest manifestation of this figure. He is related to Aleel, the harp-player in *The Countess Cathleen,* Yeats's first published play, and to Forgael, the harper in *The Shadowy Waters.* As Aleel is a foil to the stronger character of the Countess, Clarin is a foil to the Queen; and Clarin's main purpose in the plot is to clarify the Queen's conflict and thus reveal her character to the audience. Aleel is on the side of earthly love and the old gods that Countess Cathleen rejects. Clarin provokes Vivien's vengeance by refusing her love. The wandering singer who slights or insults the Queen is important in two much later plays, *The King of the Great Clock Tower* and *A Full Moon in March.* In *A Full Moon in March,* as in *Vivien and Time,* the emphasis is on the virgin Queen—beautiful, but proud, bloodthirsty, and revengeful—who takes a terrible vengeance on the man who slights her.

Clarin is also an example of another, related, character—the figure who is possessed and wanders from land to land without rest, seeking the fulfillment of his vision. Clarin and Asphodel are both led on to endless wanderings by supernatural voices, "souls of unrest" (SB23.3.172) which "possess" them. This theme of endless search is one of the most important in Yeats's canon. It is found in such early work of the 1880s and 1890s as "The Man who dreamed of Faeryland," "The Hosting of the Sidhe," "The Song of Wandering Aengus," "The Stolen Child," "Cuchulain's Fight with the Sea," and *The Land of Heart's Desire.*

In those works, however, the search appears in a specifically Irish form. Like Clarin, who is pale, grows old before his time, and wanders "haggard-eyed," the persona of "The Song of Wandering Aengus" has grown "old with wandering" in search of "a glimmering girl" and determines to "find out where she has gone, / And kiss her lips and take her hands. . . . " (P 60). Forgael in *The Shadowy Waters* (1900) wanders in search of immortal love. From Bryan O'Looney's translation of Michael Comyn's eighteenth-century Gaelic poem "The Land of Youth," Yeats took symbols of such a quest: "a young man following a girl who has a golden apple" and "a hound with one red ear following a deer with no horns" (P 591). He borrows these symbols of "The immortal desire of Immortals" (P 374) for "The Wanderings of Oisin" and the hound and deer for "He mourns for the Change that has come upon Him and his Beloved, and longs for the End of the World" (P 61) and *The Shadowy Waters* (VP 764).

Long before these poems, and in its pre-Irish form, the theme of the man who wanders searching for a phantom love has appeared in *Vivien and Time:*

> *Clarin.* By day and night crying aloud her name
> On hills and in the sombre forest
> Where shuddereth eternal night I seek
> Where pensive streamlets muse forever
> Like children in a dream so still they are
> Ever I follow the flying shadow
> But yet it flies and I must seek, still seek.
> Yonder it is on the hillside glowing
> While I live I follow without ceasing.
> I come, I come, shadow of Asphodel!
>
> [SB23.3.181]

If we need a source, we may look to Shelley's *Alastor,* although in Shelley it is the vision's bright eyes, not her shadow, that haunt the youth. The phantoms in "The Wanderings of Oisin" are "shadows" (P 367), and one also recalls the "immortal, mild, proud shadows" of *The Shadowy Waters* that "come from Eden on flying feet" (P 405). Most relevant is "The Woman of the Sidhe herself" of *At the Hawk's Well,* "The mountain witch, the unappeasable shadow" who "is always flitting upon this mountainside, / To allure or to destroy" (VPl 407). Cuchulain falls subject to her curse, gazes in "her unmoistened eyes" (VPl 407), and is told "And never till you are lying in the earth / Can you know rest" (VPl 411–12). Similarly, Asphodel is told

> Peace in the end you shall have
> And your o'erworn heart shall have rest
> When the yew and the cypress wave
> In the cold earth over your breast.
>
> [SB23.3.194]

Clarin's and Asphodel's "unrest" is partly a result of their separation. They are an example of yet another theme, the lovers who desire a perfect union but can never come together. The lovers in *The Dreaming of the Bones* are another example, as are Cuchulain and Fand in *The Only Jealousy of Emer.* Later lovers like Crazy Jane are not content with a mere physical union, remaining restless and unsatisfied because the two souls are not truly united. This theme of unsatisfied love is connected with Yeats's theory of the longing of the self and anti-self and their search for each other.

Certain of Yeats's central images appear first in *Vivien and Time.* In "A Prayer for my Daughter" (1919) Yeats prays that his daughter may flourish like a laurel tree, and the laurel has in that poem all its traditional associations with aesthetic achievement. He prays that her thoughts may be like linnets and she like a tree with "no business but dispensing round / Their magnanimities of sound" (P 189). The opening scene of *Vivien and Time* takes place in a whole grove of laurels among which the poet Clarin hears his beloved's name in wind, in bird-call, and in the notes of his "zittar." All these "magnanimities of sound" are dispensed around by the symbolic laurels:

> The enamoured nightingale hath stolen
> For a chorus thy name, my disturber,
> And the laurel fondles the sound in joy.
>
> [SB23.3.166]

Butterflies often symbolize the soul in Yeats, as in much ancient and modern symbolism. In *The Hour Glass* (1914) the Wise Man's soul, after his death, takes the form of a butterfly released by an angel. The Fool explains:

> O, look what has come from his mouth! O, look what has come from his mouth—the white butterfly! He is dead, and I have taken his soul in my hands; but I know why you open the lid of that golden box. I must give it to you. There then [*he puts butterfly in casket*], he has gone through his pains, and you will open the lid in the Garden of Paradise. [VPl 639]

"Wisdom is a butterfly" we are told by "Tom O'Roughley" (P 141), and Yeats notes that the butterfly symbolizes "the crooked road of intuition" (P 597). The "great purple butterfly" in "Another Song of a Fool" was once "a schoolmaster" (like the Wise Man of *The Hour Glass*) and has "learning in his eye" (P 170). The butterflies of "Blood and the Moon" "come in through the loopholes and die against the windowpanes" of the tower (P 597), seeming to "cling upon the moonlit skies" like souls trying to rise toward "The purity of the unclouded moon" (P 238).[31]

These uses of the butterfly-soul symbolism are prefigured in *Vivien and Time:*

> (*A Page appears at the door to R., carefully enclosing something in both his hands.*)
>
> Page. Look, look you here!
> Vivien. What have you there, my child?
>   (*The Page shows a large tropic butterfly.*
>   *The Queen lays it on the table.*)
>   'Tis dead—you should not slay these sunny things;
>   They say they're souls of long dead fairies.
>
> [SB23.3.171]

(Since fairyland is the setting of *Vivien and Time*, and she herself is a fairy queen, she is not making a distinction between the souls of fairies and those of humans. The butterfly is a dead person's soul.) Later, when Vivien, through the agency of the Page, has cast a fatal spell on Clarin and Asphodel, she addresses these unlucky souls as butterflies:

> O butterflies, butterflies ruined by a child,
> What did the laughter of thy wings for thee?
> What did the people's favour do for thee,
> Or all the fancies of thine idle harp?
>
> [SB23.3.175]

Swans, a major symbol in Yeats, also stand for the the "solitary soul," as in "Nineteen Hundred and Nineteen" (1921):

> Some moralist or mythological poet
> Compares the solitary soul to a swan;
> I am satisfied with that,
> Satisfied if a troubled mirror show it,
> Before that brief gleam of its life be gone,
> An image of its state;
> The wings half spread for flight,
> The breast thrust out in pride
> Whether to play, or to ride
> Those winds that clamour of approaching night.
>
> [P 208]

There are also striking images of swans in "The Wild Swans at Coole," "The Tower," "Leda and the Swan," "Coole and Ballylee, 1931," and elsewhere. Maud Gonne, with her "Ledaean body," is one of the "daughters of the swan" in "Among School Children" (P 216), but Vivien is the first of those daughters in Yeats's work.

The swan as incorporating a spirit goes back to the Leda myth. Irish stories about human swans include "The Children of Lir" and "The Dream of Angus Og."[32] But Yeats could have found a similar tale in "The Six Swans" in *Grimm's Fairy Tales*, and with an attractive illustration by Walter Crane. There is no human being turned swan in *Vivien and Time*, but a swan is a sort of totem for Vivien and indeed shows "an image of [her] state":

> Men saw in the heaven when I was born
> When a wild swan passed in the blinding blue
> Great was the might and the mirth of his wings
> Down 'fore their feet fell he dead in the way.
> Then wan-faced augured the gray sign-tellers
> That my life should have might like that wild wing
> That had for a soul the powers of night

> For 'twas no common bird, those old men said,
> But that lame-footed fate would o'ertake me
> When the tide of my strength was full.
> So evil augured the grey sign-tellers. . . .
>
> [SB23.3.176–77]

She defies this prophecy, believing she will triumph over her rival, Asphodel, in spite of Clarin's opposition, and in her confidence cries out "The wild swan soars" (SB23.3.181).

Later, having put Asphodel in a trance, she is "glad with triumphing" and sings a mysterious song ending hauntingly, "Now where is the wild swan's fellow?" (SB23.3.186), echoed over thirty years later by an equally haunting line in *Calvary*, "What can a swan need but a swan?" (VPl 788) and by the image of the swans paddling "lover by lover" in "The Wild Swans at Coole" (P 131).

Another of Yeats's major symbols is the fountain, perhaps derived quite early on from Shelley (E&I 81), though it is not until his essay on "The Philosophy of Shelley's Poetry" (1900) that Yeats speaks of Shelley's reading Porphyry on "intellectual fountains" and on "fountains and rivers [that] symbolize generation" (E&I 83). In "The Poetry of Sir Samuel Ferguson—I" (1886) the fountain is a symbol of the "living waters" of the "Irish cycle" (UP1 82), as it is again in "The Celtic Element in Literature" (1897): "and now a new fountain of legends, and, as I think, a more abundant fountain than any in Europe, is being opened, the fountain of Gaelic legends . . . " (E&I 186). In "At Stratford-on-Avon" (1901), Yeats uses the figure of the fountain in preferring Richard II to that "natural force" Henry V, praising "that lyricism which rose out of Richard's mind like the jet of a fountain to fall again where it had risen" (E&I 108). In "Discoveries" (1906) "Art . . . shrinks . . . from all that is of the brain only, from all that is not a fountain jetting from the entire hopes, memories, and sensations of the body" (E&I 292). The "abounding glittering jet" of the fountain of life rises in the rich man's garden in "Ancestral Houses" (P 200) and leaps high up on the mountainside where "upstanding men / . . . / Drop their cast at the side / Of dripping stone" in "The Tower" (P 198).

In *Vivien and Time* life's fountains are part not only of the imagery but of the action. Vivien cannot die "Until the fountains on the steeps have rest" (SB23.3.175), which, she thinks, can never happen because it never has. But it does happen. After her death Clarin explains that

> there was bitter frost in fairy land
> Which never happened in all time before
> And fairy souls from streams and flowers fled
> Wherefore upon the steeps the fountains rest. . . .
>
> [SB23.3.190]

In "Time and the Witch Vivien" Yeats sets the scene of Vivien's contest with Time and her resulting death in *"a marble flagged, pillared room"* which has *"A fountain in the centre"* (P 514). Just before the end Yeats makes sure that we recall this symbol of life: Vivien says, "I hear the carp go splash, / And now and then a bubble rise" (P 517). Immediately afterwards she loses the chess game and dies. It is of interest that in the Merlin romances a fountain in the forest of Briosque is a favorite haunt of Niniane's and that there she trysts with Merlin.[33]

Vivien and Time begins cheerfully in a classical laurel grove, but ends in a Dantesque "dark grove," also a symbol which Yeats would use in his later poetry. In the final scene Asphodel passes through *"A dark grove"* (SB23.3.191). She is "alone," her "whole soul bitterly athirst for peace." She is told by fairy voices that she can dwell with peace "above / All mortal things" if she neither hates nor loves. They warn her

> But quench, O thing of dust,
> Those awful flames that dart
> And gleam beneath the crust
> Of thy all-throbbing heart.
>
> [SB23.3.192]

More than forty years later, in "Blood and the Moon" (1928), Yeats has Jonathan Swift lament that "the heart in his blood-sodden breast had dragged him down into mankind" (P 237). In *The Words upon the Window-pane* (1934) Yeats shows a fascination with Swift's epitaph: "He has gone where fierce indignation can lacerate his heart no more" (VPl 942). In "Parnell's Funeral" Parnell is another solitary who has passed "Through Jonathan Swift's dark grove . . . and there / Plucked bitter wisdom that enriched his blood" (P 280). Yeats had no doubt long forgotten that in *Vivien and Time* Asphodel, too, passes "alone" through a "dark grove" seeking peace "above . . . mortal things" but escaping the "all-throbbing heart" only in death.

Vivien and Time is full of floral imagery. It runs from the beginning of the action in a laurel grove, through a profusion of flower imagery as Vivien's power rises, to the death of the flowers along with the death of Vivien and Clarin, and to the awakening of Asphodel in the dark grove of cypress and yew. Unlike the other images we have traced, however, flowers are few and far between in the later Yeats.

A glance at the concordance to Yeats's poems shows that the word "flower" appears eighteen times before 1900 (arbitrarily using that date to distinguish early from late poetry) but only three times after, the plural "flowers" nineteen times before 1900 and ten times after. Of specific flowers, the rose, which is omnipresent before 1900, appears afterwards only in "The Song of a Fool," "The Rose Tree," "My House," and "The Three Bushes." The lily appears in six poems before 1900, but later only in "The Gift of Harun Al-Rashid." The setting of *The Island of Statues* is in an enchanted garden, and an enchanted flower is central to the plot. In that work there are references to many flowers that are seldom or never mentioned again in Yeats's poetry: pansies, anemones, monks-hood, foxglove, laburnum. Daffodils appear there and in two other very early poems. Violets are found only in "How Ferencz Renyi Kept Silent." The poppy appears in five pre-1900 poems; only in "Shepherd and Goatherd" after. Laurel, on the other hand, appears only in "The Wanderings of Oisin" before 1900 but in three later poems: "A Prayer for my Daughter," "Coole Park, 1929," and "News for the Delphic Oracle." However, the pre-1900 appearance is without symbolic overtones, while the post-1900 appearances are symbolical. "Blossoms" are found only before 1900. "Blossom" and "blossoming" prosper later, but often in a general sense and as verb or verbal.

"Why can't you English poets keep flowers out of your poetry," Yeats asked Dorothy Wellesley.[34] Cutting observation of flowers out of his poetry was one way in which Yeats cured himself of superficial imitation of the English tradition. *Vivien and Time,* however, like *The Island of Statues* (written later in 1884), is still very imitative of that tradition. Yeats's inability to keep flowers out of his 1883–84 poetry is simply a sign of his times. The reader will immediately think of the garden in Tennyson's *Maud* where Maud is "Queen Rose of the rose-bud garden of girls" and of the poppies in Swinburne's "Garden of Proserpine." The poems, like the paintings of Rossetti—and Pre-Raphaelite and symbolist painting generally—are full of the flower symbolism that crowds into *The Island of Statues* and *Vivien and Time.*

The marble statues in the "Dedication" are "Like unto hawthorn white," and the person to whom the poem is dedicated has bright eyes and black hair like "the peeping pansy's face" (SB23.3.164). The play opens in a laurel grove. The heroine is a flower of the otherworld, "Asphodel." Vivien contrasts herself with Asphodel as rosemary and rue (SB23.3.171). The magic mirror tells Vivien that her power will last until the flowers are frozen, which she believes can never happen. Flowers accompany the prime of Vivien's power. In act I, scene 3, Yeats has her *"arranging flowers in a large antique vase"* (SB23.3.176). She interrupts her soliloquy, which tells us her plots, with asides to the flowers: "lie there / Among thy sister mummers of the year / O pale Narcissus" (SB23.3.177). When the Page comes in she *"takes flowers from the vase and begins arranging them in his dress"* (SB23.3.179). Countering Vivien's colorful bouquet with a hint of frost, the Page carries a wreath of "snowy blossoms" (SB23.3.179) which he will hang on a column set up to the memory of the supposedly dead Asphodel; the Page also carries a letter which brings Vivien the bitter news that Asphodel is not dead after all. For Vivien the death of Asphodel, flower of the otherworld, would be the death of death. But the "snowy blossoms" will triumph.

When Vivien, disguised as a gypsy, puts Asphodel into a trance, she does it not with a poisoned apple, as in "Snow White," but with a poisoned flower, perhaps borrowed from the "poison'd rose" of Tennyson's "Merlin and Vivien."[35] Asphodel recognizes too late that something is wrong when Vivien presents her autumn flower in springtime. Vivien triumphs over the fallen Asphodel by singing

> Every flower bows his head
> Passion worn and passion fed
> Green and gold and lustrous yellow
> Glutted with excess of sun
> All the flowers quire as one
> Now where is the wild swan's fellow?
>
> [SB23.3.186]

Act II, scene 1, returns us to the laurel copse, in which Clarin plots Vivien's death. In act II, scene 2, Vivien rejoices that "The lily wristed Asphodel has slept / These summers three" (SB22.3.65) and again that she herself "shall not bend / Until upon the steeps the fountains rest / And 'fore the sun the flowers' lips are closed" (SB22.3.66). In that scene as revised for "Time and the Witch Vivien," the only reference to flowers is to Vivien's own "roseate fingers" (P 514).

In the next scene of *Vivien and Time* we learn "That there was bitter frost in fairy land" and that "'fore the sun the flowers' lips are closed" (SB23.3.190). As the prime of Vivien's power is marked by a choiring of flowers glutted with sun, her fall is marked by the death of flowers. Act II, scene 3, gives us a glimmering Asphodel: "*Light only on Asphodel*" in a "*dark grove*" (SB23.3.191). She is the only flower left, and that flower too is to be extinguished.

> *First voice.*
> Peace in the end you shall have
> And your o'erworn heart shall have rest
> *Second voice.*
> When the yew and the cypress wave
> In the cold earth over your breast.
> (*Exit Asphodel upon her wanderings.*)
>
> [SB23.3.194]

So the play moves from a laurel grove and a profusion of flowers to a dark grove, the yew, and the cypress.

Returning to the foreshadowing in *Vivien and Time* of Yeats's later work, we note here devices of his dance plays. In his middle years, having led the Irish theatre to great achievement and having achieved distinguished stage plays of his own, Yeats withdrew to cultivate a new, private kind of drama. He urged the "Popular Theatre" to "grow always more objective" but announced that in his own work he would seek "not a theatre but the theatre's anti-self" (Ex 257), "a mysterious art, always reminding and half-reminding those who understand it of dearly loved things, doing its work by suggestion, not by direct statement, a complexity of rhythm, colour, gesture, not space-pervading like the intellect, but a memory and a prophecy: a mode of drama Shelley and Keats could have used without ceasing to be themselves, and for which even Blake in the mood of *The Book of Thel* might not have been too obscure" (Ex 255). He wished a hostess, "an audience of fifty, a room worthy of it (some great dining-room or drawing-room), half a dozen young men and women who can dance and speak verse or play drum and flute and zither" (Ex 255; one thinks of Clarin's "zittar").

There was to be "no scenery" (E&I 221). His model was to be the Noh drama of Japan where "speech, music, song, and dance created an image of nobility and strange beauty" (E&I 229). He substituted masks for make-up "to bring the audience close enough to the play to hear every inflection of the voice" (E&I 226). He decided that "the most effective lighting is the lighting we are most accustomed to in our rooms" (VPl 398–99). He regrets that he did not discover in his youth that his "theatre must be the ancient theatre that can be made by unrolling a carpet or marking out a place with a stick, or setting a screen against the wall" (VP1 415).

Could Yeats's interest in returning to drawing-room drama have been a nostalgia for the occasion in his youth when he and a group of friends presented (or at least planned to present) *Vivien and Time* at the home of Judge Wright at Howth (*MM* 35)? There are hints in the early play of the direction to come. There is little indication of scenery, although necessary props—an oak chair, the magic mirror, the horseshoe over a door, Merlin's book, magical instruments, and so on—are mentioned. The play opens in a laurel grove (at Howth this scene could have been presented outside, with rhododendrons for laurels).

The "Voices" at the end are like Yeats's later "Chorus of Musicians," and music is important in the play. Vivien both plays and sings when, disguised as a gypsy, she casts a spell on Asphodel. Later she sings again to celebrate her triumph. We are sure that, were it not for a misfortune of casting, the play would have opened with music and that Clarin would have *sung* the ominous song about the fate of the rosemary (Asphodel) and the rue (Vivien). Clarin's role begs for an actor who can play and sing. Vivien speaks of "the wild soul of his zittar" and calls him "the wild singer of wild songs" (SB23.3.177). But Yeats, who obviously played Clarin, was then (and always) almost entirely unmusical. Therefore Clarin holds the zittar unplayed in his hand and merely reads his ballad.

Masks figure in the action. When the two women first enter, Vivien holds a mask in her hand and Asphodel is masked. Asphodel's unmasking startles Clarin into his untactful praise of her beauty and causes Vivien's jealousy. Vivien continues to hold her mask in her hand when she enters in act I, scene 2, to consult her magic mirror.

Vivien and Time is clearly not a dance play, as there is no dance performed before the audience. Yet the dance is present as an idea and is important in the action. Vivien and Asphodel leave the masquerade ball to get Clarin to tell them a tale: "I am weary with the dance" (SB23.3.167), says Vivien. When she objects to the ballad he has bought "From a lean pedlar with a bag and scythe" (SB23.3.167), Clarin responds with a reference to the dance she has left:

> If mirth you need, why sought you the laurel?
> The flood tide of joy is full in the hall.
>
> [SB23.3.168]

Immediately after declaring Asphodel more beautiful than Vivien, Clarin asks her to dance: "Hear you! Again they dance! / So, Countess Asphodel, a measure, pray! (SB23.3.169). Their departure to dance together leaves Vivien alone on the stage to tell us that her love for them has changed to hate and that she will avenge herself for the slight.

The play is episodic, rather than concentrated and intense. Yet it perhaps presaged the dance plays to come. And like the Noh of Spirits, and like Yeats's own dance plays, the central scene is the manifestation of a spirit, or at least of an abstraction—Vivien's confrontation with Time.

Yeats and the Arthurian Tradition

Yeats's images, even as early as *Vivien and Time*, have the "precision of symbols" (E&I 80), as he said of Shelley's. And as with Shelley this precision arose from both meditation and a fascinated consciousness of tradition (E&I 78–86). The tradition which gives backbone to *Vivien and Time* is the Arthurian legend.

When Yeats wrote the play, sometime between the fall of 1882 and January 1884, the Arthurian tradition was still very popular in literature and, of course, had been popular for much of the century. Let us recall certain highlights. In 1832 Tennyson published "The Lady of Shalott" and planned to write "an epic or a drama of King Arthur" which he thought would take him twenty years and which took him over twice that.[36] Besides Malory's *Morte d'Arthur*, Lady Charlotte Guest's 1838 translation of the *Mabinogion* was grist for Tennyson's mill. In 1842 appeared Tennyson's "Morte d'Arthur" (written about 1835) and the lyrics "Sir Launcelot and Queen Guinevere" and "Sir Galahad." Wagner's *Lohengrin* was first performed in 1850. In 1852 Matthew Arnold published in *Empedocles on Etna and Other Poems* his "Tristram and Iseult," containing the story of Vivien and Merlin in its final section, "Iseult of Britanny."

About 1854 Dante Gabriel Rossetti discovered Malory and began using Arthurian subjects in his painting.[37] In 1856 Robert Southey's edition of the *Morte d'Arthur* appeared and was discovered by the youthful Edward Burne-Jones and William Morris: "So great did their love and veneration for this book become that [they] were almost too shy to speak of it, even among their intimate friends. It was not till a year later, when they heard Rossetti say that the two greatest books in the world were the Bible and the *Morte d'Arthur* that their tongues were unloosed."[38] In 1857 Rossetti, Morris, Burne-Jones and others joined to decorate the new Union Society at Oxford with scenes from the *Morte d'Arthur*. Burne-Jones did a *Nimuë Luring Merlin*, which, like all these paintings, later deteriorated.[39]

In 1858 Morris expressed his passionate love of the legends in *The Defense of Guenevere*. This is also the date of his one surviving oil painting, *Queen Guenevere*. Tennyson's "Nimuë," privately printed in *Enid and Nimuë: The True and the False* (1857), was revised as "Vivien" and included in the first series of *Idylls of the King* (1859), which sold 10,000 copies in a month and continued thereafter to sustain Tennyson as the most popular of English poets. In 1862 G. F. Watts painted his well-known *Sir Galahad*. And 1856 is the date of the first performance of Wagner's *Tristan und Isolde*.

Tennyson's "The Coming of Arthur," "The Holy Grail," and "Pelleas and Ettare" appeared in 1869, "The Last Tournament" in 1871, and "Gareth and Lynette" in 1872. In 1874 Tennyson greatly expanded "Vivien." To this same year belongs Burne-Jones's well-known *The Beguiling of Merlin*, which seems to use objects from both Tennyson's version (Merlin's book) and Arnold's (the flowering thorn trees—though these may have come directly from the French medieval *Romance of Merlin*). This painting was Burne-Jones's first success at his 1877 Grosvenor Gallery exhibition.

In 1882, not long before Yeats wrote *Vivien and Time*, appeared Swinburne's *Tristram of Lyonesse*. In this year also Wagner's *Parsifal* was performed. In 1885, just after the date of *Vivien and Time*, appeared "Balin and Balan," the last of Tennyson's *Idylls*.

All the writers and artists we have mentioned influenced Yeats, and had not John O'Leary pointed him towards Ireland, "The Wanderings of Oisin" of 1889 might well have been but a new treatment of Arthurian romance, the story not of Niamh but of her possible namesake Niniane. For Lucy Paton finds in Yeats's major source, *The Lay of Oisin in the Land of Youth*, "the same theme that forms the kernel of the story told of Niniane, that of a mortal's retention by a fay in an enchanted dwelling" and recognizes the name "Niamh" as the "possible original of *Niniane*."[40] Fortunately for Ireland, Yeats strove instead, in his Fenian and Red Branch tales, for what he thought he saw at last realized in Lady Gregory's *Cuchulain of Muirthemne* (1902), "a book to set beside the *Morte d'Arthur* and the *Mabinogion*" (E&I 188). Because of this new direction, we find little of Arthurian subject matter in Yeats's mature poetry and drama.

We cannot prove that Yeats, like his fictional counterpart Michael Hearne in *The Speckled Bird*, had, at an early age, read of "Merlin under the stone" in Malory's *Morte d'Arthur* (SB 9). It does seem probable, however. It seems likely, too, that he had read some Spenser. *Vivien and Time* may well be one of the works referred to when he says "I had begun to write poetry in imitation of Shelley and of Edmund Spenser, play after play . . . " (Au 66). Yeats's admission, in this same passage, that his "lines but seldom scanned" because he "spoke them slowly as [he] wrote" (Au 67), sounds much like John Butler Yeats's description of the same process in his 7 January 1884 letter to Dowden, cited earlier. Although Yeats confesses in the introduction to his 1906 edition of *Poems of Spenser* that "Until quite lately I knew nothing of Spenser but the parts I had read as a boy," those parts did include "the enchanted persecution [or "procession"] of Amoret,"[41] that is, Book III, Canto XII. If he had read Canto XII, he may also have read "as a boy" Canto III, which tells of Merlin and his cave and of the Ladie of the Lake.

Yeats may even have read a translation of Ariosto, whose Bradamant, like Spenser's Britomart, visits Merlin's cave in Canto III of *Orlando Furioso*. At seventeen Yeats loved "beyond other portraits" Titian's *Ariosto* because of "its grave look, as if waiting for some perfect final event."[42] How could he have failed to find out about Ariosto himself and to dip into his book?

John Eglinton has recorded that in 1883, while still at Erasmus High School, Yeats was an admirer of Arnold's current essays: "Yeats told us that no one could write an essay now except Herbert Spencer and Matthew Arnold."[43] It seems likely that Yeats would have known Arnold's poems as well, perhaps including the story of Merlin and Vivien from "Iseult of Brittany." We do know that he "had read as a boy" (Au 141), in a book belonging to his father, Morris's *The Defence of Guenevere* (1858), which he had liked less than *The Earthly Paradise* (1868–70).

We can assume Yeats's knowledge of Tennyson at an early age. At the High School Yeats had been required "to write an essay on 'Men may rise on stepping-stones of their dead selves to higher things'" (Au 58), lines from *In Memoriam*. Of the Metropolitan School of Art, which he entered in May 1884,[44] four months after the date he placed on *Vivien and Time*, Yeats writes "Of England I alone knew anything. Our ablest student . . . had never heard of Tennyson or Browning, and it was I who carried into the school some knowledge of English poetry . . . " (Au 81).

As we have said, Tennyson's "Merlin and Vivien" was probably the direct source of *Vivien and Time*, which almost seems a sequel to it in which the beguiler is beguiled. In "Merlin and Vivien" a young witch overcomes an old wizard, gaining the secret of his magic book. In *Vivien and Time* the same young witch attempts to win his hour-glass from another old wizard, Time (a "fierce magician" [P 514] in "Time and the Witch Vivien"), and forfeits her life. Yeats's spelling of the name is the same as Tennyson's, whereas Arnold had spelled it "Vivian."

Vivien exhibits the same deplorable lack of respect for age in both Tennyson and Yeats. Tennyson describes her triumph:

> Then crying "I have made his glory mine,"
> And shrieking out "O fool!" the harlot leapt
> Adown the forest, and the thicket closed
> Behind her, and the forest echo'd "fool."
>
> [*Works* 388]

In "Time and the Witch Vivien" Vivien calls Time "a little, light old man," greets him "Ha, ha! ha, ha, ha! / The wrinkled squanderer of human wealth," mocks him with her triumph over Merlin ("Young girls' wits are better / Than old men's any day, as Merlin found"), and ascribes Time's victory at dice to "Chance, and not skill" (P 514–17).

Yeats's Vivien is a nicer person than Tennyson's, who is essentially evil, a lamia—serpentine, and with a death's head showing through her beauty: "How from thy rosy lips of life and love, / Flashed the bare-grinning skeleton of death!" (*Works* 386). In Tennyson, Vivien's pride craves honor from Lancelot and Guinevere even if she has to win it through blackmail:

> . . . Ah little rat that borest in the dyke
> Thy hole by night to let the boundless deep
> Down upon far-off cities while they dance—
> Or dream—of thee they dream'd not—nor of me
> These—ay, but each of either: ride, and dream
> The mortal dream that never yet was mine—
> Ride, ride and dream until ye wake—to me!
> Then, narrow court and lubber King, farewell!
> For Lancelot will be gracious to the rat,
> And our wise Queen, if knowing that I know,
> Will hate, loathe, fear—but honor me the more.
>
> [*Works* 374–75]

Although Vivien does not need a motive to do evil, she gains one in Arthur's rejection of her advances and in the Camelot gossip about her resulting embarrassment (*Works* 375).

Being jealous and murderous herself, Tennyson's Vivien assumes these motives in others. When Merlin describes a chaste lady whose eyes "Waged . . . unwilling tho' successful war / On all the youth," Vivien replies,

> . . . Thy tongue has tript a little: ask thyself.
> The lady never made *unwilling* war
> With those fine eyes: she had her pleasure in it,
> And made her good man jealous with good cause.
> And lived there neither dame nor damsel then
> Wroth at a lover's loss? were all as tame,
> I mean, as noble, as their Queen was fair?
> Not one to flirt a venom at her eyes,
> Or pinch a murderous dust into her drink,
> Or make her paler with a poison'd rose?
>
> [*Works* 382]

That poisoned rose is like the autumn flower with which Yeats's Vivien puts Asphodel into a trance. We have seen that both Yeats's Vivien and his Margaret Leland are jealous and even murderous creatures (latently in Margaret's case). In this they are like Tennyson's Vivien. Yet, as one nineteenth-century critic put it, Tennyson had "invented a Vivienne unknown to any previous writer, the creature and invention of his own brain."[45] None of the various tales of Vivien and Merlin which Paton summarizes have a Vivien as accomplished in evil as is Tennyson's or even Yeats's.[46] Arnold's Vivian is a "false fay,"[47] but no example of her falseness is given except her betrayal of Merlin. Swinburne's

Nimue, only briefly mentioned, is a saint, and in any case Yeats probably did not read in *Tristram of Lyonesse* (1882) how "The heavenly hands of holier Nimue . . . / Should shut [Merlin] in with sleep as kind as death"[48] until shortly before 1 August 1887 when he writes to Katharine Tynan of having read the book "lately" (CL1 29). Surely Yeats got Vivien's bad nature from Tennyson's Vivien.

A common motif in "Merlin and Vivien" and *Vivien and Time* is Merlin's magic book. The book is not mentioned in Malory, nor in Spenser, where the sage is busily "writing strange characters in the ground" (*The Faerie Queene* III.iii.14) like *Ille* in Yeats's "Ego Dominus Tuus" (P 160). There is a "triple claspèd book" which the wise Melissa consults before showing Bradamant the future in Harrington's Ariosto, but Merlin himself consults no book.[49] There is no book in Arnold, nor in Swinburne.

Yeats may simply have associated magic book and magician since his father read Scott's *The Lay of the Last Minstrel* to him when he was a child (Au 46; the book of the magician Michael Scott figures largely in the action). And in Burne-Jones's *The Beguiling of Merlin*, probably based on the Early English Text Society translation of the French medieval *Romance of Merlin*, Nimuë consults a book.[50] Nevertheless the prominence of a magic book in both Tennyson's poem and Yeats's is a definite link. Tennyson's book is most impressive:

> Thou read the book, my pretty Vivien!
> O ay, it is but twenty pages long,
> But every page having an ample marge,
> And every marge enclosing in the midst
> A square of text that looks a little blot,
> The text no larger than the limbs of fleas;
> And every square of text an awful charm,
> Writ in a language that has long gone by.
> So long, that mountains have arisen since
> With cities on their flanks—thou read the book!
> And every margin scribbled, crost, and cramm'd
> With comment, densest condensation, hard
> To mind and eye; but the long sleepless nights
> Of my long life have made it easy to me.
> And none can read the text, not even I;
> And none can read the comment but myself;
> And in the comment did I find the charm.
> O, the results are simple; a mere child
> Might use it to the harm of any one,
> And never could undo it. . . .
>
> [*Works* 383]

In *Vivien and Time* it is indeed a "mere child" who recites the spell from the book—now an enormous volume that becomes fiery hot when the spell is read. Vivien's Page does not know the evil he is doing and cannot reverse it once the spell is broken.

Another bit of evidence that Yeats is thinking principally of Tennyson's "Merlin and Vivien" is that he, like Tennyson, has Vivien imprison Merlin in an oak, rather than a hawthorne, as do Arnold, Burne-Jones, and Swinburne. "No taste have I for slumber 'neath an oak" (P 515) says Time in "Time and the Witch Vivien." This seems a direct allusion to Tennyson's poem.

Vivien and Time and "Time and the Witch Vivien" have clearly visualized situations. Yeats would have been aware of—and would have seen if he could—representations by Pre-Raphaelite and symbolist artists of the subject of his play.

It has been noted above that after Rossetti discovered Malory in 1854 the Pre-Raphaelites and their followers frequently treated Arthurian material. Yeats says that when he was seventeen (1882–83) he "was already an old-fashioned brass cannon full of shot" (Au 116), and it is well to remember that Pre-Raphaelitism and symbolism were a considerable part of what he was loaded with. He was "in all things Pre-Raphaelite" (Au 114). His father had told him about Rossetti and Blake when he was fifteen or sixteen, and Rossetti's *Dante's Dream* at Liverpool fascinated him at about the same time (Au 114–15). His father's friends during the family's first stay at Bedford Park (1879–81) "were painters who had been influenced by the Pre-Raphaelite movement" (Au 44).

Therefore we may be sure that when he created the enchantress who is the heroine of *Vivien and Time* and "Time and the Witch Vivien" he had very much in mind the enchantresses painted by Pre-Raphaelite and symbolist painters. We may begin with a "portrait" of Vivien herself.

In 1863 Frederick Sandys painted a *Vivien*, head proudly lifted against a background of peacock plumes. She wears a rich necklace and a gown patterned with interlocking forms. Her right hand holds a sprig of flowers and leaves, and her left hand relinquishes (or reaches toward) a fruit.[51] The same model (probably Keomy, a gypsy girl who was Sandys's mistress for a time) posed for his *Morgan le Fay* (1862–63), in which the witch is making incantations in a corner full of "*Magical instruments*" (P 514) like those in "Time and the Witch Vivien."[52] It is not hard to imagine this as a picture of Vivien herself conjuring, especially as the model of Sandys's *Vivien* was used: the leopard skin Sandys's Morgan le Fay wears hangs over the back of a chair in act I, scene 1, of *Vivien and Time* (SB23.3.166). Yeats's father visited Sandys's studio in June 1868, showed him his pictures, and received his praise

Figure 1. J. B. Yeats, Illustration for "King Goll. An Irish Legend," by W. B. Yeats
(*From* The Leisure Hour, *September 1887; by courtesy of the British Library*)

Figure 2. Frederick Sandys, *Vivien*, 1863
Oil on canvas, 25" × 20½"
(*Published by permission of the City of Manchester Art Galleries*)

Figure 3. Frederick Sandys, *Morgan le Fay*, 1862–63
Oil on panel, 24¾" × 17½"
(*Published by permission of Birmingham Museums and Art Gallery*)

Figure 4. Walter Crane, Frontispiece to *The Necklace of Princess Fiorimonde* (From Mary Augusta De Morgan, The Necklace of Princess Fiorimonde [London: Macmillan, 1880])

Figure 5. Sir Edward Burne-Jones, *Merlin and Nimuë*, 1861
Gouache, 25" × 19¾"
(*Crown copyright Victoria and Albert Museum*)

Figure 6. Sir Edward Burne-Jones, *The Beguiling of Merlin*, 1874
Oil, 72½" × 43¼"
(*The Lady Lever Art Gallery, Port Sunlight, Cheshire*)

Figure 7. Sir Edward Burne-Jones, *Witch's Tree*, 1882–88 (*From Edward Burne-Jones,* The Flower Book [*London: Fine Art Society, 1905*]; *by courtesy of the Jones Library, Amherst, Massachusetts*)

Figure 8. Moritz Retzsch, *Die Schachspiele* [Chess Games] (*By permission of the British Library*)

Figure 9. J. Noel Paton, *Death and Life-in-Death*
(*From Samuel Taylor Coleridge,* The Rime of the Ancient Mariner [London: Art-Union of London, 1863])

Figure 10. Pierre Puvis de Chavannes, *Death and the Maidens* (*The Reaper*), 1872 Oil on canvas, 57½" × 46⅛" (*Sterling and Francine Clark Art Institute, Williamstown, Massachusetts*)

and encouragement as well as an invitation for further visits, so that there would have been a family acquaintance with Sandys's work.[53] A drawing, *Morgan le Fay,* appeared as a supplement to *The British Architect* in October 1879, four years before we believe Yeats to have been writing his play.[54] Burne-Jones, too, did a *Morgan le Fay,* a gouache of 1862, very cool and beautiful, though much touched-up since the original date. Morgan le Fay, like Vivien in Yeats's play, is surrounded by magical flowers.[55]

In Yeats's play Vivien sees herself as a successor to Circe: "Great Circe, Circe, now thy fame is fled / Since mine was born . . ." (SB23.3.175). And Circe is another enchantress painted by the Pre-Raphaelites. Yeats could certainly have known, or at least known about, Burne-Jones's *The Wine of Circe* (1863–69), exhibited at the Old Water-colour Society in 1869 and then attacked in the *Art Journal,* though one of the best works of the period and the inspiration of a poem by Rossetti. The room in which Circe bends to poison the bright wine for her "charmèd cup" (SB23.3.165) was originally as Gothic as that in Sandys's *Morgan le Fay* but in the end became classical. "The ships had been moved back, light flooded the room, and the design was controlled less by the need to create atmosphere than by carefully balanced linear rhythms."[56] Yeats, interestingly enough, also chooses a classical scene for his play, even though his characters and certain appurtenances are indeed medieval. His "Dedication" sings of a palace built of "dreamland marble" (SB23.3.161) with pillars and statues. Vivien arranges flowers *"in a large antique vase"* (SB23.3.176). The scene of "Time and the Witch Vivien" is *"A marble-flagged, pillared room."* Though *"Magical instruments"* are collected *"in one corner,"* there is *"A fountain in the centre"* (P 514). Such a scene recalls classical interiors painted at about the date of Yeats's play by Lord Leighton, by Sir Lawrence Alma-Tadema, and by Sir Edward J. Poynter. Walter Crane's frontispiece to Mary A. De Morgan's *The Necklace of Princess Fiorimonde*,[57] though not an interior, shows us a lady like Vivien whose "image" and "beautiful . . . roseate fingers" are reflected, along with "the little golden greedy carp" (P 514), in a marble fountain. Marble statues, like those which figure in the "Dedication," line the walk, and a pillared temple is in the distance. These pictures are mentioned here, not as influences, but to show how representative of their time *Vivien and Time* and "Time and the Witch Vivien" were.

One year before Yeats wrote *Vivien and Time* several of the motifs he was to borrow from "Snow White" and "Sleeping Beauty" appeared in illustrations by Walter Crane to *Household Stories, from the collection of the Brothers Grimm,* translated by Lucy Crane: a frontispiece of the sleeping Briar Rose being discovered by the Prince; a full-page picture of the evil Queen giving Snow White the poisoned apple, a head-piece of Snow White in a trance, and a tail-piece of the Queen looking proudly and cruelly into her magic mirror.[58] Yeats had read both Grimm and Anderson as a boy in Sligo (Au 47), but he would have been interested in these illustrations by a follower of the Pre-Raphaelites for a book from which he was constantly borrowing themes for his play. Yeats later met Crane "constantly" (Au 140) at William Morris's suppers.

The Sleeping Beauty was, of course, one of Burne-Jones's favorite themes. In the early 1860s he had designed a set of tales illustrating Perrault's story. A "small *Briar Rose* series" was done in 1870–73. And in 1873 he began a series of four larger canvases finished only in 1890. Another of his favorite themes was Merlin and Nimuë. He chose "Merlin imprisoned beneath a stone by the Damsel of the Lake" as subject for his mural in the ill-fated Oxford Union series of 1857.[59] In 1861 he did a gouache of *Merlin and Nimuë,* in which the two stand near the open tomb. This is the most dramatic of his handlings of the theme. The crisis is at its climax—Merlin is not yet defeated. Nimuë, her back to him, holds the magic book and glances back at him, while he, gripped with sudden tension, realizes too late that she will take advantage of his trust. Dark hills and glimmering water and sky frame the lonely scene.[60]

The well-known oil *The Beguiling of Merlin* is dated 1874, though finished and first exhibited in 1877.[61] The gray-haired Merlin sinks down, falling into his last sleep, but fixing glazing eyes on Vivien, who stands erect among triumphant blossoms, her back to Merlin as she holds the book of power safely out of his reach, her head turned towards him as she observes, with a basilisk stare, the effect of her magic. Her right knee is bent, and she will hurry away when satisfied that he is helpless. Merlin sinks like a corpse among flowers as the ancient hawthorn tree overwhelms the scene with fresh blossoms. Its serpentine branches, mediating between the tree and the blossoms, seem the struggles between the sexes and between age and youth. Ironically, the figure of the erect young woman is doubled in the bole of the old tree, while declining branches of flowers double the fall of Merlin, easing him gently down. Merlin's left index finger points, unconsciously, towards a blue-white iris springing up in the foreground and perhaps announcing a resolution of the two principles. This iris counters Merlin's declining age with erect new growth. Its simple thrusting up out of the ground counters also the twisted poses of Nimuë and the tree. Nimuë's head is bent like the tree's crown as she turns toward Merlin. As we have said earlier, the story of *Vivien and Time,* like the story of *Merlin and Vivien,* shows the struggle of youth and age. The flowers and youth win in Burne-Jones's representation of the latter; the flowers are frozen and Time triumphant in Yeats's play.[62]

In 1882 Burne-Jones started a group of "water-colour designs for a flower book based on the visual images inspired by flowers."[63] "Witch's Tree" again shows an erect Vivien and a reclining Merlin in the hawthorn tree. Vivien, crowned, stands at the left holding a stringed instrument by which, rather than a book, she has put Merlin to sleep. Merlin is much older than in the previous conceptions, white-bearded and in a black robe. He is motionless, sound asleep, and his mouth is open, suggesting a gentle snore. Vivien, in autumnal brown, is facing Merlin, bending towards him quietly like a mother towards a sleeping child before she tip-toes from the nursery. Although there is ambiguity—she may be waiting to see if her poison has worked—there is none of the tension of *The Beguiling of Merlin*. The serpentine branches only to rise to support the unthreatening old man. The hawthorn blossoms actually have begun to cover his robe. Moreover, they are growing between us and Vivien's back, binding her in with her ancient lover. She will have to push them aside if she leaves, which as yet she had made no motion to do. The design is altogether more gentle and restful than that of *The Beguiling of Merlin*. One could do worse than sleep forever in that bower as the music dies away and the hawthorn blossoms mount everywhere. There is little likelihood that Yeats could have seen any of this series, done 1882–98, before finishing his play. But it is interesting that so near to the same date the poet and the painter were surrounding the Vivien story with symbolic flowers.

Burne-Jones's depictions are beautiful representations of how the youthful Vivien traps wise old Merlin in his own snares. Yeats would later see his enchantress as the *Leanhaun Shee* (fairy mistress) of Celtic literature. She is Niamh of "The Wanderings of Oisin," the perpetually young fairy with whom Oisin lives for 300 years. On leaving her and touching the soil of Ireland he becomes an ancient man exiled in mortality. Or Yeats would see her as the Woman of the Sidhe in *The Only Jealousy of Emer*, who wished to carry off the aging Cuchulain. But the subject of our present play is not the story of "Merlin and Vivien" but of *Vivien and Time*. Instead of the beguiling of aged wisdom by youthful beauty we get the sequel to that story in which an aged figure—Time—swiftly defeats all the youthful beauty's plots and overcomes her. In *Vivien and Time* Yeats combines two archetypal plots. He ends the story of the enchantress with the story of Death and the Maiden.

Somewhere there must be the perfect illustration for the climax of Yeats's play. The scene of the young woman playing a game of chance or skill with hoary Time is immediately recognizable and visually evocative. We envision it, and we have seen it before. But where? Certainly it is related to the Death and the Maiden motif. One thinks of Schubert's song and of late medieval and Renaissance pictures of women being accosted by grisly skeletons. Often the women primp before a mirror, like Vivien. And often the skeletons carry Time's hour-glass.[64]

Missing in all these pictures is the theme of trying to defeat the holder of the hour-glass in a game of chance or skill. However, Wirth shows a fifteenth-century copper plate engraving of a premonitory skeleton playing chess with an old king while a court of secular and clerical figures watch and the Angel of Death, holding an hour-glass, presides. The King turns away from the board as Death is about to make the winning move.[65]

Yeats may have known some treatment of this motif such as the drawing "Die Schachspiele" by Moritz Retzsch described by George Eliot in *Daniel Deronda* (1876): "Most of us remember Retzsch's drawing of destiny in the shape of Mephistopheles playing at chess with man for his soul, a game in which we may imagine the clever adversary making a feint of unintended moves so as to set the beguiled mortal on carrying his defensive pieces away from the true point of attack."[66]

The nearest pre-1884 analogue we have so far been able to find for the situation in "Time and the Witch Vivien" in which a woman plays dice or chess with Time or Death is section III of "The Rime of the Ancient Mariner," and there the female Life-in-Death plays dice with Death not for her own life, but for the Mariner's. What is more, she wins!

> And is that Woman all her crew?
> Is that a DEATH? and are there two?
> Is DEATH that woman's mate?
>
> *Her* lips were red, *her* looks were free,
> Her locks were yellow as gold:
> Her skin was as white as leprosy,
> The Night-mare LIFE-IN-DEATH was she,
> Who thicks man's blood with cold.
>
> The naked hulk alongside came,
> And the twain were casting dice;
> The game is done! I've won! I've won!
> Quoth she, and whistles thrice.[67]

Yeats's Vivien does not win the dice-throw, nor is she supernatural. Yet she is a witch, and she indeed provides a life-in-death for her victims, making them wander forever in search of a phantom.

Although in *The Road to Xanadu* John Livingston Lowes cites Gothic horror stories in general, the only specific source he gives for

Coleridge's incident is the tale "of one Falkenberg, who, for murder done, is doomed to wander forever on the sea, accompanied by two spectral forms, one white, one black. . . . And in a ship with all sails set, the two forms play at dice for the wanderer's soul."[68] This is not at all the situation in Yeats's play, but that situation could have been suggested by Coleridge's poem as remembered in an illustration. Illustrators inevitably leave out of the composition the Mariner for whose soul the dice game is played and concentrate on Death and the woman. Thus the situation in the illustrations looks closer than is the text to the Death and the Maiden pictures, with the added element of the dice game. Of seven illustrated editions published before 1884 one might point to that by J. Noel Paton, an associate of the Pre-Raphaelites.[69] The jubilance of Life-in-Death would be like that of Vivien had she won her wager with Time.

To conclude, we may look at two pictures superficially very much alike. The general theme of Time (or Death) and the Maiden is treated by Burne-Jones in a 1860 decoration on the panel of his upright piano. Seven maidens droop in melancholy poses listening to one of their number play a lute. Sunflowers, also in varying poses, stand behind them. At the doorway, pulling the bell-rope, stands a crowned and shrouded Death, a scythe over his arm.[70] We mention this to point up the contrast with the very beautiful *Death and the Maidens* (or *The Reaper*) of 1872 by Puvis de Chavannes,[71] a painter for whom Yeats later expressed great admiration (Au 550). The point is not that Yeats knew either picture, but that Puvis has taken the youth-age alternation one step beyond the victory of Time. As Vivien defeats age in the Merlin and Vivien story, and is in turn defeated by Time in "Time and the Witch Vivien," so Time in turn is defeated, at least momentarily, in Puvis's picture. Time or Death, the old man with the scythe, has indeed cut swathes of flowers, and the forest to the right of the picture is dark with shadow. But in the center six maidens move happily in the sun, and they have taken the flowers Time has cut down and are admiring and playing with them. Time's havoc merely enriches the perpetual present in which—to quote Wallace Stevens—"maidens die, to the auroral / Celebration of a maiden's choral."[72] At their feet the grim reaper lies asleep—at least for the moment.

So much for *Vivien and Time*. John Butler Yeats's portrait of Yeats as "King Goll" was done almost four years after the date of Yeats's first play. And it illustrates a poem written after Yeats had decided to devote himself to Irish subjects. But since it shows the poet with harp in hand, it may serve to represent Clarin, the first of many portraits in Yeats's poetry of himself as bard. Unfortunately, he is ripping out the strings instead of playing them properly, but then Clarin in *Vivien and*

Time, being acted by unmusical Yeats, can only hold, not play, the instrument and only speak, not sing, the words.

After writing *Vivien and Time* Yeats first mentions Arthurian matter in his published poems and plays in *The Island of Statues* (written after *Vivien and Time* in the summer of 1884; published in 1885). The third sleeper awakened from enchantment by Naschina asks "Doth still the man whom each stern rover fears— / The austere Arthur—rule from Uther's chair?" (P 481). Yeats liked this effect enough to use it in the 1906 revision of *The Shadowy Waters*. Aibric, falling under the enchantment of Forgael's harp, murmurs "What name had that dead king? Arthur of Britain? / No, no—not Arthur" (P 424).

In the [1 August 1887] letter to Katharine Tynan quoted above, Yeats contrasts "the aristocratic young ladies in the Idyls of the King" with Swinburne's Mary Tudor. Tennyson's heroines are "less heroic" than those of Swinburne, Morris, and Rossetti and "less passionate and splendid but realized as far as they go more completely—much more like actual every day people . . ." (CL1 30). If Vivien may be thought of as a heroine, this description includes her. In his 1892 review of Tennyson's last book, Yeats recalls that *The Idylls of the King* was a triumph (UP1 252).

By 1893 it is clear that in Yeats's view Malory, along with Chaucer and the ballads, represented in English literature the stage of Homer in Greek literature, that all-important "period of narrative poetry" (UP1 269–70) out of which the periods of drama and of lyric poetry grew. This conception had developed but had not changed when Yeats wrote in *A Vision* (1925) that "The period from 1005 to 1180 is attributed in the diagram to the first two gyres of our millenium, and what interests me in this period, which corresponds to the Homeric period two thousand years before, is the creation of the Arthurian Tales and Romanesque architecture" (AV-A 198).

In 1895 Yeats deplores the present age of criticism, a literature of "wise comments" in which "Arthur and his Court are nothing, but the many-coloured lights that play about them are as beautiful as the lights from cathedral windows." Attacking the "criticism of life" in Victorian treatments of the heroic stories, he hopes for an age of imagination or revelation like that of the ancients or the Elizabethans which "created beings who made the people of this world seem but shadows" (E&I 196–97). From 1896 to 1902 or 1903 Yeats was actively engaged with his friends in creating Celtic mysteries based on the four sacred symbols of Celtic heathendom.[73] Yet this activity was a Grail quest: "The Four Jewels . . . foreshadowed the Christian symbolism of the Saint Grail, whose legends Willie loved to trace to Ireland."[74]

The final version of *The Speckled Bird* (February 1902–May 1903) gives fictional accounts based on Yeats's work on the mysteries with MacGregor Mathers. A convert draws

> a series of diagrams representing the ascent of the soul above the slopes of a sacred mountain towards the castle of the Grail, the stages of [this] ascent corresponding to its ascent through earth and water and air, the castle itself being the divine fire.
> Another day while they were elaborating a diagram of a symbolical wood where Arthur's knights were to hunt symbolical creatures, Michael thought he saw a faint flicker of fire on the ceiling, and then Maclagan saw the whole room become full of fire. [SB 80]

"The poems of the Grail, that are so plentiful," lack "the rich life that one feels behind the great poems" because

> the poets of the Grail have had no initiation behind them to fix the images of their poems and to so weave image to image that, when one is named, all float up in the mind and create so great a reverie about [the] dish and the[?] cup and about the more ancient images that are behind them and about the illusions and dangers of the quest that a common beauty would all but weave all the poems into one great epic. [SB 206]

The mysteries were to create a new literature. "Young poets and painters" were to "come to this order of the Grail" whose myth "is as interwoven with the scenery and the history of England and Wales, as the myths of Greece were with the scenery and history of Greece." In the pictures or poems of the genius of this group, "Men will see . . . , besides the charm that his genius gives him, the fanaticism of the saints or of those that fling themselves upon spears" (SB 207).

No doubt William Morris was one of the "poets of the Grail" who failed to base his art on a religious initiation. In "The Happiest of Poets" (1902), Yeats asserted that Morris "wrote indeed of nothing but of the quest of the Grail, but it was the Heathen Grail that gave every man his chosen food, and not the Grail of Malory or Wagner; and he came at last to praise, as other men have praised the martyrs of religion or of passion, men with lucky eyes and men whom all women love" (E&I 55). Spenser, too, had missed the Grail of Malory. In Yeats's 1902 introduction to his selection from Spenser, Yeats argued that, "Full of the spirit of the Renaissance, at once passionate and artificial, looking out upon the world now as craftsman, now as connoisseur, he was to found his art upon theirs rather than upon the more humane, the more noble, the less intellectual art of Malory and the Minstrels" (E&I 356).

The new Celtic movement was to be a resurgence of that Celtic fountain, which "of all the fountains of the passions and beliefs of ancient times in Europe . . . alone has been for centuries close to the main river of European literature" and "has again and again brought 'the vivifying spirit' 'of excess' into the arts of Europe." Here in "The Celtic Element in Literature" (1897) Yeats declares that "the legends of Arthur and his Table, and of the Holy Grail, once, it seems, the cauldron of an Irish god, changed the literature of Europe, and, it may be, changed, as it were, the very roots of man's emotions by their influence on the spirit of chivalry and on the spirit of romance . . ." (E&I 185). Only the Scandinavian tradition (in Wagner, Morris, and the early Ibsen) has rivalled in "passionate element" the "still unfaded legends of Arthur and of the Holy Grail; and now a new fountain of legends . . . is being opened, the fountain of Gaelic legends . . ." (E&I 186). Moreover, this process is occurring at a time "when the imagination of the world is ready as it was at the coming of the tales of Arthur and of the Grail for a new intoxication. . . . The arts by brooding upon their own intensity have become religious, and are seeking, as I think Verhaeren has said, to create a sacred book" (E&I 187).

As part of the new "religious" movement based on old legends, particularly the Celtic, Yeats welcomed in an 1898 review Ernest Rhys's *Welsh Ballads*. He quoted one poem which remembered "the world's great mystery,— / The grave of Arthur." He praised most another Arthurian translation: "'The House of Hendré,' which is inspired by some legend of a poet who saw in a vision the seven heavens, and Merlin and Arthur there, and the heroes and the poets about them, and his own seat waiting, and so longed for death. . . ." This he thought "the best of the original poems" with "a melancholy, like that of curlews crying over some desolate marsh . . ." (UP2 93-94).

When in the late 1890s Yeats first knew Lady Gregory, "the *Morte d'Arthur* was her book of books" (UP2 467), and undoubtedly she stimulated him to read Malory in the period 1899-1902.[75] In a 1902 postscript to "The Celtic Element in Literature" he claims to have found in her *Cuchulain of Muirthemne* "a book to set beside the *Morte d'Arthur* and the *Mabinogion*" (E&I 188).

These same books, the *Morte d'Arthur* and the *Mabinogion*, are the first to interest the boy Michael Hearne in the final version of *The Speckled Bird*. In them he seeks not amusement but belief. He has a more religious than literary interest, yet he thinks "not indeed of devil or angel, God or saint, but[?] of Merlin under the stone" (SB 9). God the Father in a certain religious picture looks to him like Merlin or Taliesin (SB 12). He delights most in "the story of the Grail and the stories of Merlin and Morgan le Fay . . ." (SB 9).

Yeats himself had experience of "unintentionally" casting "a glamour, an enchantment" (in other words, a mild hypnosis) over friends. In "Magic" (1901) he based on this fact a belief "that men could cast intentionally a far stronger enchantment, a far stronger glamour, over the more sensitive people of ancient times, or that men can still do so where the old order of life remains unbroken. . . . Why should not enchanters like him in the *Morte d'Arthur* make troops of horse seem but grey stones?" (E&I 42). The "wizard that changed a troop of horses into grey stones" is one of the Arthurian images in *The Speckled Bird* which "expressed by . . . extravagance an energy or a magnificence or a mystery not in the sober images of life" (SB 9-10). That Yeats did not get his wizard from the *Morte d'Arthur*, as he misremembered, but from Whitley Stokes's 1890 *Lives of the Saints, from the Book of Lismore* (SB 10n15), only shows how thoroughly Yeats had confounded the Irish and the Arthurian traditions.

"Under the Moon" (P 82-83), first published on 15 June 1901, seems a *tour de force*, an advertisement of Yeats's program for placing *Cuchulain of Muirthemne* beside the *Morte d'Arthur* and the *Mabinogion*. The evocative list of names juxtaposes people and places from Arthurian tales, from the *Mabinogion*, and from Irish myth and legend. The first images, however, are Arthurian:

> I have no happiness in dreaming of Brycelinde,
> Nor Avalon the grass-green hollow, nor Joyous Isle,[76]
> Where one found Lancelot crazed and hid him for a while. . . .

Brycelinde, the wood Broceliande in which Vivien beguiled Merlin, is thus the most prominent image in the poem, but Vivien is not named as one of the "women whose beauty was folded in dismay" that Yeats is trying in the poem not to think about.

In "Speaking to the Psaltery" (1902), Yeats tells us that "Sir Ector's lamentations over the dead Launcelot out of the *Morte d'Arthur*" were among the verses spoken by Florence Farr as she "sat with a beautiful stringed instrument upon her knee, her fingers passing over the strings" (E&I 13). Yeats's preoccupation with "cantillation" at this period is another form of the fascination which Arthurian ballads on the lips of a troubadour had for him from first to last. It ends only with the posthumous publication of "The Statesman's Holiday," a parody of his "early sentimental poems" (Ex 452):

> Here's a Montenegrin lute
> And its old sole string
> Makes me sweet music
> And I delight to sing:
> *Tall dames go walking in grass green Avalon.*
>
> [P 583]

It begins with Clarin-Yeats, who in *Vivien and Time* speaks the ballads he cannot sing.

Also in 1902, Yeats added to *The Celtic Twilight* a section on "Miraculous Creatures." These contemporary Irish phenomena in the "Enchanted Woods" are "of the race of the white stag that flits in and out of the tales of Arthur, and of the evil pig that slew Diarmuid where Ben Bulben mixes with the sea wind" (Myth 65). (Again Yeats has melded contemporary spiritualistic phenomena with both Irish and Arthurian myth.) Followed by a white bracket and a lady on a white palfrey, the stag bounds into the room at the wedding celebration of Arthur and Guinevere (Malory III.v) and is the cause of numerous adventures, in one of which the lady is kidnapped and on her return proves to be Nimuë (III.xiv). The beguiling of Merlin by Nimuë takes place in the very next chapter (IV.1).[77] The white stag was a male symbol in a dream Mrs. Yeats had one night in January 1919 when Yeats himself dreamed of a female symbol, the Glencar waterfall.[78] "Towards Break of Day" was the result:

> But she that beside me lay
> Had watched in bitterer sleep
> The marvellous stag of Arthur,
> That lofty white stag, leap
> From mountain steep to steep.
>
> [P 185]

Yeats's determination to graft the Irish onto the Arthurian comes out even in his 1905 formula for that most important mark of the Irish Renaissance, the Anglo-Irish idiom as it appeared in the plays of Lady Gregory and of Synge: "the beautiful English which has grown up in Irish-speaking districts, and takes its vocabulary from the time of Malory and of the translators of the Bible, but its idiom and its vivid metaphor from Irish" (E&I 299).

Yeats's quest for wisdom would always take the form of a quest for love, his quest for love that of a quest for wisdom. In a note to *The Wind Among the Reeds* (1899), which was published a year before *The Shadowy Waters* (1900), Yeats claims to have found in the *Encyclopedia Britannica* that "Tristram, in the oldest form of the tale of Tristram and Iseult, drank wisdom, and madness the shadow of wisdom, and not love, out of the magic cup" (P 623).[79] This may explain why *The Shadowy Waters*, which reminds us so much of Wagner's *Tristan und Isolde*, nevertheless has, in comparison to the opera, much more emphasis on the supersensual and less on the sensual.[80]

Nevertheless there is no asceticism in Yeats's play. AE, preferring the earlier end of *The Shadowy Waters*, commented that "Merely because . . . [love] changes from a mortal world into an immortal [it] does not change from sexual to spiritual. It can only do so by sacrifice and experience. . . ."[81] But Yeats was finally and unashamedly seeking not a merely spiritual love, but one which stands, immortally, "In all the vigour of its blood" (P 269), as he wrote in "Tom the Lunatic" (1932).

As Yeats was glad to connect wisdom with the great lover Tristram, so he was glad to connect love with the wise Merlin. Other than *Vivien and Time,* Yeats's most interesting citation of the story of Merlin and Vivien, or in this instance "Niniene," is of William Wells Newell's *King Arthur and the Table Round* (1897). He alludes to it in 1914, 1925, and 1935—always as from Chrétien de Troyes, although it is actually from the *Huth Merlin.*[82] A digression here may help us to understand the importance of this citation. In early unpublished versions of *The Shadowy Waters* Yeats has his hero Forgael reject Dectora. He seeks an immortal love, and when he sees that Dectora is not an immortal he goes celibate to death and eternity.[83] In the published versions Forgael and Dectora seek the other world together. AE guesses that "when the poet came himself to love, the thought of that lonely journey to the Everliving grew alien to his mood."[84]

Yeats's meeting Maud Gonne may not, however, have had more effect than his becoming in the early 1890s a member of a cabalistic society, The Order of the Golden Dawn, and a student of the work of William Blake. Yeats's thought in *The Shadowy Waters* is cabalistic: "The reunion of God and His *Shekhinah* constitutes the meaning of redemption. In this state, again seen in purely mythical terms, the masculine and feminine are carried back to their original unity, and in this uninterrupted union of the two, the powers of generation will once again flow unimpeded through all the worlds."[85]

"Swedenborg, Mediums, and the Desolate Places" (1914) contains Yeats's earliest allusion to this tale. Yeats is distinguishing Swedenborg, who "but half felt, half saw, half tasted the kingdom of heaven" (Ex 42), from Blake. The "impulse towards what is definite and sensuous . . . went out of Swedenborg when he turned from vision . . . whereas Blake carried it to a passion and made it the foundation of his thought" (Ex 43). In Blake's work, although we find there "the peaceful Swedenborgian heaven," we achieve that heaven "by no obedience but by the energy that 'is eternal delight,' for 'the treasures of heaven are not negations of passion but realities of intellect from which the passions emanate uncurbed in their eternal glory.'" For Blake, "those who have come to freedom" live "above good and evil, neither accused, nor yet accusing, . . . their senses sharpened by eternity." These souls are higher than those exalted by theology. "Merlin, who in the verses of Chrétien de Troyes was laid in the one tomb with dead lovers, is very near and the saints are far away" (Ex 44). Stirred by natural "as by human beauty, he saw all Merlin's people, spirits 'of vegetable nature' and faeries whom we call 'accident and chance.' He made possible a religious life to those who had seen the painters and poets of the romantic movement succeed to theology . . ." (Ex 45).

In the 1925 *A Vision* Yeats summarizes:

> When Merlin in Crétien de Troyes loved Ninian he showed her a cavern adorned with gold mosaics and made by a prince for his beloved, and told her that those lovers died upon the same day and were laid "in the chamber where they found delight." He thereupon lifted a slab of red marble that his art alone could lift and showed them wrapped in winding sheets of white samite. The tomb remained open, for Ninian asked that she and Merlin might return to the cavern and spend their night near those dead lovers, but before night came Merlin grew sad and fell asleep, and she and her attendants took him "by head and foot" and laid him "in the tomb and replaced the stone," for Merlin had taught her the magic words, and "from that hour none beheld Merlin dead or alive." [AV-A 197]

The chamber carved from the rock, the gold mosaics, the tomb covered with a red cloth embroidered with beasts worked in gold are all described by Newell.[86]

This passage is Yeats's lengthiest reference to the tale of Merlin and Vivien (or Ninian). It appears in section four of "Dove or Swan," Yeats's account of the historical aspects of his "system," in the section "A.D. 1050 to the Present Day" (AV-A 196–215).[87] Perhaps Yeats sees the romantic movement as understanding at last "something [which] must have happened in the courts and castles . . . that could not find its full explanation for a thousand years" (AV-A 196–97). Romance replaced theology. A Byzantine bishop saw in a certain female singer "a beauty that would be sanctified," while in another singer Harun Al-Raschid saw a beauty "which was its own sanctity, and it was this latter sanctity, come back from the first Crusade or up from Arabian Spain or half Asiatic Provence and Sicily, that created romance. What forgotten reverie, what initiation it may be, separated wisdom from the monastery and, creating Merlin, joined it to passion" (AV-A 197).

The initiation and reverie which created Merlin and joined wisdom to passion were, Yeats thought, missing from modern poems of the Grail: "The poets of the Grail have had no initiation behind them to fix the images of their poems and to so weave image to image that, when one is named, all float up in the mind and create so great a reverie . . ." (SB 206). And we have seen that the purpose of the Celtic mysteries was to provide again that initiation and reverie.

Yeats reinforced the example of Merlin in the tomb of the dead lovers with the examples of Parsifal's replacing church ceremony with the love trance and of his praying to his lady rather than to God or the Virgin when going into battle (AV-A 198).[88]

In his essay on "The Mandukya Upanishad" (1935) Yeats has harmonized the love trance with Tantric worship, "where a man and woman, when in sexual union, transfigure each other's images into the masculine and feminine characters of God." He speaks of married people who practice "a meditation, wherein the man seeks the divine Self as present in his wife, the wife the divine Self as present in the man," and asks "Did this worship, this meditation, establish among us romantic love, was it prevalent in Northern Europe during the twelfth century?" (E&I 484). The love trances of Gawain and Parsifal are here his primary examples of romantic love, with Merlin as a supporting example:

> In the German epic *Parsifal* Gawain drives a dagger through his hand without knowing it during his love-trance, Parsifal falls into such a trance when a drop of blood upon snow recalls to his mind a tear upon his wife's cheek, and before he awakes overthrows many knights. When riding into battle he prays not to God but to his wife, and she, falling into trance, protects him. One thinks, too, of that mysterious poem by Chrétien de Troyes, wherein Vivien, having laid Merlin, personification of wisdom, by the side of dead lovers, closes their tomb. [E&I 484-85]

Vivien and Time, then, is an example of the fascination with the stories of Arthur—and particularly with the figure of the magician Merlin—which Yeats felt all his life. Merlin and Arthur are not necessary to the bare plot of Yeats's first play. They are brought in because of his early awareness of the need of myth to support the meaning of his story and because of his great and lasting interest in the Arthurian tradition. But *Vivien and Time* is unique in Arthurian literature. Everyone knows what happened to Merlin. But what, in the end, happened to Vivien? Only Yeats, so far as we know, adds this tale to the Arthurian cycle.

A Description of the Manuscripts of *Vivien and Time*

National Library of Ireland Ms. 30,357 is a maroon notebook measuring 18 cm (7³/₃₂") wide by 22.8 cm (8³¹/₃₂") high and has on the cover in black ink in Yeats's hand, "Viven [sic] and Time / a dramatic poem / January the 8th / 1884." This stiff paper cover is textured with tiny diamond shapes (about .15 cm). On all four sides, about 1.1 cm in from the edge and parallel to each edge, a border line about .2 cm wide is impressed into the cover. At each corner two of these lines cross at right angles. In the center of the cover is impressed a monogram of the letters "M S S" superimposed one on another. In the lower right-hand corner the signature "W. B. Yeats" appears in the same black ink. The same signature, in a faded grey-brown ink, appears on the inside of the front cover.

The notebook paper is a rather heavy (20 lb.?) laid with line and chain marks but no watermarks. Sheets originally measuring 35.2 cm (13⅞") wide were folded in the middle to make folios 17.6 cm (6¹⁵⁄₁₆") wide. The height is 22.9 cm (9"). This white paper is lined every .9 cm (1¹⁄₃₁") in a violet blue, 23 lines to a page, with a top margin of about 2 cm (²⁵⁄₃₂") and a bottom margin of about 1 cm (¹³⁄₃₂"). The sheets are sewn at the center fold. At present, counting some stubs, there are 42 folios. But folios 20–21 and 23–24 are detached from those with which they were originally joined and are loose in the notebook. This is significant in that it is just before folio 25 that the scene between Vivien and Time, now restored, would have appeared. The removal of the pages containing that scene has apparently caused the separation of the loose folios. Folios 8, 28, and 38–42 are mere stubs, the pages having been cut out. Marks on the stub of folio 8 show that both recto and verso had been written on, but there seems no break in the continuity. We may assume that folio 8 was discarded because of a preferred version written on folio 9. There are no marks on the stub of folio 28, but the same situation may have existed there. There is now no break in the continuity between folio 27 and folio 29. Folios 29 and 30, on the other hand, give differing versions of the last lines of the play and Asphodel's exit.

Why folios 38–42 were cut out is unknown. The play ends with folio 30; the rest of the notebook is blank, except for a piece of pink stationery laid in between folio 30 and folio 31 which gives a slightly different version of folio 21, Vivien's curse on Asphodel and Clarin. The stationery is a paper of about 20 lb. weight, with some rag content, no line, chain, or watermarks. A sheet measuring 23 cm (9¹⁄₁₆") wide has been folded to make two folios 11.5 cm (4¹⁷⁄₃₂") wide. The height is 17.85 cm (7¹⁄₃₂"). The same grey-brown ink is used on this inserted paper as in most of the notebook. Divergences are noted.

This is a fair copy, probably one created for the rehearsal which J. B. Yeats mentions in his 7 January 1884 letter to Dowden. It is unlikely, considering the January 8th date, to be the manuscript lent to Dowden before January 7th. Yeats has carefully corrected his spelling errors by going over them with a black crayon wax pencil and in other places in black ink. He has also made a few changes of substance in both media.

The pages missing from Ms. 30,357, containing act II, scene 2, are found in National Library of Ireland Ms. 30,460. There are five leaves, six pages. The first leaf is folded to make two pages. The others are single, having been torn from their mates in the notebook, with which they match perfectly when the group is slipped in before folio 25. The paper, ink, and handwriting are all identical to those in the notebook. A red stain at the very bottom left of the last three pages matches the same stain on folios 25 ff. of the notebook. There is thus no doubt that the pages are from the notebook. They contain all of act II, scene 2, down to the stage direction "(*She dies.*)."

Both these manuscripts were until recently in the collection of Michael B. Yeats, where they were catalogued as MBY 357 and MBY 460.

Textual Notes to *Vivien and Time*

Words in italics are spelled and punctuated as in Yeats's manuscripts.

1. *dreamers*
2. *charmèd*   By mistake Yeats used the acute instead of the grave accent, "charmèd," to give syllabic value to "-ed."
3. *sky s*   Yeats may have meant "sky's," but "skies" seems more likely.
4. *For a chorus, thy name my disturber*
5. *scythe*
6. *planet*   (no end stop)
7. *shadow'ed*
8. *that*   The word seems accidentally blotted rather than cancelled.
9. *squirrels*   A "dray" is a squirrel's nest.
10. *deamons*   It is more likely that Yeats meant the eye of a "demon" or devil than the eye of a "daemon" in the sense of a god, attendant spirit, or the genius of a place.
11. *imputence*   Yeats probably means "impudence" rather than "impotence" or "impatience."
12. *boar*   An alternative reading is "bone."
13. *wone*   Probably Yeats's spelling of "won," not "wone" meaning "moan."
14. *O scarce*   See discussion above of "Or scarce" as probably intended.
15. *had how long*
16. *fell*

Notes to the Commentary

1. This essay copyright ©1987 by David R. Clark and Rosalind E. Clark. *Vivien and Time* and all previously unpublished materials by W. B. Yeats copyright © 1987 by Anne Yeats and Michael Butler Yeats and are published here with their permission. Our thanks are due to the Yeats family for many kindnesses and courtesies. We thank them, the Macmillan Publishing Co., Inc. (New York), and the Macmillan Press, Ltd. (London) for permission to quote from Yeats's published works. The courtesy of A. P. Watt Ltd. is greatly appreciated.

80 David R. Clark and Rosalind E. Clark

We thank former Directors Alf MacLochlainn and Patrick Henchy, Director Michael Hewson, and the staff of the National Library of Ireland, also the staffs of the University of Massachusetts Library, the Amherst College Library, the Mead Art Gallery Library, the Smith College Library, the Hillyer Art Gallery Library, the Jones Library (Amherst), the Cushwa-Leighton Library of St. Mary's College (Notre Dame), the Library of the National College of Art and the National Gallery Library (Dublin), the University of Cambridge Library, and the Frank Melville, Jr. Memorial Library, State University of New York at Stony Brook, where the William Butler Yeats Archives are held.

David Clark thanks the American Council of Learned Societies, the American Philosophical Society, and the University of Massachusetts Research Council for recent grants for research on Yeats.

This edition was first conceived with the late Liam Miller, to whom we owe especial thanks. Other individuals to whom we owe thanks are Richard Allen, Mary A. Clark, Richard Fallis, Richard J. Finneran, Mary FitzGerald, John Friedman, Narayan Hegde, Roy and Erica Leslie, Lewis Lusardi, James and Gloria McGuire, Arpena Mesrobian, Micheál O Aodha, Colin Smythe, and Richard and Sigrid Weber.

The late Mrs. W. B. Yeats was kind to both of us and first showed Yeats's early unpublished plays to David Clark and encouraged him in "sorting them out."

"Sailing from Avalon" is dedicated to Mary A. Clark.

2. *The Wanderings of Oisin and Other Poems* (London: Kegan Paul, Trench & Co., 1889).

3. Yeats wrote the play for Laura Armstrong at Howth. Although the Yeats family moved to Howth in late 1881, Yeats did not meet Laura until the autumn of 1882 (William M. Murphy, *Prodigal Father: The Life of John Butler Yeats, 1839–1922* [Ithaca and London: Cornell University Press, 1978] 123, 132; cf. CL1 xii). Autumn 1882, then, is the earliest date for the composition of *Vivien and Time*.

The "Dedication" of *Vivien and Time* is dated "January the 8th 1884." There is no sign that the "Dedication" is of a different date from the rest of the play. On the cover of the notebook containing the play appears "Viven [sic] and Time / a dramatic poem / January the 8th / 1884." On 7 January 1884 J. B. Yeats wrote Edward Dowden asking for the return of the manuscript (*J. B. Yeats: Letters to His Son W. B. Yeats and Others 1869–1922*, ed. Joseph Hone [New York: Dutton, 1946] 52). 7 January 1884, then, is the last date for the completion of the play. The dating "1882–83" for the writing of the play will therefore refer to the period between autumn 1882 and 7 January 1884. We will respect Yeats's date of 8 January 1884 for the completion of the play including the "Dedication."

J. B. Yeats must have been mistaken when he claimed that his son was "sixteen years old" when he wrote *Vivien and Time* (Marguerite Wilkinson, "A Talk with John Butler Yeats about His Son William Butler Yeats," *Touchstone* 6 [Oct. 1919]: 10–17, quoted by Murphy, 569n42), as Yeats celebrated his seventeenth birthday on 13 June 1882, before he met Laura Armstrong.

4. *Poems* (London: T. Fisher Unwin, 1895), v; VP 845.

5. Thomas Parkinson, "Some Recent Work on Yeats: From Great Modern Poet to Canonical Classic," *Southern Review* 15.3 (July 1979): 742–52, esp. 748.

6. Richard Ellmann, *Yeats: The Man and the Masks* (New York: Norton, 1979) 46. Hereafter cited in the text as *MM*.

7. *J. B. Yeats: Letters* 52.

8. Dedication to *Fairy and Folk Tales of the Irish Peasantry*, ed. W. B. Yeats (London: Walter Scott; New York: Thomas Whittaker; Toronto: W. Gage and Co., 1888) v.

9. Mary Catherine Flannery, *Yeats and Magic: The Earlier Works* (New York: Barnes & Noble, 1978) 16.

10. This citation indicates that the passage is found on p. 163 of the third volume of hardcopy derived from reel 23 in the William Butler Yeats Archives, Frank Melville, Jr. Memorial Library, State University of New York at Stony Brook. This is the most accurate method of citing Yeats's manuscripts at present.

    In our commentary, quotations from the manuscript have been regularized in accord with our edited text.

11. *J. B. Yeats: Letters* 52.

12. Murphy 132, citing a letter from John Butler Yeats to John Quinn on 3 December 1917 (Berg Collection, New York Public Library). For Yeats and Laura Armstrong, see also Gloria Kline, *The Last Courtly Lover: Yeats and the Idea of Woman* (Ann Arbor: UMI Research Press, 1983), esp. 57–60 and 63–66.

13. Murphy 569n43.

14. Murphy 569n44, citing letters from John Butler Yeats to Lily Yeats (24 Dec. 1915) and to W. B. Yeats (12 Feb. 1916), both presumably in the collection of Michael B. Yeats.

15. Murphy 573n19. See also his "William Butler Yeats's *John Sherman*: An Irish Poet's Declaration of Independence," *Irish University Review* 9.1 (Spring 1979): 97–98.

16. We differ from the more traditional view that Sherman is subjective and Howard objective, as argued, for example, in JSD 27–31.

17. *Burne-Jones: The Paintings, Graphic and Decorative Work of Sir Edward Burne-Jones 1833–98* (London: The Arts Council of Great Britain, 1975) 27. Hereafter cited as *Burne-Jones*.

18. Lucy Allen Paton, *Studies in the Fairy Mythology of Arthurian Romance* (Boston: Ginn, 1903) 247. Hereafter cited as Paton.

19. G. D. West, *An Index of Proper Names in French Arthurian Prose Romances* (Toronto: University of Toronto Press, 1978) 81.

20. *Histoire de Grimaud*, ed. Eugène Hucher, in *Le Saint-Graal* (Paris: Le Mans, 1875–78) 3: 593, 595, 598, 600.

21. Roger Lathuillère, *Guiron le Courtois, Etude de la tradition manuscrit et analyse critique*, Publications romances et français 86 (Genève, 1966) sec. 262; *Les Prophécies de Merlin*, ed. from MS 593 in the Bibliothèque Municipal of Rennes by Lucy Allen Paton, Modern Language Association of America Monograph Series 1 (1926–27; New York, 1966) 394, 400.

22. Ernest Langlois, *Table des noms propres de toute nature compris dans les chansons de geste imprimées* (Paris: E. Bouillon, 1904), lists "Clarin" as appearing in *Rolant*, ed. Stengel, 63, 504b, and in *Anseis de Cartage*, 5684.

23. "Palmyra," *Encyclopaedia Britannica* (1962) 17:163.

24. *Odyssey* 11:539. See also 24:1.

25. Ellmann quotes the opening passage of II.ii (*MM* 35–36).

26. See Virginia Moore, *The Unicorn: William Butler Yeats' Search for Reality* (New York: Macmillan, 1954) 208–9; but also George Mills Harper, *Yeats's Quest for Eden* (Dublin: Dolmen Press, 1966).

27. *Drama of the English Renaissance*, ed. M. L. Wine (New York: Modern Library, 1969) 690. Hereafter cited as Wine.

28. Wine 688.

29. Wine 763.

30. Richard Ellmann, *The Identity of Yeats*, 2nd ed (New York: Oxford University Press, 1964) 23.

31. In *The Shadowy Waters*, Yeats draws on what could be considered an Irish version of the butterfly symbol: Etain is changed to a fly (a "silver fly" in the 1900 text), and Aengus makes a magic harp "That she among her winds might know he wept" (P 407).

32. P. W. Joyce, *Old Celtic Romances: Tales from Irish Mythology* (1879; New York: Devin-Adair, 1962) 1–26; Lady Gregory, *Cuchulain of Muirthemne* (1902; Gerrards Cross: Colin Smythe, 1970) 118–21.

33. Paton 205.

34. LDW 173. Yeats's question provoked Dorothy Wellesley to several questionable assertions: that Yeats strongly disliked flowers; that he had a "lack of interest in natural beauty for its own sake"; that "most of the Celtic poets are not concerned with nature at all"; that Yeats did not draw inspiration from details of nature but only from the massed effects a painter sees; that "his lack of observation concerning natural beauty was almost an active obsession" which dims "most poems of his concerned with Nature"; and that his poor sight made this "racial characteristic" more serious. Any of these assertions which are not simply incorrect are non-sequiturs because Yeats was talking about flowers in poetry, not flowers in life. And flowers in poetry must have a meaning beyond their being just flowers. The symbolic rose gets into Yeats's poetry, early and late, because it is symbolic. It may be an actual rose, but actual roses which are not symbolic have, he felt, no place in verse. In the early manuscripts of *The Shadowy Waters*, for example, there are enough roses to satisfy even Dorothy Wellesley, yet they are all symbolic. Forgael throws himself on heaps of roses to get inspiration from their scent. They are "Danaan roses," roses of the Children of Danu, the Sidhe. In some versions heaps of apple-blossoms replace the roses. See *Druid Craft: The Writing of* The Shadowy Waters, ed. Michael J. Sidnell, George P. Mayhew, and David R. Clark (Amherst: University of Massachusetts Press, 1971) 87–88, 169. The apple-blossoms too are presumably supernatural and related to the dream life, though suggested by Maud Gonne's complexion: "Her complexion was luminous, like that of apple-blossom through which the light falls, and I remember her standing that first day by a great heap of such blossoms in the window" (Au 123). That Yeats used the massed effects a painter sees, that "lack of observation concerning natural beauty was almost an active obsession," if true, show that he wanted to use nature for the purposes of art. "Art is art because it is not nature," he quotes Goethe (Ex 88).

35. *The Works of Tennyson*, ed. Hallam, Lord Tennyson (New York: Macmillan, 1913) 373–88, esp. 382. Hereafter cited in the text as *Works*.

36. *The Poetical Works of Alfred Lord Tennyson*, intro. Eugene Parsons (New York: Thomas Y. Crowell, n.d. [ca. 1900]) 705.

37. William Gaunt, *The Restless Century: Painting in Britain 1800–1900* (Oxford: Phaidon, 1978) 235.

38. Philip Henderson, *William Morris: His Life, Work, and Friends* (London: Thames and Hudson, 1967) 29. Hereafter cited as Henderson.

39. Henderson 43–45.

40. Paton 244, 242.

41. E&I 382–83. This edition gives "enchanted procession" where all earlier texts give "enchanted persecution." Although Yeats places this persecution/procession of Amoret in "the Fourth Book of *The Faerie Queene*" (E&I 383), he must mean the "maske of Cupid" in III.xii.

42. Au 116. The portrait that Yeats knew as *Ariosto* is now called *Portrait of a Man* (National Gallery, London).

43. John Eglinton, "Dublin Letter," *The Dial* 72 (March 1922): 300. Quoted in Thomas L. Dume, "William Butler Yeats: A Survey of His Reading," diss., Temple University, 1950, 217; hereafter cited as Dume.

44. Murphy 139. The records for 1884 of the Metropolitan School of Art (now the National College of Art) show that Susan M. Yeats, Elizabeth C. Yeats, and Wm. B. Yeats, all "Artisans" and all of 10 Ashfield Terrace, Harolds Cross, each paid a fee of £1.2.6 in May 1884. Courtesy of Richard Weber, National College of Art, Dublin. Murphy notes that Yeats's sisters entered the school in May 1883 (139).

45. S. Humphreys Gurteen, *The Arthurian Epic* (New York: G. P. Putnam's Sons, 1895) 184.

46. Paton 204–27.

47. "Iseult of Brittany" (l. 161), in *Poetry and Criticism of Matthew Arnold*, ed. A. Dwight Culler (Boston: Houghton Mifflin, 1961) 105.

48. Algernon Charles Swinburne, *Tristram of Lyonesse and Other Poems* (London: Chatto & Windus, 1882) 30–31.

49. Ariosto's *Orlando Furioso*, sel. from trans. of Sir John Harrington, ed. Rudolf Gottfried (Bloomington and London: Indiana University Press, 1971) 73–74.

50. Burne-Jones 51.

51. *Vivien*, oil on canvas, 25" × 20.5", dated 1863 (Manchester City Art Gallery). Cf. *Frederick Sandys 1829–1904* (Brighton: Brighton Museum and Art Gallery, 1974), catalogue no. 63. Hereafter cited as *Sandys*.

52. *Morgan le Fay*, oil on panel, 24.75" × 17.5" (City Museum and Art Gallery, Birmingham). *Sandys* catalogue no. 58.

53. Murphy 57 and 556n13.

54. William E. Fredeman, *Pre-Raphaelitism: A Bibliocritical Study* (Cambridge: Harvard University Press, 1965) 297. Another striking enchantress is Sandys' *Medea* (1868), oil on panel, 24.5" × 18.25" (City Museum and Art Gallery, Birmingham). *Sandys* catalogue no. 72. This has been reproduced photographically as the frontispiece to Col. A. B. Richardson's poem "Medea" in 1869.

55. *Morgan le Fay* (1862), gouache, 86.5 × 48 cm. (London: Borough of Hammersmith Public Libraries). Cf. *Burne-Jones All Colour Paperback*, intro. May Johnson (London: Academy Editions, 1979), plate 7; hereafter cited as Johnson.

56. *The Wine of Circe* (1863–69), gouache, 70 × 101.5 cm. (private collection). *Burne-Jones* catalogue no. 105. Reproduced in black-and-white in *Sir Edward Burne-Jones* (London: George Newnes; New York: Frederick Warne & Co., n.d.), plate 42.

57. London: Macmillan, 1880.

58. London: Macmillan, 1882.

59. Martin Harrison and Bill Waters, *Burne-Jones* (New York: G. P. Putnam's Sons, 1973) 35. Hereafter cited as Harrison and Waters.

60. *Merlin and Nimuë*, gouache, 64 × 50.8 cm (Victoria and Albert Museum). *Burne-Jones* catalogue no. 27. This watercolor was owned by the Newcastle industrialist James Leathart. It had been exhibited by the Old Water-colour Society in the year of Yeats's birth.

61. *The Beguiling of Merlin*, oil, 186 × 111 cm. (Lady Lever Art Gallery, Port Sunlight, Cheshire). *Burne-Jones* catalogue no. 129; color reproduction between pp. 8–9. Owned by Frederick Leyland; exhibited in the Grosvenor Gallery, 1877; and in the Exposition Universelle, Paris, 1878.

62. See the interpretation of the painting in Harrison and Waters 110–13, much elaborated upon here.

Around 1873 Burne-Jones had made a study for the head of Nimuë which he thought better done than that in the finished painting. There are no Medusa-like cords binding her hair, her brow is less tense (or less overhung by her hair), her eyes more frankly observant, and her lips more sensuously parted. "Study for the head of Nimuë in *The Beguiling of Merlin*" (ca. 1873), gouache, 76.2 × 50.8 cm. (Delaware Art Museum). *Burne-Jones* catalogue no. 130.

63. See Johnson, plates 39 (*Ladder of Heaven*), 40 (*Wake Dearest*), 41 (*Golden Shower*), 42 (*Adder's Tongue*), 43 (*White Garden*), 44 (*Traveler's Joy*), 45 (*Witch's Tree*), and 46 (*Fire Tree*). All are watercolors 16.5 cm. in diameter, done 1882–98 and now in the British Museum.

64. Jean Wirth, *La Jeune Fille et la Mort: Recherches sur les thèmes macabres dans l'art germanique de la Renaissance* (Genève: Librairie Droz, 1979), esp. figures 8, 42, 44, 55, 62–67, 69–70, 72–73, 76, 129, 131, 140, 142–44; hereafter cited as Wirth. Wirth traces (2–3, 87–93) the descent of the poem by Matthias Claudius which Schubert set to music as "Der Tod und das Mädchen" back through an old ballad called "Lenore," popularized by Bürger, of which Scott did a version called "William and Mary," echoed in "The Rime of the Ancient Mariner" (J. B. Beer, *Coleridge the Visionary* [New York: Collier, 1962] 155–56). Wirth finds the late medieval source in graphic artists such as Hans Baldung Grien, who treated the theme about 1515. Wirth also cites sixteenth-century German plays on the subject (91). The Death and the Maiden theme persists in the nineteenth century and is well enough known in 1819 to get into George Cruikshank's political cartoon of a skeleton "Radical Reform" raping the maiden Britannia (*Graphic Works of George Cruikshank*, ed. Richard A. Vogler [New York: Dover, 1979], figure 17).

65. Wirth, figure 14: Maître B R à l'Ancre, *Partie d'échecs avec la mort* (cuivre). See also p. 32.

This theme persists in our own time in Ingmar Bergman's film *The Seventh Seal*, in which the central situation is a game of chess between Death and the knight who is the protagonist. Bergman, a minister's son, derived the situation from old church paintings (Jörn Donner, *The Films of Ingmar Bergman* [New York: Dover, 1976] 138). The knight says that he knows from pictures that Death plays chess. One such picture is a wall painting by Albertus Pictor in Taby Church, Upland, Sweden. This information was provided by Professor John Friedman.

66. George Eliot, *Daniel Deronda* (Chicago and New York: Belford, Clarke, & Co., 1885) 421 (chapter 37).

67. *The Best of Coleridge*, ed. Earl Leslie Griggs (New York: Ronald Press, 1947) 47.

68. John Livingston Lowes, *The Road to Xanadu: A Study in the Ways of the Imagination* (Boston and New York: Houghton Mifflin, 1927) 277.

69. *The Rime of the Ancient Mariner*, illustrated David Scott (London and Edinburgh, 1837); E. H. Wehnert, B. Foster, et al. (London, 1857); J. Noel Paton (London: 1863); W. Collins (Glasgow, 1875); Gustave Doré (London, 1876); [Vest Pocket Series] (Boston, 1876); G. Doré, B. Foster, et al. (Boston, 1884).

70. Victoria and Albert Museum. Cf. Raymond Watkinson, *Pre-Raphaelite Art and Design* (Greenwich, Conn.: New York Graphic Society, 1970), figure 67.

71. Oil (Sterling and Francine Clark Art Institute, Williamstown, Massachusetts). Reproduced in color in Robert L. Delevoy, *Symbolists and Symbolism* (New York: Rizzoli, 1978) 117.

72. "Peter Quince at the Clavier," *Collected Poems of Wallace Stevens* (New York: Alfred A. Knopf, 1955) 92.

73. SB xxv; Lucy Shephard Kalogera, *Yeats's Celtic Mysteries*, diss., Florida State University, 1977, 9.

74. Maud Gonne, "Yeats and Ireland," *Scattering Branches: Tributes to W. B. Yeats*, ed. Stephen Gwynn (New York: Macmillan, 1940) 23.

75. Dume 266.

76. In *Prolegomena to the Study of Yeats's Poems* (Philadelphia: University of Pennsylvania Press, 1957) 80, George Brandon Saul notes that "'Joyous Isle' . . . may be found in the 'Agravain' portion of the Prose Vulgate *Lancelot*: Yeats's reference implies a confusion of the story of Lancelot and Pelles' daughter." John Rhys's *Studies in the Arthurian Legend* (Oxford: Clarendon, 1891) has been suggested as Yeats's source (P 631, note to 86.2–3).

77. See also P 646 (note to 198.23) for a white stag connected with Arthur in the *Mabinogion*.

78. See George Mills Harper and Sandra L. Sprayberry, "Complementary Creation: Notes on 'Another Song of a Fool' and 'Towards Break of Day,'" *Yeats* 4 (1986): 69–85.

79. Yeats seems to have misremembered his source (see P 623).

80. In 1899 Yeats wrote that ". . . Richard Wagner's dramas of 'The Ring,' are, together with his mainly Celtic 'Parsival' and 'Lohengrin,' and 'Tristan and Iseult,' the most passionate influence in the arts of Europe" (UP2 125).

81. *A Tower of Polished Black Stones: Early Versions of* The Shadowy Waters, ed. David Ridgley Clark and George Mayhew (Dublin: Dolmen Press, 1971) xi.

82. William Wells Newell, *King Arthur and the Table Round: Tales chiefly after the Old French of Crestien of Troyes* . . . (Boston and New York: Houghton Mifflin; Cambridge: Riverside Press, 1897) 2:134–39; hereafter cited as Newell. Yeats's mistake was easy to make, especially in light of the title. Most of the book *is* taken from Chrétien, and the introductory chapters concentrate on him, leaving an impression in the reader's mind that all the stories were his. In a vaguely worded note at the end of the book, however, we learn of the "Merlin" episode: "The romance is edited by G. Paris and J. Ulrich, Paris, 1886." If one reads the whole note carefully, one can deduce that the "romance" is not by Chrétien. The note ends "The story recites, that . . . Arthur became the father of Modred. . . . This relation . . . was . . . created by minstrels in order to heighten the tragic situation, and foreign to the story as known to Crestien" (2:258–59). Dume explains (276n298) that the Paris and Ulrich edition is of the *Huth Merlin*, not of a Chrétien romance at all.

83. *Druid Craft* 72.

84. *Song and Its Fountains* (New York: Macmillan, 1932) 11.

85. Gershom G. Scholem, *On the Kabbalah and Its Symbolism* (New York: Schocken Books, 1969) 108.

86. Newell 2:137–39.

87. The section was rewritten as part five in the 1937 *A Vision*, without significant change in the passage about Merlin (AV-B 285–300).

88. Yeats refers on several occasions to Wolfram von Eschenbach's *Parsival:* Ex 113 (1903); Ex 214–15 (1906); Au 151 (1922); AV-A 198–99 (1925); E&I 484 (1935). According to Dume (337), he read it in Jessie L. Weston's 1894 translation.

The Three Deaths of Yeats

Hugh Kenner

It's been noted more than once, and by Hazard Adams most recently, that the poems of W. B. Yeats make up a book; Adams describes it as "an antithetical book with a narrative-mimetic plot, the main character of which is a fictive figure who eventually names himself Yeats."[1] He does so when he chants near the very end, "In Drumcliff churchyard Yeats is laid" (P 327).[2] Having said that, "Yeats" goes on to utter no fewer than eighteen additional poems, a record utterance for someone whom gravediggers' spades have by his own testimony thrust beneath the sod. "Art thou there, truepenny?" (*Hamlet* I.v.150). Yes, world without end, he's there. He has proved it by bringing off the same trick twice before. It's the hedgehog's one trick against the fox's many, the trick, *in extremis*, of a cunningly managed death.

For prior to the death of record, 28 January 1939, William Butler Yeats had managed more paper deaths than one. (My count is two, hence three lives; then the coroner's death, and a fourth life.) It was not an outlandish idea; to go and come back was theosophical routine which we'll not investigate though he and Maud Gonne both believed it. For the soul to be set free "at the last servile crescent"—a phrase he wrote, so to speak, from experience—was to be turned loose into a mysterious chaos, speaking but "what's blown into the mind" (P 166), until the time was ripe for a fresh journey. How often Yeats spoke what's blown into the mind admirers can't help but know. *On the Boiler* is a salient instance. I'll suggest that on such occasions he deemed himself licensed because dead.

The first of Yeats's three lives spans, approximately, the period New Critics used to designate "early Yeats." New Critics were responding to a new alertness of language they detected in anything Yeats was publishing by the time of, say, *The Wild Swans at Coole*. Thus

Rose of all Roses, Rose of all the World!

[P 37]

was Pre-Raphaelite in a way no student of Cleanth Brooks would be caught dead with; whereas

> the down-turn of his wrist
> When the flies drop in the stream
>
> [P 148–49]

—that is the Real Language of Men. It does not croon, and it admits words like "wrist" and "flies," which for vulgarity both of sound and of denotation Pre-Raphaelitism would not have been caught dead with, either. Imagine the Blessed Damozel taking cognizance of even trout-flies! Or uttering a noise like "wrist"!

It's easy to mock New Critical criteria, especially if, like me, you're a grateful sometime student of Brooks; the movement did tend to suppose that Rossetti wrote the wrong kind of poem, Donne the right kind, and that a poet's education, in the generation of Yeats, meant outgrowing the one to mature into the other. It wasn't noticed that the "right" kind of poem was simply the kind New Critical terminology had a grip on: that in excluding Rossetti it excluded William Carlos Williams as well, not to mention all of Pound save *Mauberly*. One of its heuristic triumphs remains its reclamation of Yeats from the Celtic Twilight, permitting a generation of sophomores to be exposed to "The Tower." (Why "The Tower"? Because the same reprint fee used to be charged for any Yeats poem irrespective of length; so if you were putting an anthology together you'd pay the same money for "The Tower" as for "Spilt Milk," and might as well buy 195 lines as 4. Yeats the epigrammatist got discounted in those years.)

The two-model Yeats we inherited from the 1940s had the advantage of pointing to a truth but the disadvantage of not explaining it correctly. For the New Critics were never quite agreed on when Early Yeats ceased and Late Great Yeats commenced, Whereas William Butler Yeats was perfectly clear. He'd engineered that transition when he accomplished his first death sometime in 1909. Thereafter "Yeats" was someone Yeats could write about, a poet of the same name, now folded into history. That former Yeats had

> filled the eyes
> Or the discerning ears

while his successor was

> Delighted to be but wise
>
> [P 136]

—having dubiously "improved" in his new incarnation.

For note how, early in the new century, we detect Yeats I, just turned forty, designing himself a tombstone; this appeared as *The Poetical Works* in 1906–7, and was soon supplemented by something more elaborate, a sort of Albert Memorial better known as the 1908 *Collected Works:* one volume of poems, three of plays, two of fictions, two of essays. That was to be his legacy, and 1060 sets were printed.[3] The latest-written of the poems in it dates from 1905, when he was forty, and tells how he

> grew to be out of fashion
> Like an old song.
>
> [P 83]

Collected Works! The ominous sound of finality is reinforced by the emphases of *Autobiographies.* That project, in public progress from 1916 clear to 1938, may be described as a fictional life of Yeats I, written by Yeats II, whom the ambience Yeats I had inherited never ceased to fascinate. The narrative, it's notable, stops with the death of Synge (1909), and Yeats may well have had an eye on *A Portrait of the Artist as a Young Man* when he rounded the book with excerpts from a diary. That let the last pages be written in the present tense, as if to signify a narrative finally arrived at Now: moreover the last Now Yeats I had known.[4]

Another preoccupation of Yeats II was his namesake's *Poems* of 1895, which as everyone knows he kept tinkering with from reprint to reprint. As late as 1927, whoever asked in a shop for the Poems of W. B. Yeats would be handed the current edition of that long-ago work, the sixty-two-year-old public man being quite content, apparently, to be remembered as sometime author of "The Wanderings of Oisin," *The Countess Cathleen,* and *The Land of Heart's Desire,* and just forty lyrics in an unexplained twofold grouping: "Crossways," "The Rose."[5] Casual readers needn't ever know what he and his intimates knew, that the boundary between those groups was less aesthetic than autobiographical, commemorating as it did the moment Maud Gonne entered his life.

So Yeats about 1909 turned into a vanished self for the middle-aged Yeats to commemorate, edit, ponder, and fantasize about. The reasons could only have been complex; we may list a few. The *Poetical Works* and the *Collected Works* afford one clue; Yeats was getting sufficiently removed from the manner he'd long perfected to feel, when he re-read a poem like "Innisfree," almost as though someone else had written it. That removal may have been grounded in apprehension about starting to repeat his effects. *The Wind Among the Reeds* (1899) does rather overdo the vocative case,[6] and some of the finest poems in the early manner ("The Fish," "He remembers forgotten Beauty," "He wishes for the Cloths of Heaven") are jostled by several of the most embarrassing ("The Travail of Passion," "The Lover speaks to the Hearers of his Songs in Coming Days," "He wishes his Beloved were Dead").

Then the long struggle to make something coherent of *The Shadowy Waters* may have set him wondering whether there was something after all to the tradition that such a kind of poet as he was shouldn't persist past forty. Shelley and Keats hadn't lived to find out, but Wordsworth was a dreadful example. Also, troubles with *The Shadowy Waters* had sent him to Ben Jonson, in whom he'd discovered the *public* language he was to use in "The Fascination of What's Difficult"[7] and "Upon a House shaken by the Land Agitation." The poet of *The Wind Among the Reeds* doesn't fuss about Land Agitations. This has to be someone else.

As the need for a public language indicates, he'd lost his old faith in an Irishry whose consciousness could be raised by continued intercourse with the best the poetic imagination could offer. The folly of that was crystal clear by 1907, the *Playboy* year. The one thing you could usefully do with a public that wore noisy boots and brought tin trumpets into the Abbey was deride it. (And the Lane Pictures episode! Lord!) Coping with all that, Yeats's soul was caught in a servile crescent.

Time to leave: to make room for Yeats II and a new beginning.

Yeats II had nothing like the 1895 *Poems* to offer. He defined himself by stages, tentatively: some memoirs, to establish his chief credential, continuity with Yeats I; an identification with The Tower, which meant that unlike Yeats I he had truck with neither Dublin nor London, a trick especially neat when he was serving as a Senator of the new Republic; an occult work, the first *A Vision,* to establish that unlike Yeats I (who claimed only intermittent moments of vision), he enjoyed intercourse with sources of revelation; and a mastery of diction Yeats I had never dreamt of, permitting as it did every kind of effects from "The drunkards, pilferers of public funds" (P 151) to "Vague memories, nothing but memories" (P 153). (But nothing like "Cover it up with a lonely tune" [P 535]: that order of magic was dead with the first Yeats.)

He showed signs of system, not only *A Vision* but "The Phases of the Moon," and hinted that it could order piece-meal offerings. Yes, Yeats II was the systematizer Yeats I hadn't been. Beneath and beyond the wonderful cohesion of poem after poem—"Sailing to Byzantium,"

"The Tower," "Leda and the Swan"—we sense the promise that, given patience, all will one day unite in a tranced moment of insight. And the clock is ticking, and his soul is "fastened to a dying animal" (P 193). He knows, though, that he's living in another kind of time than the kind that drags down imagination, that dragged down Wordsworth:

> Never had I more
> Excited, passionate, fantastical
> Imagination, nor an ear and eye
> That more expected the impossible—
> No, not in boyhood when with rod and fly,
> Or the humbler worm, I climbed Ben Bulben's back
> And had the livelong summer day to spend.
>
> [P 194]

Yeats would not have written "the humbler worm" save to summon up the age of Wordsworth, when self-consciousness about diction could be of that order; he writes it now in defining his distance from Wordsworth, who'd cried at thirty-four

> Whither is fled the visionary gleam?
> Where is it now, the glory and the dream?
> ["Ode: Intimations of Immortality," ll. 56–57]

Yeats is affirming that it's here, it's here. For he had evaded the Wordsworthian fate by his stratagem of a second coming. There had been point, after all, in the 'nineties maxim that your art's attention should be bent upon your life. Thirty, forty . . . somewhere in that range is the Romantic Poet's cutoff, and he'd evaded it by starting a new life.

. . . Except that the attached animal continued to die on its former schedule. Nothing to be done about that (though the Steinach business was a try). By the time he was putting *The Tower* volume together we may divine him sensing time running out. It was time that he wrote his will, for one thing. In another poem he was "the parting guest" (P 211); on another page he's exhorting himself, via Sophocles, to "endure what life God gives and ask no longer span" (P 226); and *The Tower* ends with him

> Wound in mind's wandering
> As mummies in the mummy-cloth are wound.
> [P 230]

That's all pretty funereal, and may be connected with the lung hemorrhages, the fever and exhaustion, of 1927. Thereafter he'd spend every winter on the Mediterranean, and he seems to have thought *The Tower* (1928) would be his last book, with "All Souls' Night" (though written in 1920) for a noble finale, a last leavetaking from cherished—occult—friends, less celebrated than Synge and Lady Gregory, called up from the grave and soon to be joined beyond it. Alas for such plans, he didn't die.

1909, 1929; yet the sun rose still, the indifferent sun. There's a tentativeness about his collections of the 1930s, even about their titles: *A Winding Stair and Other Poems; Parnell's Funeral and Other Poems;* finally just *New Poems.* It's as though the old cunning architect of volumes had been caught by a need to improvise. As he had, if *The Tower* (as I propose) had been meant for a grand finale. But he hadn't died. Hence titles that buy time, till he realized that he'd best register a second death. "And Other Poems" says "no leisure for unity here." "New Poems" says "grab-bag," and here and there a shrillness has been noted. An unforeseen Yeats III is doing what he can: coping with what he'd most feared, a dribbling off into miscellany, and worrying whether the long-gathered Sacred Book may have to be abandoned shapeless.

Then, apparently in the very last days of his life, when for sure there could be no doubt that his time wasn't long, he had one of his most profound inspirations. That was when he drew up a table of contents for *Last Poems* (if that title wasn't his it's in his spirit), and made the year-old "Under Ben Bulben" begin it. This third time he will die for sure! Dead beyond peradventure on the first page, he'll open the last book by intoning "Swear" like King Claudius's ghost; and posterity he'll cast as Hamlet, instructing it to deal sternly with the ignoble.[8]

What that gesture did was proclaim his third, his "physical" death; after that, his survival, chanting

> Under bare Ben Bulben's head
> In Drumcliff churchyard Yeats is laid . . .
>
> [P 327]

and from beyond the grave he chants of fierce horsemen riding from mountain to mountain, of the mysterious rites of the old black tower where they hear the shaking bones of dead men buried upright, of the weird reception Cuchulain had in the underworld—this last told in the *terza rima* of Dante, a lost detail as it were of the *Commedia*. And he sings of the empty coat upon its hanger—all his coats empty now—and prefigures yet another birth, from "where all the ladders start" (P 348), and is even audacious enough to end it all (P 348) with a longing to be "young again" (and hold her in his arms).

That is the third death, for once coincident with empirical record. That is also the brief career of Yeats IV, the translunar poet, the subterranean voice. It's recovered for us by the arrangement of *Last Poems* in the Finneran edition, where the posthumous status of fully eighteen poems is at last recorded. It's guided by it that we recover the two previous deaths, the one deliberated in 1909, the other inadvertent about 1930. And what freedom he permitted himself when he was "dead"! *On the Boiler* is one instance. And it's a "Wild Old Wicked Man" who'll have us know that

> An old ghost's thoughts are lightning
>
> [P 318]

and who chants, not once but five times,

> . . . fol de rol de rolly O.
>
> [P 313–14]

Fancy that in *The Wind Among the Reeds!* For *New Poems* (1938) is a wild book, best read as instancing the license he accorded himself when he came to terms, as he had in 1910, with the fact that, being "dead," he could say or sing absolutely anything at all and be answerable to no human criterion. When it comes to dying there's no substitute for experience.

How literally is all this to be believed? (But how literally is Yeats to be believed?) Were I writing his biography I'd say flatly (1) that at some time he came to regard his famous first self as having died as of 1909: indeed came to make that fact (fancy?) the focus of much autobiographical effort; (2) that he thought of *The Tower,* when he was compiling it, as probably a final book; (3) that he was consequently hard put to make a coherence of subsequent collections; and (4) that he triumphantly designed *Last Poems,* in a table of contents drawn up on his deathbed, as a sequence of utterances from beyond the grave. Those are the nodepoints, between which we spin the tale as we fancy. You've read my version.

Notes

1. "Constituting Yeats's Poems as a Book," *Yeats* 4 (1986): 1.
2. Cf. "I, the poet William Yeats" in "To be carved on a Stone at Thoor Ballylee" (P 190).
3. "The announcement of the *Collected Works* set the literary gossips of Dublin saying that Yeats would write no more, or very little." Joseph Hone, *W. B. Yeats, 1865–1939*, 2nd ed. (London: Macmillan, 1962) 225.

4. A coda rather than an ending, *The Bounty of Sweden* serves to let Nobel recognition confirm the integrity of work a Yeats by then vanished had done in his 20s and 30s. So with Swedish blessing the pre-1909 Yeats has folded into history.

5. To some extent Yeats was doubtless constrained by the fact that the rights to *Poems* were held first by T. Fisher Unwin and later by Ernest Benn. In arranging for the first edition, Yeats had asked of Unwin "That the book be yours *for 4 years* & then return to me" (CL1 403). The publisher apparently agreed—"Unwin has accepted all my terms" (CL1 408)—but the contract may have been later modified, perhaps with the second edition of *Poems* (1899). Yeats's note expressing unhappiness with Benn (B 156–57) suggests that in the 1920s he had little control over the rights to the volume.

6. "O sweet everlasting voices, be still"
"O curlew, cry no more in the air"
"O cloud-pale eyelids, dream-dimmed eyes"
"O women, kneeling by your altar-rails long hence"
[P 55, 62, 67, 71]

Of the thirty-seven poems now grouped as *The Wind Among the Reeds*, sixteen at least go through motions of *address*, with or without an "O." This count omits several mixed instances.

7. Compare "the day's war with every knave and dolt, / Theatre business, management of men" (P 93) with Jonson's "Come leave the loathed stage, / And the more loathsome age" ("Ode to Himself," *Poems*, ed. Ian Donaldson [London, New York, Toronto: Oxford University Press, 1975] 354.)

8. As Curtis Bradford argued in *Yeats's 'Last Poems' Again*, Yeats Centenary Papers 7 (Dublin: Dolmen Press, 1966) 261, "Yeats speaks not only 'Under Ben Bulben' from the tomb, he speaks all his *Last Poems* from the tomb."

Sailing the Seas to Nowhere: Inversions of Yeats's Symbolism in "Sailing to Byzantium"

Edward Lense

> *Poetry concerns itself with the creation of Paradises. I use the word in the plural for there are as many paradises as there are individual men—nay—as many as there are separate feelings.*
> J. B. Yeats to W. B. Yeats, 10 May 1914

When his father made this comment in a letter to him,[1] Yeats had already been creating Paradises in his work for thirty years and would continue to do so until the end of his life. Each of his versions of Paradise was, furthermore, based on "a separate feeling"; for Yeats, the Other World in any of the forms he gave it was the expression of *one* emotion, a concentration of feeling entirely different from the partial and shifting emotions of this world. Byzantium in "Sailing to Byzantium" (P 193–94) is one such form of the Other World; what makes it unique is that the emotion it embodies is bitterness and a thorough rejection of life in this or any other world. Byzantium is "paradise" for the speaker of the poem, but certainly it is the paradise of an individual and unlikely to appeal to anyone else.

There is no mistaking the speaker's bitterness: because he is an old man, he loathes his body, a "dying animal" that traps him in the physical world; he rejects the sexually potent young, who in their "sensual music" generate more bodies to add to the sprawling mass of procreation that the old man perceives as the antithesis of the order he sees in art; finally, he rejects the entire natural world, announcing that in the next life "I shall never take / My bodily form from any natural thing" (P 194). After such a series of negations, there is nothing left for the Other World to embody but pure forms, static works of art divorced from human content. The speaker himself will become not a living being but a machine, since any organic life implies change and the stasis he seeks is absolute. All this is clear from the text of the poem in isolation, but the lyric is deeply embedded in the context of Yeats's other work; in that larger perspective, it is apparent that the old man is rejecting not only this world but also the Other World as Yeats's generally conceived of it. His way of rejecting the Yeatsian Other World is through a precise inversion of Yeats's usual terms: where other forms of the Other World are, in one way or another, perfected forms of human life, Byzantium is the abnegation of all human life; where other forms of the Other World are full of a vivid energy shared by their inhabitants, Byzantium is a static world of art in which the perfect inhabitant is merely a conduit for time, the succession "Of what is past, or passing, or to come." Further, the old man sets up Byzantium, especially in the image of the golden bird, as a direct parody of Yeats's other versions of Paradise. Not only is Byzantium different in spirit from almost every alternative form of the Other World, it is presented in the usual terms turned inside-out: the sexual dance of the Other World, the source of creative energy that crowds the world with its forms, is here a burning-away of physical form, while the discarnate soul, which Yeats almost always represented as a bird, is here a machine that mimics the form of bird but is not alive.

By way of this antithetical imagery, then, the old man challenges Yeats's own conception of the Other World and achieves a pure bitterness, a "separate feeling" unmixed with any other emotion, that enables him to reject all aspects of this world without qualification. In so doing, the old man is rejecting not only his own body and the bodies of the young around him, but the whole spiritual order that impels the soul through a succession of bodies in search of its inherent human form, the form it had before the world was made. The soul's journey, in Yeats's system, carries it through both this world and the Other World; it is limited to neither one nor the other, but must alternate between them in various states of being. While the soul might eventually escape altogether from the Great Wheel, the cycle of incarnations, it can never choose one moment of the cycle and stay there. This, however, is exactly what the old man wants to do and asserts that he *will* do. Such an assertion challenges the entire system and, more importantly to "Sailing to Byzantium" itself, reveals the depth of the old man's bitterness toward life. He is without hope that there can ever be a natural form that will be pleasing to his soul, and this lack of hope makes him the anti-type of many other speakers in Yeats's poems, such as the Self in "A Dialogue of Self and Soul" who, in spite of his knowledge of the difficulties of human life, is "content to live it all again / And yet again" (P 236) in the hope that he can find enlightenment through the experiences of life.

The Self's affirmation of human life is part of a consistent pattern in Yeats's work that Helen Vendler has called, after a phrase in "Under Ben Bulben," the "profane perfection" of mankind: "the Platonic sacred is violently matched with the incarnate human," and this yoking of apparent opposites is, in part, what gives Yeats's images of the Other World their special force.[2] It is difficult for a soul to escape from the scenes of human life: even Byzantium, as Vendler points out, is a human city with a secular ruler, the Emperor, and the golden bird itself is placed firmly at his court, with human beings, not discarnate spirits, as the audience for its song. However, to define the terms of the old man's rejection of that way of perceiving the Other World, it is first necessary to look at the Other World in its usual guises as Tír na nÓg and the Fifteenth Phase of the Moon, and at the image, central to much of Yeats's poetry, of the discarnate soul as a bird. The precision of the old man's use of these images is crucial to the success of "Sailing to Byzantium" as parody and, consequently, to the reader's understanding that this speaker's bitterness is not an ordinary emotion based on experience alone, but an absolute rejection of life in this or any world.

Yeats's most frequent model for the Other World was Tír na nÓg, the Land of the Young, in Celtic mythology. Such a land is, by its nature, "no country for old men" because it embodies the physical vigor and the pursuits of youth, exactly those things the old man most despises. The first two lines of "Sailing to Byzantium" might just as well be describing the Country of the Young; it is only at the word "dying" that the old man is definitely talking about the physical world, since Tír na nÓg differs from the physical world only in the absence there of death, suffering and old age. Tír na nÓg is not a land of ghosts, or of unfamiliar, esoteric forms, but simply this world raised to perfection. It is also, in both Irish tradition and Yeats's poems and plays, the *source* of this world's energies. Forgael's description of this quality in *The Shadowy Waters* (1906 version) is quite traditional:

> Where the world ends
> The mind is made unchanging, for it finds
> Miracle, ecstasy, the impossible hope,
> The flagstone under all, the fire of fires,
> The roots of the world.
>
> [P 413]

The "fire of fires" anticipates the old man's vision of "God's holy fire," but is actually the opposite in its effect: where the fire of Byzantium burns away the familiar forms of nature and creates, the old man hopes, forms "out of nature," this fire burns with the energy that creates the forms of the physical world.

Yeats liked to point out that the folk-belief in Tír na nÓg ran parallel to more esoteric ideas about the perfection of the human form in the Other World. Commenting on Swedenborg's visions of the Other World, which were very similar to his own, he wrote:

> In the west of Ireland the country people say that after death every man grows upward or downward to the likeness of thirty years . . . and stays always in that likeness; and these angels move always towards "the springtime of their life" and grow more and more beautiful, "the more thousand years they live," and women who have died infirm with age, and yet lived in faith and charity, and true love towards husband or lover, come "after a succession of years" to an adolescence that was not in Helen's mirror, "for to grow old in heaven is to grow young." [Ex 38-39]

Or, as Aherne puts it in "The Phases of the Moon," "All dreams of the soul / End in a beautiful man's or woman's body" (P 165). The weight of tradition is behind Aherne's statement, and it is also in harmony with the whole pattern of Yeats's personal system. But the transformation that the old man longs for is antithetical to this process: he will not take on the form of "any natural thing," let alone that of a young human body, since that of all natural forms is the one he feels most alien to himself. His blanket condemnation of both this world and Tír na nÓg in the opening lines of the poem, then, shuts off the possibility that his soul can dream like other souls, and prevents him from making the journey to Tír na nÓg. For him, becoming young again would be pointless because he denies the idea that the soul's inherent form is a human one, or that anything human can remain when the "dying animal" of a physical incarnation is burned away. The human form, he implies, belongs to his body, not his soul.

Nonetheless, he *does* make a journey, and naturally it is the mirror-image of the traditional voyage to Tír na nÓg. He is going east, not west, not into the heart of nature but, as he says in an early draft, "from nature towards Byzantium" (Bradford 99). By traveling in this way he is very precisely turning Yeats's traditional imagery inside-out. Yeats often represented the journey to Tír na nÓg in terms of the traditional Irish *imram:* like Bran or St. Brendan, Yeats's hero generally travels west to the islands of the Other World. *The Shadowy Waters* is an *imram*, as is *The Wanderings of Oisin*. Since Irish tradition also represented Tír na nÓg as present alongside the physical world, and accessible to a human being through special insight, Yeats at times set some characters, like Red Hanrahan, on a visionary quest among the scenes of ordinary life. In any case, no one sails east except in the Byzantium poems, and no one but the old man is so indifferent to the journey itself. The voyage from this world to the Other World, whether in traditional narratives or Yeats's poems and plays, is essentially a process in which the voyager changes from a creature of this world into a supernatural being. Sometimes, as in *The Shadowy Waters*, the process is a matter of leaving the physical world farther and farther behind; more often, the process involves a physical transformation into a bird. *The Shadowy Waters* has both images, since Forgael uses the man-headed birds on their way to Tír na nÓg to steer his ship; "Sailing to Byzantium" also has both the sea-voyage and the golden bird that the old man has chosen as the ideal form for his soul. But there is nothing gradual about the old man's journey—as he speaks it is already done, and disposed of in a few words: "therefore I have sailed the seas and come / To the holy city of Byzantium."

That Yeats should describe the journey in such a compressed way is important because it negates his usual emphasis on the process of changing worlds. It is clear that the old man has not been transported to Byzantium through a supernatural flash of insight, since he has indeed "sailed the seas"; Yeats gives just enough information to show that there *has* been a long process at work, and that the old man is speaking from a particular moment in the midst of it. This balance between the static present of the poem and the sequence of events that leads up to the present and will (perhaps) continue in the old man's transformation was a matter to which Yeats paid great attention while writing the poem. Successive drafts bring up "sun-browned pleasant mariners," a "Danish merchant," and the dolphins that eventually appear in "Byzantium" (Bradford 99–101), but Yeats pared them all away to ensure that the speaker would be heard at only one moment, in Byzantium, as static as the figures in the gold mosaic of a wall. The voyage has been taken in record time, but the speaker is not yet transformed: he is still an old man trapped in his body, praying for release. Neither the journey nor the release is described in the poem, though both are essential to the *imram*, whether in tradition or in Yeats's work.

I have discussed this inversion of Yeats's usual practice at some length because it is central to the poem, especially to the poem as it stands in relation to the rest of Yeats's writing about the Other World and the cycle of incarnations. When Yeats wrote about the soul's progress from one state of being to another, he was writing about an integral part of a larger process. His imagery, particularly in the esoteric system of *A Vision*, always implies continual change; the interpenetrating gyres and the phases of the moon show an individual soul, or the course of history, to be in a state of constant tension, caught between past and future, moving inexorably through predetermined cycles. The periods between incarnations are no exceptions: the soul in its passage through the Other World is caught up in its own eddy of the larger gyres just as surely as it is caught up in history while subject to the material world. The peculiar stasis of "Sailing to Byzantium," then, sets it firmly apart from Yeats's other poems about the Other World, with their emphasis on perpetual motion; here, even the "sages standing in God's holy fire" are, as the speaker addresses them, quite still.

Should the sages emerge from their stillness and "perne in a gyre," they will (the old man hopes) be doing something quite contrary to Yeats's usual imagery of the gyres, since, at all other times, the gyres are Yeats's metaphor for the force that drives each soul forward in an endless cycle. The old man prefers to see this motion as a one-way expulsion from life, but there is little support for this idea in the rest of Yeats's poetry. On the contrary, a more "orthodox" way of imagining the gyres in action in the Other World is exactly what the old man would find most appalling. In *The King of the Great Clock Tower*, for example, the attendants define these gyres as a sexual dance:

> *Second Attendant:*
> They dance all day that dance in Tir-nan-oge.
> *First Attendant:*
> There every lover is a happy rogue;
> And should he speak, it is the speech of birds.
> No thought has he, and therefore has no words,
> No thought because no clock, no clock because
> If I consider deeply, lad and lass,
> Nerve touching nerve upon that happy ground,
> Are bobbins where all time is bound and wound.
>
> [VPl 398]

This is a far more typically Yeatsian approach to Paradise. Although these lines have a cluster of images exactly parallel to "Sailing to Byzantium," the images work in a way precisely opposed to the old man's wishes and expectations but in accordance with the principle that the Other World is the heart of nature, the source of the forms and energies of this world. On the basis of this play, or Ribh's or Crazy Jane's visions, the old man may be about to find the young in one another's arms forever.

However irregular, in Yeatsian terms, the journey to Byzantium and the old man's interpretation of the dance of the Other World might be, his image of the golden bird is the strangest, and most striking, feature of the poem. It is through this image that the old man reveals the full extent of his bitterness and rejection of life: his form in the Other World will not only be "out of nature," but a direct parody of a natural form. Not only will he be a machine, but a machine in the shape of a bird that will, like the miraculous bird of "Byzantium,"

>   scorn aloud
> In glory of changeless metal
> Common bird or petal
> And all complexities of mire or blood.
>
> [P 248]

This shape is an appropriate choice, since the soul's normal form between incarnations, in Yeats's poetry, is that of a supernatural bird. The soul in this form is in transition, preparing to move on to a new body or to a period in the Other World. However, the old man, true to his desire for stasis, wants to remain frozen in this intermediate state rather than consent to another life in a human body. His seeing such an existence as a state of Paradise, rather than as a grotesque punishment in Hell, is the full expression of his bitterness and brings the poem to a startling and powerful emotional climax. At the same time, the image is bizarre enough to serve the old man as a mockery of all the many birds that sing in Yeats's Other World as well as the "birds in the trees" of this world. Just as the journey to Byzantium parodies the traditional voyage to Tír na nÓg by keeping to its basic form but running it in reverse, the golden bird keeps the outward form of the Yeatsian soul-as-bird but inverts the normal content of that image: the golden bird is not a form taken on by a living soul, but a form created from outside it, like the mechanical birds made by Grecian goldsmiths, and it moves not because it is alive but because it is controlled by outside forces. Instead of being one of the "bobbins where all time is bound and wound," it will be moved by time without participating in time. In other words, the old man's soul will be effectively dead, while his bodily form will perpetually mimic the actions of living beings.

But the golden bird is specifically a bird in form, and it parodies not only natural birds but also one of Yeats's favorite images. His recurrent use of birds as emblems of the discarnate soul and as dwellers in Paradise is well-known and has been thoroughly studied by James L. Allen,[4] so there is no need to examine it here in detail. What is most important about this image, in relation to "Sailing to Byzantium," is that the miraculous bird of Yeats's image-system represents an individual soul that has changed its form but not its essential nature: it is still the same soul as when it wore a human form, and still part of the cycle of incarnations. It has reached, if only momentarily, an ideal form, but translation to the Other World has not changed it into something wholly new or necessarily immutable.

Often Yeats used the image of the soul-bird as a link between this world and the Other World, making its flight analogous to the sea-journey of an *imram*. He pictures a flock of such birds floating toward Tír na nÓg in "The White Birds":

> I am haunted by numberless islands, and many a Danaan shore,
> Where Time would surely forget us, and Sorrow come near us no more;
> Soon far from the rose and the lily and fret of the flames would we be,
> Were we only white birds, my beloved, buoyed out on the foam of the sea!
>
> [P 42]

These are, as Richard Ellmann has noted, "special birds, close to the discarnate species in 'Sailing to Byzantium,'"[5] but they are hardly unique to this poem. In his early work, Yeats often used such birds to link his own versions of Paradise with Irish tradition. Sometimes, as in "The White Birds," they are more or less decorative, and sometimes they are deliberately archaic touches, like the two swans that represent Baile and Ailinn reborn in Tír na nÓg and flying "Linked by a gold chain each to each" (P 400). However, like Tír na nÓg itself, Yeats's soul-birds were not simply Irish coloration; rather, they were central to his imagination and remained part of his personal imagery. In, for example, the late play *The Death of Cuchulain*, the soul's transformation into a bird works exactly as in the early poems and plays:

> There floats out there
> The shape that I shall take when I am dead,
> My soul's first shape, a soft feathery shape,
> And is not that a strange shape for the soul
> Of a great fighting-man?
>
> [VPl 1060]

However strange this transformation might seem to Cuchulain, it is inevitable in Yeats's system of imagery, in which the overall pattern of a soul's progress through the cycle of incarnations is far more important than the events of any particular life on the way.

Aside from being an emblem of the state between incarnations, a supernatural bird can mark those moments when the Other World is closest to this world, particularly moments of mystical ecstasy. Such ecstasies, in Yeats's work, make the Other World momentarily tangible and allow the visionary to see into the hidden workings of the spiritual realm. The old man is praying for just such a vision: he wants the sages to "perne in a gyre," that is, reveal to him their fundamental motion. However, when Yeats combines such visions with images of supernatural birds, the visions are generally sexual in origin. So, for example, when the woman of "A Woman Young and Old" is closest to the Other World, it is at a moment of sexual climax: "And now we stare astonished at the sea, / And a miraculous strange bird shrieks at us" (P 272). At a similar moment, Solomon explains to Sheba that their intercourse has almost brought the world to an end by projecting the Other World onto it:

> A cockerel
> Crew from a blossoming apple bough
> Three hundred years before the Fall,
> And never crew again till now,
> And would not now but that he thought,
> Chance being at one with Choice at last,
> All that the brigand apple brought
> And this foul world were dead at last.
> He that crowed out eternity
> Thought to have crowed it in again.
>
> [P 177]

Such images are natural in Yeats's poetry because he portrays life as driven onward by intense passions, passions that are themselves reflections of the force that drives the soul through its incarnations. Sexual love is common to both this world and the Other World, following the Hermetic axiom of "as above, so below"; but in keeping with the principle that all things have greater vigor in the Other World, the passion of discarnate spirits is more intense than bodies can allow. Here, the young are in one another's arms; there, according to the hermit Ribh, ". . . whole is joined to whole; / For the intercourse of angels is a light / Where for its moment both seem lost, consumed" (P 284). This image is close to that in *The King of the Great Clock Tower*, "nerve touching nerve upon that happy ground," (VPl 991) but it is also close to the old man's plea to the sages to "consume my heart away" (P 193). The difference is that the old man's passion, as intense as any lover's, is for an end to incarnations, while sexual intercourse, human or divine, must lead to perpetual renewals of the body. The old man is turning away from a spiritual order that he can repudiate only by inverting the language and imagery through which Yeats normally describes ecstasy and spiritual power.

The old man is trapped, then, not only by his aging body but by the nature of the entire universe as Yeats envisions it, both in his poems and plays and in his esoteric system. The old man's last refuge is to re-define Paradise, to make it a realm not of living spirits, which must share the qualities of human life, but of perfect works of art. However, his perception of art is no more in keeping with the body of Yeats's work than his perception of re-birth or sexual passion. The first stanza of "Sailing to Byzantium" defines art rather narrowly as the product of "intellect" opposed to the self-limiting passions of the body: "Caught in that sensual music all neglect / Monuments of unageing intellect." This separation of mind and body runs counter to Yeats's fusion of art, intellect, and the human form in his description of Byzantium in *A Vision*:

> I think if I could be given a month of Antiquity and leave to spend it where I chose, I would spend it in Byzantium a little before Justinian opened St. Sophia and closed the Academy of Plato. I think I could find in some little wine-shop some philosophical worker in mosaic who could answer all my questions, the supernatural descending nearer to him than to Plotinus even, for the pride of his delicate skill would make what was an instrument of power to princes and clerics, a murderous madness in the mob, show as a lovely flexible presence like that of a perfect human body. [AV-B 279]

Yeats's choice here of "a perfect human body" as the ideal form for a work of art is no more arbitrary than is that of the golden bird of "Sailing to Byzantium." Yeats, speaking in his own voice, affirms everything the old man denies: for Yeats the human form is the eternal form of the soul, so it is natural for him to depict the achievement of a work of art, a bridge between this world and the supernatural world, in terms of the body. Further, since the body is the means by which the soul experiences all the events of life in this world, a perfect body can also represent what Yeats called "Unity of Being," that mingling of intellect, passion, and acceptance of fate which he saw as the highest state of awareness attainable in life, and which is the opposite of the old man's strict division between body and mind. Yeats saw the art of the Italian Renaissance, and of Byzantium, in this light. In the Renaissance, which corresponds in history to the Fifteenth Phase of the Moon, artists, according to Yeats, found that

> the human norm, discovered from the measurement of ancient statues, was God's first handiwork, that "perfectly proportioned human body" which had seemed to Dante Unity of Being symbolized. The ascetic, who had a thousand years before attained his transfiguration upon the golden ground of Byzantine mosaic, had turned not into an athlete but into that unlaboring form the athlete dreamed of: the second Adam had become the first. [AV-B 291–92]

The "perfectly proportioned human body" of the Renaissance, which Yeats saw as a recurrence of the ideal forms on the "golden ground of Byzantine mosaic," is not far from the perfect body of Tír na nÓg. Art, for Yeats, was always a means of embodying the ideal; the old man shares this perception of art, but his ideal is the antithesis of the human form. In rejecting that form, he must also reject Yeats's understanding of the content of Byzantine art and turn it into its opposite.

Even the old man's choice of Byzantium as the place where he will be transformed parodies a specific element of Yeats's system and so is consistent with his parody of the Irish *imram* as a means of getting to the Other World and with his choice of a mechanical bird as the eternal form for his soul. Throughout the poem, then, the old man alludes to ideas and images integral to Yeats's work, but inverts them. The element of parody in the speaker's rhetoric, however, does not make "Sailing to Byzantium" an aberration in Yeats's poetry; rather, the old man's precise use of Yeatsian symbols binds the poem to the many other works in which Yeats defines his versions of the Other World, and, by calling them up in order to reject them, reinforces the power of the old man's rejection of life. As part of the design of Yeats's work, the old man is the anti-type of the speakers who affirm the human body as the inherent form of the soul and thereby affirm human life with all its pain. Suffering and the acceptance of suffering are closely balanced in Yeats's work, but while his affirmations are not easily won, they *are* won in the other poems, in the plays, and in *A Vision*; the old man is the one speaker whose despair is so absolute that it leads him, by his own choice, entirely out of life and into a form that is a mockery of life.

This analysis of the poem's context has, necessarily, led away from "Sailing to Byzantium" itself and toward those images and ideas which the old man turns into their opposites. The poem does not depend on this context for its force; rather, this context strengthens the old man's cry of pain through the poem's many analogues of form and imagery, creating around it a series of echoes that are still in one voice. Yeats introduced nothing unique or unusual, in terms of his personal imagery, in this poem—the journey to the Other World, the gyres, the soul as a bird are all very familiar in his work, and even Byzantium as a world of art is a symbol carefully defined elsewhere. He *did* make the poem unique in its power by reversing the meaning of all those images, thereby making it even more negative in its full context than in isolation. That absolute negation adds to the already considerable weight of the speaker's bitterness at the decay of his body, and makes it clear that he is not just an old man speaking from a black mood, but a man whose rejection of life is so final that only the creation of a special Paradise, in complete opposition to Yeats's vision of the spiritual world, can fully express his pain.

Notes

1. *J. B. Yeats: Letters to His Son W. B. Yeats and Others 1869–1922*, ed. Joseph Hone (London: Faber, 1944) 179.
2. Helen Vendler, "Sacred and Profane Perfection in Yeats," *The Southern Review* 9.1 (Jan 1973): 105–16.
3. Curtis Bradford, "Yeats's Byzantium Poems: A Study of Their Development," *Yeats: A Collection of Critical Essays*, ed. John Unterecker (Englewood Cliffs, N. J.: Prentice-Hall, 1963) 99. Hereafter cited as Bradford.

4. James L. Allen, "From Traditional to Personal Myth: Yeats's Golden Bird," *Canadian Journal of Irish Studies* 5.2 (1979): 1–30.
5. Richard Ellmann, *The Identity of Yeats*, 2nd ed. (New York: Oxford University Press, 1964) 70.

Reassessing Arthur Symons's Relationship with Lady Gregory

Bruce D. Morris

For far too many years a hardened amber of secondary sources has preserved the half-truth that Arthur Symons blamed Lady Gregory for Yeats deserting lyric poetry and, as a result, disliked her intensely. Yet there is no real evidence that Symons developed this hostility until after 1908 when a catastrophic mental breakdown left him more and more superstitious, withdrawn, and irrationally fearful. In fact, a careful examination of contemporary sources, including unpublished letters and anonymous reviews, reveals that even though Lady Gregory may have entertained some reservations about Symons's influence on Yeats's style, their relations were, in general, quite cordial before 1908.

The basis for much of this confusion is a 22 October 1912 letter from J. B. Yeats to his daughter Lily in which appears a reported conversation between Symons and Agnes Tobin, the young American poet and translator who had visited him frequently during his prolonged convalescence in Brooke House sanatorium: "It seems that 'Arthur' hates Lady Gregory," explains JBY, "and moans at the mention of her." "Well, Arthur," accuses Tobin, "it was your fault." "Yes, I know," admits Symons. "It was I who brought him to Coole, and as soon as her terrible eye fell upon him I knew she would keep him, and he is now lost to lyrical poetry." J. B. Yeats completes this portrait of a paranoid by adding that Symons insists on calling Lady Gregory the "Strega" (Italian for "witch").[1]

The temptation to abstract so colorful an anecdote from its proper psychological context proved too strong first for Joseph Hone and, later, for A. Norman Jeffares, both of whom reached the same hasty conclusion: Symons, like Maud Gonne, and several of the poet's other Irish friends, disapproved of Yeats's famous collaboration with Lady Gregory.[2] And George Moore appeared to confirm that this animosity was mutual when he recalled in *Hail and Farewell* how Lady Gregory "seemed to dread that the inspiration the hills of Sligo had nourished might wither in the Temple,"[3] where Yeats shared a flat with Symons during the winter of 1895/96. But Moore is unreliable at best, and Hone and Jeffares might have known better than to accept at face value a statement made by Symons in 1912 when his recovery was as yet very far from complete.

Neither Symons nor Lady Gregory have recorded their reactions following an initial encounter at Coole in August 1896, but those first impressions could not have been particularly negative, for if we can still trust Symons's memory as late as 1940, he and Yeats lunched with her there on three successive occasions.[4] We now know for certain, though, thanks to the following letter from one of Lady Gregory's albums, that by the summer of 1898 Symons was already passing on, at Yeats's request, an incident from recent European history illustrating the predicament of those in Ireland, like Douglas Hyde and herself, who were attempting to revive the indigenous language and literature.

[mid-August 1898]
Fountain Court
The Temple

Dear Lady Gregory

I had begun to write to Yeats, when it occurred to me that this letter may not reach him in time. If, therefore, he is still with you, will you tell him that I shall expect him here to dinner on Sunday?

He asks me to tell you more precisely a story which was told me by Count Lützow.[5] I am afraid I don't remember the exact details, but the point was that owing to the spread of German, the Czech language so nearly died out, at all events as a literary language, in Bohemia, that one of a small company of learned men, gathered together to discuss the possibilities of its revival, glanced up at the ceiling and said, "If that ceiling were to fall, the Bohemian language would be at an end!" Unfortunately I don't remember exactly when this occurred: certainly during the present century, and I should think not more than 50 years ago, if that. The native Bohemian literature completely died out for two centuries, and has only lately revived again. I remember Lützow showing me, last May, an article comparing the fortunes of Bohemia with Ireland in an Irish paper with a Gaelic name and the front page in Gaelic: you may know it.

Yours sincerely,

Arthur Symons[6]

True, in 1899 Symons did politely decline Lady Gregory's invitation to visit her and Yeats in Ireland that summer, but his excuses seem quite plausible: in June he needed to stay in London to correct proofs of *The Symbolist Movement in Literature,* and in August he was already scheduled to attend the Wagner festival at Bayreuth.[7] So if there was any substantive conflict between Symons and Lady Gregory at the beginning of their relationship, it most likely reflected a debate already in progress between Symons and Yeats themselves: Symons arguing that the "nomadic life" was the best of all possible lives for an artist, Yeats countering that "an artist worked best among his own folk and in the land of his fathers."[8]

It is easy to understand why Lady Gregory, who, it will be remembered, was already collecting tales of peasant beliefs, should have sided with Yeats, who had returned to Ireland during the summer of 1896 with the specific intention of discovering in the folk imagination an antidote fo the lacquered, artificial style he noticed developing in his story *Rosa Alchemica* (Mem 100–1). As she later confided to Moore (who, for once, lets her speak in her own voice), "Yeats came to Coole every summer because it was necessary to get him away from the intellectual distractions Arthur Symons had inaugurated." "All Yeats's early poems," she went on, "were written in Sligo, and among them were twenty beautiful lyrics and Ireland's one great poem, *The Wanderings of Usheen*—all these had come straight out of the landscape and people he had known from boyhood" (HF 204). Moore took these "intellectual distractions" to mean such "alien influences" as Villiers, Verlaine and Maeterlink that Symons, as editor of the internationalist *Savoy*, was translating and interpreting for Yeats, whose own knowledge of French was slight. But by 1902 Symons too had rejected artifice and was making his own "amends to nature"; and although his admiration for most of the writers of the Celtic Revival was tempered by a distrust of their formulaic mannerisms,[9] he was nonetheless still promoting the works of Lady Gregory with great enthusiasm.

Several signs of their generally good relations have survived, some already familiar, others heretofore overlooked. Lady Gregory herself, for one, recalls dining with Symons and Thomas Hardy in June 1904 during the London Stage Society's rehearsals of Yeats's *Where There Is Nothing*.[10] And Ann Saddlemyer has published an 11 February 1903 letter in which Symons offers Lady Gregory help in getting *Riders to the Sea* into the *Fortnightly Review* before the play was scheduled for publication in book form.[11] Until now, though, it was not known that Symons, despite his initial failure with Lady Gregory's *Cuchulain of Muirthemne*, was eventually able to place in the *Athenaeum* an appreciative review of her next book, *Poets and Dreamers*.

On 5 August 1902 Symons wrote to Yeats, who was then staying at Coole Park, complaining, "You will have seen a review, not altogether amiable of Lady Gregory's book in last week's 'Athenaeum': I don't know who can have written it, or why I was not allowed to write something in its place."[12] After sneering at "the fantastic and grotesque elements of Celtic legend, which either puzzle or annoy the English mind," the anonymous reviewer had attacked Lady Gregory's use of dialect in *Cuchulain of Muirthemne* as "no more than a specimen of suitable English style, coloured by a few Irish idioms, some of which tend to become tedious by frequent repetition."[13] Yet this setback did not deter Symons for long. As the following letter from the Berg Collection shows, when her *Poets and Dreamers* came out in 1903, Symons, with the same persistence that characterized his struggle to find James Joyce a publisher,[14] quickly seized this new opportunity to continue his campaign on Lady Gregory's behalf.

[n.d.]
134 Lauderdale Mansions
  Maida Vale. W.

Dear Lady Gregory

   I am very glad to have your book, & I have already read Raftery, & the beautiful nativity play, & the wonderful ballad on p. 64, & a few other things; & I am writing to ask the Athenaeum if I may review it. I fear they will again send your work to someone more likely to take the purely English view of things Irish. But I would like to get it. I could do something better about it than I could have done about the other book.
   The cover looks very nice; would not a cover wholly of linen be good?

Very truly yours

Arthur Symons[15]

This time the *Athenaeum* must have replied in the affirmative, for the unsigned review reprinted in the appendix which follows was included in the 23 May 1903 issue.[16] It is definitely by Symons, since in it Lady Gregory's "grave, quaint, simple, and sinewy language" is compared favorably to the "living speech" of the Irish peasants Symons had actually encountered himself while vacationing with Yeats in Galway, Sligo, and on the Aran Islands during the summer of 1896. Here again, as he had done earlier with contemporary Provençal and French Symbolist poets, Symons attempts to educate the English reading public concerning a new literary "movement," in this case, the nascent Irish Literary Renaissance, which he then locates within a broader European intellectual tradition that included, oddly enough, Heine, Villon, Catullus, and Tolstoy. Even if we ignore the correspondence that preceded it, this one review—and the private conversations it suggests—would justify beginning to speak of an Arthur Symons-Lady Gregory friendship that was cut short, like so many other positive features of Symons's creative life, by the catastrophe of 1908.

Appendix

Poets and Dreamers: Studies and Translations from the Irish. By Lady Gregory. (Murray.) [Reprint]

In this book the Irish peasant is for the first time allowed to speak for himself. In "Cuchulain of Muirthemne" Lady Gregory had already invented a new form of English: the first really faithful transcript of the speech of the Irish peasant, as he thinks in Irish and speaks in English. Here, in these folk-tales collected from old men and women on the roads, and from the cabins of poor people, and from the workhouses, and in these songs, ballads and plays translated from Irish, we have a grave, quaint, simple, and sinewy language, which is not a consciously naïve or experimental thing, but a living speech, which the present writer has heard spoken, in exactly this form and with just these subtly indicated cadences, in Galway, in Sligo, and on the islands of Arran. Here, then, is the genuine dialect. And, unlike the lingo which could only express a low and farcical kind of humour, this real dialect is able to say all that words can say of the dreams and faiths that are in the hearts of the people. What more, indeed, can we ask of the sincerity of words than what we find in these three stanzas translated from a Western ballad called 'The Grief of a Girl's Heart'?—

> "It is late last night the dog was speaking of you; the snipe was speaking of you in her deep marsh. It is you are the lonely bird through the woods; and that you may be without a mate until you find me.
>
> "It was on that Sunday I gave my love to you; the Sunday that is last before Easter Sunday. And myself on my knees reading the Passion: and my eyes giving love to you for ever.
>
> "You have taken the east from me; you have taken the west from me; you have taken what is before me and what is behind me; you have taken the moon, you have taken the sun from me; and my fear is great that you have taken God from me!"

Lady Gregory's book is made partly or translations, partly of folk-stories taken down from the lips of the people, with a slight, but sufficient thread of her own spinning to bind all together. Folk-lorists will find new material, where the general reader will find fresh entertainment, in the 'Workhouse Dreams' and in 'Herb-Healing' and in 'Mountain Theology.' In the long chapter on Raftery we have a record, with translations and quaint peasant comments, of the blind poet-fiddler of Galway, the last of a long tradition, who died sixty years ago, and whose poems, though he never wrote them down, are still repeated from mouth to mouth. The prose translations of "a few of the more homely ballads" of the West add something definitely worth having to the prose and verse translations in Dr. Hyde's remarkable book 'The

Love-Songs of Connacht,' published ten years ago: a book containing some of the most difficult successes in verse translation which have been done in our time.[17] But it is perhaps in the translations of the poems and plays of Dr. Hyde himself that the English reader will find the most interesting part of an exceptionally and variously interesting book.

In the preface to his book of Irish poems, 'Ubhla de'n Craoibh' ('Apples from the Branch'), Dr. Hyde says:—

> "I would like better to make even one good verse in the language in which I am now writing than to make a whole book of verses in English. For if there should be any good found in my English verses, it would not go to the credit of my mother, Ireland, but of my stepmother, England."

It is impossible for an Englishman to compare the merit of Dr. Hyde's verse as verse, in Irish and in English, and to say whether a writer who has so nimble a tread in English has a lighter or a heavier step in Irish. But at least the Irish which Dr. Hyde writes is not, as with the poets of Munster, a kind of learned language, but a language actually spoken in the country, in no more than a slightly rougher form. To the partisans of the other school he seems an incorrect writer, willing to use words and constructions that have come into the language from English; not sternly conservative, a writer of Irish as it should be spoken. But it is just because he is a poet and a man of deep human feeling that he writes, as nearly as possible, in the language of the people; and his writing is simple, and it speaks straight. Here, in Lady Gregory's English, is a poem that, in the original, must be a great poem:—

> There are three devils eating my heart—
> They left me, my grief! without a thing:
> Sickness wrought, and Love wrought,
> And an empty pocket, my ruin and my woe.
> Poverty left me without a shirt,
> Barefooted, barelegged, without any covering;
> Sickness left me with my head weak
> And my body miserable, an ugly thing.
> Love left me like a coal upon the floor,
> Like a half-burned sod, that is never put out.
> Worse than the cough, worse than the fever itself,
> Worse than any curse at all under the sun,
> Worse than the great poverty,
> Is the devil that is called "Love" by the people.
> And if I were in my young youth again,
> I would not take, or give, or ask for a kiss!

In that poem, read in English prose, there is a fierce personal quality which Lady Gregory compares with the quality of Villon or Heine. Something of Villon there may be, the Villon who spoke of "winter, when the wolves live on wind"; but something also more like Catullus than Heine.

There are four one-act plays by Dr. Hyde in this volume. Two of them, 'The Twisting of the Rope' and 'The Marriage,' have humour, a delightful naturalness, and also a touch of mystery or irresponsibility. But in 'The Lost Saint' and in 'The Nativity' there is a beauty wholly of the imagination, and they are full of pity and tenderness. Both are made out of simple materials. They are close to the earth, and to humble and sincere minds. They have an instinctive, and unsought *naïveté*. They are genuinely dramatic and the drama seems to awaken of itself rather than to be plotted for a purpose. Some such work as this, surely, is what Tolstoy understands by true art; and, though Tolstoy's definition is a local and not a universal one, it defines an admirable and beautiful thing, which here, for once, stands before us. This work is too literally a living growth to be torn apart and divided into specimens. It is not so much that there are fine poetical things in it, that there are beautiful speeches, as that each of the two plays is itself a poem. If Lady Gregory's book contained no more than those last fifty pages it would be a book which has added something to English literature.

A word may be said on the original binding of the book in sacking and sugar-paper. The printing—which, like the binding, was done in Ireland—cannot compare for a moment with the English printing of 'Cuchulain of Muirthemne'; but the binding has a simplicity and a suitability of its own, which give it not only a more novel aspect than that of 'Cuchulain,' but also an aspect of homely peasant-beauty.

Notes

1. J. B. Yeats: *Letters to His Son W. B. Yeats and Others 1869–1922*, ed. Joseph Hone (London: Faber, 1944) 179.

2. Joseph Hone first presented this view in his *W. B. Yeats: 1865–1939* (London: Macmillan, 1943) 138, and it was then repeated by A. Norman Jeffares in *W. B. Yeats: Man and Poet* (New Haven: Yale University Press, 1949) 147. See also William M. Murphy, *Prodigal Father: The Life of John Butler Yeats (1839–1922)* (Ithaca and London: Cornell University Press, 1978) 193.

3. George Moore, *Hail and Farewell: Ave, Salve, Vale*, ed. Richard Allen Cave (Washington D.C.: Catholic University of America Press, 1985) 548. Further references are cited parenthetically in the text as *HF*.

4. Arthur Symons, TLS to Joseph Hone, 12 February 1940, Ms. 5919, National Library of Ireland, Dublin. In this poorly punctuated letter, written when he was seventy-five years old and nearly blind, Symons told Hone, "It was in 1896 Yeats first met Lady Gregory, She wrote to Edward Martyn Asking him to bring Yeats and myself to lunch at Gort, we lunched with Lady Gregory on three seperate [sic] occasions I did not stay at Lady Gregory's I left Yeats with Edward Martyn and returned to London alone. I did not go to Ireland again."

5. Count Franz Heinrich Hieronymus Valentin von Lützow (1849–1916), author, historian and Bohemian patriot.

6. Before offering the original of this black-bordered ALS for sale at Phillips in 1978, Colin Smythe, the executor of the Gregory literary estate, made a transcription of it, which he has kindly consented to be reproduced here.

7. Arthur Symons, ALS to W. B. Yeats (early June 1899); copy in the Yeats Archive, Frank Melville, Jr. Memorial Library, State University of New York at Stony Brook.

8. During a BBC broadcast delivered in December 1954, Max Beerhohm describes Yeats and Symons publicly debating this question at a supper party given by Leonard Smithers, probably in January 1896, to celebrate the first number of the *Savoy:* "Shaking back the lock from his brow, [Yeats] turned to Symons and declared that an artist worked best among his own folk and in the land of his fathers. Symons was rather daunted but stuck to his point. He argued that new sights and sounds and odours braced the whole intelligence of a man and quickened his powers of creation. Yeats, gently and firmly, would have none of this." Quoted in Roger Lhombreaud, *Arthur Symons: A Critical Biography* (London: Unicorn, 1963) 123.

9. Arthur Symons, ALS to "Seumas O'Sullivan" (James Starkey), 19 February 1905, Ms. 4630/68, Trinity College, Dublin. In this letter Symons criticizes Starkey, and, by implication, the whole Revival, for playing "on rhythms too capriciously—as even Yeats does, and as all the Irish writers have learnt from him to do," as well as for what Symons deemed, "a *too* consistent vagueness."

10. *Seventy Years: Being the Autobiography of Lady Gregory*, ed. Colin Smythe (New York: Macmillan, 1976) 139.

11. Arthur Symons, ALS to Lady Gregory, 11 February 1903, TCD Ms. 4424/122 in *Theatre Business: The Correspondence of the First Abbey Theatre Directors: William Butler Yeats, Lady Gregory and J. M. Synge*, ed. Ann Saddlemyer (University Park and London: Pennsylvania State University Press, 1982) 39–40. Here Saddlemyer also gives Synge's diary entry for 10 February 1903: "Dined with Lady Gregory. Play read out afterwards to A. Symons etc."

However, Symons was even more favorably impressed with Synge's work when, a few weeks later, he attended one of Yeats's Monday evenings and listened to Lady Gregory recite *The Shadow of the Glen;* so impressed, in fact, as the following letter provided by Colin Smythe shows, that he suggested sending a copy of this play to Henry Newbolt (1862–1938), then editor of the *Monthly Review.*

March 12 [1903]
134 Lauderdale Mansions
  Maida Vale. W.

Dear Lady Gregory

I saw Newbolt yesterday, and spoke to him about Synge's new play (which struck me as being in some ways even better than the other). He has promised to read it if it is sent to him, though he does not much care for plays. Will you post it to The Editor Montly Review 50a Albemarle Street.

Was not Pixie Smith, in her little song, perfect and delightful on Monday night? and was not Mrs. Eliott deplorable?

Yours very truly

Arthur Symons

12. Arthur Symons, ALS to W. B. Yeats, 5 August 1902; copy in Yeats Archive, Frank Melville, Jr. Memorial Library, State University of New York at Stony Brook.

13. Rev. of *Cuchulain of Muirthemne* by Lady Gregory, *Athenaeum* (2 August 1902): 146–47. This review is listed by E. H. Mikhail as item 744 in *Lady Gregory: An Annotated Bibliography of Criticism* (Troy, NY: Whitston, 1982) 109.

14. See Karl Beckson and John M. Munro, "Letters from Arthur Symons to James Joyce: 1904–1932," *James Joyce Quarterly* 4 (1967): 91–101.

15. Arthur Symons, ALS to Lady Gregory, n.d., Berg Collection, Astor, Lenox and Tilden Foundations, New York Public Library. The "wonderful ballad on p. 64" is "The Grief of a Girl's Heart," which Symons quotes in his *Athenaeum* review as an example of "the genuine dialect" of the Irish peasant.

16. Rev. of *Poets and Dreamers* by Lady Gregory, *Athenaeum* (23 May 1903): 157. This review is listed as item 1219 in Mikhail's bibliography and is reproduced in the appendix to this article by special permission of Mr. Brian Read, the executor of the literary estate of Arthur Symons.

17. Douglas Hyde, *The Love-Songs of Connacht* (London: T. Fisher Unwin, 1893).

Gaiety Transfiguring All That Dread: The Case of Yeats

C. A. Patrides

Yeats's "Lapis Lazuli" (P 294-95) is indisputably one of the most impressive poems in twentieth-century literature. Yet it begins with a stanza which is sufficiently unpoetic to persuade one that the poetry does not matter:

> I have heard that hysterical women say
> They are sick of the palette and fiddle-bow,
> Of poets that are always gay,
> For everybody knows or else should know
> That if nothing drastic is done
> Aeroplane and Zeppelin will come out,
> Pitch like King Billy bomb-balls in
> Until the town lie beaten flat.

The poetry apparently matters not as poetry but in relation to the thematic designs it argues aesthetically. Responding negatively at the outset of "Lapis Lazuli," the poetry retreats in pointed refusal to sustain a vulgar attack upon itself, the common enough claim that poets are indifferent to the adversities incidental to reality. In this sense, "gay" is equivalent to uninvolved, uncaring, unresponsive. But the next stanza transmutes the word into a term suggestive of commitment, steady vision, constant purpose:

> All perform their tragic play,
> There struts Hamlet, there is Lear,
> That's Ophelia, that Cordelia;
> Yet they, should the last scene be there,
> The great stage curtain about to drop,
> If worthy their prominent part in the play,
> Do not break up their lines to weep.
> They know that Hamlet and Lear are gay;
> Gaiety transfiguring all that dread.

> All men have aimed at, found and lost;
> Black out; Heaven blazing into the head:
> Tragedy wrought to its uttermost.
> Though Hamlet rambles and Lear rages,
> And all the drop scenes drop at once
> Upon a hundred thousand stages,
> It cannot grow by an inch or an ounce.

In their appeal to the essential unity of human experience, the lines constitute one of the great defences of poetry. They also constitute an ambitious effort to subordinate whatever appertains to tragedy under the banner of an imperative gaiety beyond prosaic theories whether propounded categorically by Aristotle in *Poetics* or endorsed axiomatically by overeager generic taxonomists. Given the poem's distinctly apocalyptic overtones, we might suspect that Yeats resolves the complexities of the argument by referring them to a time beyond death. But the stage is decidedly that of the immediate present: "the last scene" will soon become the first one as the performance of our several plays is repeated again and yet again "Upon a hundred thousand stages." "Heaven blazing into the head" appears, indeed, to direct us to an afterlife, but in fact specifies the moment of illumination when, even as Hamlet rambles and Lear rages, we comprehend that tragedy "wrought to its uttermost" has already inverted itself to behave after the fashion of a *commedia* beyond tragedy.

"Lapis Lazuli" exhibits an uncommon commitment to art as an omnipresent reality, even where the artifacts themselves have vanished altogether. "No handiwork of Callimachus," we are told later in the poem, "stands." But no matter, since the creativity of one artist is matched by the creativity of another, their ongoing activities communally linking each to each through a pervasive gaiety:

> All things fall and are built again
> And those that build them again are gay.

The figures carved on the lapis lazuli—and, through the figures, the artist who created them—are finally imagined seated "on the mountain and the sky," their response to "the tragic scene" below them by now inevitable:

> One asks for mournful melodies;
> Accomplished fingers begin to play.
> Their eyes mid many wrinkles, their eyes,
> Their ancient, glittering eyes, are gay.

Life's adversities are not naively disregarded. The final melodies heard are indeed "mournful," and the scene does remain "tragic." But from the still point of Yeats's turning world emanates the assurance that while tragedy does abound, gaiety abounds no less.

"Lapis Lazuli" is a poem that Yeats regarded highly, "almost the best I have made in recent years" (L 859), he said once. It is among other things his most brilliant articulation in poetry of ideas he set forth in prose on a number of occasions. But Yeats's critical prose may not be approached in the same way one approaches the critical judgments of, say, T. S. Eliot. There is no sparkle in Yeats to qualify sententious views often sententiously stated; most emphatically, his considerable critical output may not ever be treated but seriously, even too seriously. On the other hand, the apparent norm is subject to so many exceptions that one often suspects the exceptions to be themselves the norm. Yeats's critical prose should be read in the light of one's conclusions about his other prose works, notably *A Vision*. It may be that the arcane knowledge of that improbable work, imparted by extraterrestrial "communicators" but frustrated by (who else?) the "frustrators," is a seriously intended exposition of motifs earnestly upheld. But it may also be that every aspect of it is placed at the service of a comic outlook, its prefatory *Packet for Ezra Pound* representative of the sustained ingenuity later acknowledged by Pound not without some irritation ("Once out at Rapallo I tried for God's sake to prevent him from printing a thing. I told him it was rubbish. All he did was print it with a preface saying that I *said* it was rubbish"[1]). If *A Vision* is indeed comic in its essential orientation, it could be said to partake of two substantial antecedents of as much levity as seriousness: first, the Renaissance lists of fabulous books compiled by Rabelais and Donne and Sir Thomas Browne, among others; and secondly, the older tradition known as "Menippean satire," its characteristic a jocularity fully congruent with the gravity appropriate to philosophical discourse.

The several likely interpretations of *A Vision* suggest that Yeats's critical prose may also be multiform, possibly playful, and, if playful, tentative to a degree not commonly appreciated. Yeats wrote his prose with a poetic sensibility totally absent from Eliot's temperate rhetorical patterns. We are in consequence utterly captivated; but we are utterly confounded, too, by inconsistencies and obscurities at least as frequent as they are in the plays and in the later poems. As in poetry at its finest, however, the inconsistencies in Yeats's prose appertain to a predetermined tentativeness; and the obscurities, to an admission of the mystery at the center of life as of literature. The theoretical premises hazarded by Yeats in connection with tragedy and comedy are in this respect instructive in the extreme.

Tragedy for Yeats revolves about "personality," comedy about "character"; the one is general, universal, and transcendent, the other specific, particular, and visible; the one through deeply felt passions unites man to man or to nature or to both, the other—ever passionless—separates us into individuals. Such sharp lines of demarcation serve well enough in theory, for the sake of explication, but ultimately they are not responsible to reality's complexities. Yeats perceived the issue readily. "We may not," he wrote in one essay, "find either mood in its purity" (E&I 243). "In practice," he declared on another occasion, "most works are mixed: Shakespeare being tragi-comedy" (Au 471). The invocation of Shakespeare—"always a writer of tragi-comedy" (E&I 240)—is crucial in that he was Yeats's perennial court of appeal, an indispensable precedent where the dramatic practice repeatedly obliges theories to submit to the realities of reality. Now and then, Shakespeare was grouped with another "realist," Sophocles:

> It is only by extravagance, by an emphasis far greater than that of life as we observe it, that we can crowd into a few minutes the knowledge of years. Shakespeare or Sophocles can so quicken, as it were, the circles of the clock, so heighten the expression of life, that many years can unfold themselves in a few minutes, and it is always Shakespeare or Sophocles, and not Ibsen, that makes us say, 'How true, how often I have felt as that man feels'; or 'How intimately I have come to know those people on the stage'. [Ex 195–96]

Thus in 1905; and a quarter of a century later, in 1931, Yeats confirmed yet again how naturally his mind connected the two dramatists:

> Oedipus brings upon himself the curse of the gods because of an involuntary sin, but in the second play he wanders an outcast from road to road, a blind old man, attended and protected by his two daughters as Lear was protected by Cordelia. So great has been his suffering that the gods have come over to his side and those that he curses perish and those that he blesses prosper.[2]

A third statement, made in 1938 within sight of Yeats's death, links Sophocles and Shakespeare with particular reference to the transfiguring power of "gaiety," here equated with "joy":

> The arts are all the bridal chambers of joy. No tragedy is legitimate unless it leads some great character to his final joy. Polonius may go out wretchedly, but I can hear the dance music in 'Absent thee from felicity awile', or in Hamlet's speech over the dead Ophelia, and what of Cleopatra's last farewells, Lear's rage under the lightning, Oedipus sinking down at the story's end into an earth 'riven' by love? [Ex 448–49]

Primary as the example of Shakespeare ever was for Yeats, the numerous statements centered exclusively on one poet are ultimately our best measure of the theoretical premises of the other. Two of these statements must be quoted at some length, alike crucial as they are. One forms part of "A General Introduction for my Work" (1937):

> The heroes of Shakespeare convey to us through their looks, or through the metaphorical patterns of their speech, the sudden enlargement of their vision, their ecstasy at the approach of death: 'She should have died hereafter,' 'Of many thousand kisses, the poor last,' 'Absent thee from felicity awhile.' They have become God or Mother Goddess, but all must be cold; no actress has ever sobbed when she played Cleopatra, even the shallow brain of a producer has never thought of such a thing. The supernatural is present, cold winds blow across our hands, upon our faces, the thermometer falls, and because of that cold we are hated by journalists and groundlings. There may be in this or that debate painful tragedy, but in the whole work, none. I have heard Lady Gregory say, rejecting some play in the modern manner sent to the Abbey Theatre, "Tragedy must be a joy to the man who dies." Nor is it any different with lyrics, songs, narrative poems. . . . [E&I 522–23]

The other statement, written many years earlier as part of "Poetry and Tradition" (1907), demonstrates even more strikingly the transformation of the argument under the impact of Yeats's poetic sensibility:

> Shakespeare's persons, when the last darkness has gathered about them, speak out of an ecstasy that is one-half the self-surrender of sorrow, and one-half the last playing and mockery of the victorious sword before the defeated world.
> It is in the arrangement of events as in the words, and in that touch of extravagance, of irony, of surprise, which is set there after the desire of logic has been satisfied and all that is merely necessary established, and that leaves one, not in the circling necessity, but caught up into the freedom of self-delight: it is, as it were, the foam upon the cup, the long pheasant's feather on the horse's head, the spread peacock over the pasty. If it be very conscious, very deliberate, as it may be in comedy, for comedy is more personal than tragedy, we call it fantasy, perhaps even mischievous fantasy, recognising how disturbing it is to all that drag a ball at the ankle. This joy, because it must be always making and mastering, remains in the hands and in the tongue of the artist, but with his eyes he enters upon a submissive, sorrowful contemplation of the great irremediable things, and he is known from other men by making all he handles like himself, and yet by the unlikeness to himself of all that comes before him in a pure contemplation. It may have been his enemy or his love or his cause that set him dreaming, and certainly the phoenix can but open her young wings in a flaming nest; but all hate and hope vanishes in the dream, and if his mistress brag of the song or his enemy fear it, it is not that either has its praise or blame, but that the twigs of the holy nest are not easily set afire. The verses may make his mistress famous as Helen or give a victory to his cause, not because he has been either's servant, but because men delight to honour and to remember all that have served contemplation. It had been easier to fight, to die even, for Charles's house with Marvell's poem in the memory, but there is no zeal of service that had not been an impurity in the pure soil where the marvel grew. Timon of Athens contemplates his own end, and orders his tomb by the beached verge of the salt flood, and Cleopatra sets the asp to her bosom, and their words move us because their sorrow is not their own at tomb or asp, but for all men's fate. That shaping joy has kept the sorrow pure, as it had kept it were the emotion love or hate, for the nobleness of the arts is in the mingling of contraries, the extremity of sorrow, the extremity of joy, perfection of personality, the perfection of its surrender, overflowing turbulent energy, and marmorean stillness; and its red rose opens at the meeting of the two beams of the cross, and at the trysting-place of mortal and immortal, time and eternity. [E&I 254–55]

The statement is not only magnificent in itself. In its aspiration to account for both the origins and the effect no less of dramatic art than of the arts generally, it is a magisterial corrective to the theories of mere critics like Aristotle. Where theorists are confined but to the reason of things, Yeats as a creator of literature advances beyond reason ("after the desire of logic has been satisfied") to address the nature of "the great irremediable things," their "mingling of contraries" seen as the only proper acknowledgment of the transfiguration of sorrow by joy, of dread by gaiety, and—now imaginatively reconstituted—of tragedy by comedy.

Comedy, gaiety, joy: was Yeats so naive that he overlooked "the anguish of the morrow," as Eliot said of the experiential life of Donne, "the ague of the skeleton"?[3] But that would have been very odd indeed, especially for an Irishman! The foundation is not joy but sorrow, not comedy but tragedy. "We begin to live," wrote Yeats, "when we have conceived life as tragedy" (Au 189). The tragedy that is life once fully accepted, however, the immediate consequence is joy and gaiety and comedy, even loud laughter:

> There is in the creative joy our acceptance of what life brings, because we have understood the beauty of what it brings, or a hatred of death for what it takes away, which arouses within us, through some sympathy perhaps with all other men, an energy so noble, so powerful, that we laugh aloud and mock, in the terror or the sweetness of our exaltation, at death and oblivion. [E&I 322]

Possibly the most persistently reiterated of Yeats's convictions, "tragic joy" was habitually predicated in connection with Sophoclean and Shakespearean drama, as already noted. But it was also predicated in connection with drama generally ("In all the great tragedies, tragedy is a joy to the man who dies; in Greece the tragic chorus danced" [OBMV xxxiv–xxxv]) and, in an ever-expanding circle, literature at large as well as the arts barring none. It is in this sense, no doubt, that Yeats remarked in a characteristically striking phrase that "the arts are an extension of the beatitudes" (L 832). The generalization may not be writ large in the arts; but it certainly is in his own poetic practice.

Twentieth-century drama surprises, we know, by its obsessive concern with the myths that had sustained Greek drama. T. S. Eliot in England, for instance, was anticipated by O'Neill in the United States, while the eyes of almost every major dramatist in France—Gide, Cocteau, Giradoux, Sartre, Anouilh, Ionesco—were also fixed firmly on ancient Athens. Yeats, too, responded to Greek myths; but in his own fashion. His poetry attests to his fascination particularly with "the Trojan matter," which yielded remarkable achievements of the order of "Leda and the Swan"; and if on the whole his plays eschewed the myths of Greece for those of Ireland, Athenian drama remained always within reach, be it in connection with *The King's Threshold*, whose construction Yeats thought "rather like a Greek play" (L 409), or in connection even with *Purgatory*, whose principal analogue is—demonstrably, I would claim—the Aeschylean dramatization of the curse on the House of Atreus. Most tellingly, however, Yeats's drama includes two plays often disregarded as translations when they are, in fact, versions deliberately adjusted to carry his own emphases. I mean, of course, *King Oedipus* (first performed 1926) and *Oedipus at Colonus* (1927).

Oedipus fascinated Yeats. As we marked earlier, Oedipus was numbered among the "great" who, like Lear, suffer intensely, confront their destinies with "joy," and bend in their favor even the will of the gods. A lengthy passage in *A Vision* raises several tantalizing questions not calculated to delight Ezra Pound ("What if Christ and Oedipus or, to shift the names, Saint Catherine of Genoa and Michael Angelo, are the two scales of a balance . . . ?") In advance, however, Yeats attempted yet again to define the greatness of Oedipus and, in close juxtaposition as always, of Lear. The meditation follows Oedipus as he enters the heart of the sacred wood at Colonus:

> until amidst the sound of thunder earth opened, "riven by love," and he sank down soul and body into the earth. I would have him balance Christ who, crucified standing up, went into the abstract sky soul and body, and I see him altogether separated from Plato's Athens, from all that talk of the Good and the One, from all that cabinet of perfection, an image from Homer's age. When it was already certain that he must bring himself under his own curse did he not still question, and when answered as the Sphinx had been answered, stricken with the horror that is in *Gulliver* and in the *Fleurs du Mal*, did he not tear out his own eyes? He raged against his sons, and this rage was noble, not from some general idea, some sense of public law upheld, but because it seemed to contain all life, and the daughter who served him as did Cordelia Lear—he too a man of Homer's kind—seemed less attendant upon an old railing rambler than upon genius itself. He knew nothing but his mind, and yet because he spoke that mind fate possessed it and kingdoms changed according to his blessing and his cursing. Delphi, that rock at earth's navel, spoke through him, and though men shuddered and drove him away they spoke of ancient poetry, praising the boughs overhead, the grass under foot, Colonus and its horses.

But here the perspective changes, however imperceptibly, and we focus on another reason for Yeats's partiality to Oedipus, the single communion sensed to be enjoyed by legendary Greece and legendary Ireland: "I think that he lacked compassion, seeing that it must be compassion for himself, and yet stood nearer to the poor than saint or apostle, and I mutter to myself stories of Cruachan, or of Cruachmaa, or of the road-side bush withered by Raftery's curse" (AV-B 27–29).

The communion sensed is that of the convergence of the mystery at the heart of one culture on the mystery at the heart of another. The "comedy" that informs both Sophoclean plays on Oedipus did not interest Yeats. It may even have escaped his attention, intent as he was to transmute Oedipus into a primeval entity sprung from the prehistoric world of Homer, the boundless rage assertive of the boundlessness of "all life," the fear induced in others apocalyptic of a numinous presence, the readiness to enter the wood at Colonus declarative of a transcendent joy ("in Greece the tragic chorus danced"). It need therefore not surprise that Yeats in *King Oedipus* so amended the original that the protagonist's recovery from despair is expedited, and so altered the great choric odes—the only parts of Yeats's play actually in verse—that the accent falls primarily on "mystery." Yet his version of *Oedipus at Colonus* is dedicated to "mystery" even more, on that occasion not without ample warrant from Sophocles, but often—intentionally, it may be said—stretching that warrant quite beyond the breaking point. Ironically, Yeats's ignorance of Greek helped; for dependent as he was mainly if not exclusively on the translation by Sir Richard Jebb, he must have felt free to shape his phrases as he deemed advisable. Thus, when Oedipus early in the play suggests to the Chorus that he is fated to bring good fortune to Colonus and to Athens, a faithful translation of the Chorus' response would read:

> Old man,
> This argument of yours compels our wonder.
> It was not feebly worded. I am content
> That higher authorities should judge this matter.
>
> [ll. 292–95]

But Yeats's version reads: "You have spoken words that fill me with awe. I cannot understand, for they are full of hints and mysteries, but it is for my betters to find out their meaning" (VPl 860). "Full of hints and mysteries" is obviously an interpolation; but so in a sense is "awe," much more powerful as it is than either "wonder" or the original Greek ἀνάγκη. Late, when Oedipus remarks of the oracular pronouncement from Delphi reported by Ismene, he would say according to our faithful translation, "I have heard the prophecies / Brought by this girl; I think they fit those others / Spoken so long ago, and now fulfilled" (ll. 452–54); but Yeats deviates in a deliberate effort to endow Oedipus with a divine aura: "I meditate upon the new prophecies the girl has brought, and when I speak, Phoebus Apollo speaks" (VPl 865). Equally, transfixed as Yeats always was by the manner of Oedipus's absorption into the afterworld, the earth "riven by love" as he said in *A Vision*, the corresponding phrasing in his play was designed to call attention to itself: "the foundations of the earth were riven to receive him, riven not by pain but by love" (VPl 897). As with the version's prose, so with its poetry: the choric songs—again the only parts to have been put into verse—remove Yeats's version even further from the original play. In one instance, as the time for the death of Oedipus approaches, Yeats bypasses Sophocles altogether: the Chorus' passionate cry—"This blind old ragged, rambling beggarman / Calls curses upon cities, upon the great, / And scatters at his pleasure rich estate" (VPl 892)—is but a redaction of the interpretation of Oedipus in *A Vision* ("kingdoms changed according to his blessing and his cursing"). In another instance, Sophocles's superb poem to Athens (ll. 668–719) is changed utterly, the argument once more reconstituted, the images reduced and redirected, the tone adjusted to the evolved vision of the beauty and the concord of the god-protected natural order (VPl 872–73; reprinted in *The Tower* as "Colonus' Praise"). The "mystery" is not thereby negated; it is amplified, in that "the fury and the mire of human veins" is but one aspect of reality, by no means exclusive, much less final.

The complex realism of Yeats's Oedipus plays represents an achievement attained gradually and laboriously. Initially committed to "beauty" in opposition to the realism advocated at its best by Ibsen, Yeats's early plays were as he described his early poems to have been, "almost all a flight into fairyland from the real world, and a summons to that flight" (L 63). Once determined "to substitute more and more the landscapes of nature for the landscape of art," he did not gain "the real world" by losing fairyland; on the contrary, the path to the one was increasingly recognized to be by way of the other, not unlike the practice—or what Yeats understood to be the practice—of Spenser. He revised tirelessly, in the case of *The Countess Cathleen* on and off over some three decades. But as a result he learned, through experience, the need to shape his plays from within, not in the light of any predetermined theory that might misdirect him to sharply differentiated categories like tragedy and comedy. One consequence is that *Deirdre* (1906), theoretically a tragedy, conforms in practice to Yeats's views on comedy; and another, that *The Player Queen* (1919), initially conceived as tragedy, was eventually changed into a "wild comedy, almost a farce, with a tragic background" (L 588), to quote Yeats's intentionally impossible "definition." It was clearly the voice of experience that pronounced the remarkable judgment already cited, "In practice most works are mixed: Shakespeare being tragi-comedy" (Au 471).

The example of Shakespeare guided Yeats throughout his life. It must be stressed that Yeats responded to Shakespeare without anxiety, as major talents do. The elements he absorbed selectively, constructively, imaginatively, conditioned his own practice in fundamental ways. Certainly his conception and presentation of the Fool in a number of plays was vitally affected by Shakespearean precedents. Touchstone in *As You Like It*, Feste in *Twelfth Night*, and especially the Fool in *King Lear*, are the forefathers of the Yeatsian fools notably in the first of the five Cuchulain plays, *On Baile's Strand*, as well as in such very different plays as *The Hour Glass* and *The Herne's Egg*.

The first play to signal Yeats's adjustment of the Shakespearean Fool to his purposes, *On Baile's Strand* draws on Irish mythology for its subject, on Greek drama for some of its rhythms, and on Shakespeare for the means to connect the primary plot of the conflict between King Cuchulain and the High Commander Conchubar with the secondary plot involving the Fool and the Blind Man. As always in Yeats, "plot" must be understood in the highly economic fashion, and consequently the extremely suggestive way, that he dramatized all his subjects. The "means" that connect plot with plot, moreover, are equally elliptic, adapted from Shakespeare after careful consideration of their service to Yeats's objectives. Studies of *On Baile's Strand* have so far led us to the conclusion that the conflict between the Fool and the Blind Man is "complementary" to that in the primary plot; it is indeed a counterpoint to the main action, "an ironic, almost burlesque, commentary on the main theme," which the play's revision some four years later explicitly changed into "a mock play within the serious play."[4] Different though the design and the effect of *On Baile's Strand* are from those of *King Lear*, the parallels in their structures are evident enough. But the parallels in terms of individual characters are even more engrossing. To see Yeats's Fool as a descendant of the Fool in *Lear* is to realize that, by the same token, the Blind Man is a relative of Lear himself in the first instance and of Gloucester in the second, blind as both are metaphorically and in one case literally too. The proliferating analogies include the moments of mere amusement that shift abruptly, terrifyingly, into visions of horror. Yeats's Fool sings:

> When you were an acorn on the tree-top,
> Then was I an eagle-cock;
> Now that you are a withered old block,
> Still am I an eagle-cock.

"Listen to him, now," protests the Blind Man. "That's the sort of talk I have to put up with day out, day in" (VPl 519). So he does; yet, all the same, the song of the Fool is as pertinent to the unfolding action of *On Baile's Strand* as are the nonsense verses of the Fool in *Lear*, their veiled raillery a comment on the presumption of eagle-cocks like Cuchulain and the Blind Man in Yeats's play, or Lear and Gloucester in Shakespeare's. In Yeats's play, of course, the Fool's song and the Blind Man's protest are immediately followed by Cuchulain's shattering recognition that he had killed his own son. Within that abruptly changed context, we are invited to regard the Fool as wise enough to have perceived the folly of others, but wiser still to have refused openly to declare that folly. Like his predecessor in *Lear*, he chooses indirection, its emphasis obviously on appearance at the expense of reality and perhaps—if we wish to be brutally explicit—on deception. The play's complications will be resolved solely in line with one's own response to the outlook also averred in one of Yeats's shorter poems: "O what am I that I should not seem / For the song's sake a fool?" (P 282).

The Hour Glass (prose version, 1903; poetic one, 1913) shifts the balance from what seems to be to what most patently is. But the play affirms reality in spite of its protagonist, the Wise Man, who credits only the visible: "There's nothing but what can see when they are awake" (VPl 595). He teaches, in consequence, that the soul and the afterlife and God are "nothing"; yet the angel who eventually comes to claim his soul promises to spare him confinement in Hell provided one person is found who, impervious to the Wise Man's teaching, still believes. In the original legend, the Wise Man finds a child; in Yeats's play, he finds Teigue the Fool. But Teigue is unlike the Fools of Shakespeare or the Fool of *On Baile's Strand* in that he is primarily intent on securing pennies; otherwise he prefers to say "nothing." Even as his silence divides him from his predecessors, however, the reiterated motif of "nothing" is joined to the more substantial motif of "folly" to proclaim the decisive impact of *King Lear*. Within Yeats's play the silence of the Fool manoeuvers the Wise Man into a journey of self-discovery that concludes with an eloquent confession of his limitations. Not surprisingly, the play's first version was subtitled "A Morality"; even less surprisingly, Yeats was apparently willing to have the Fool wear a mask, "which makes him less a human being than a principle of the mind" (VPl 645).

The third of Yeats's plays to make extensive use of a Fool, *The Herne's Egg* (1938), was described by Yeats himself as "the strangest wildest thing I have ever written" (L 845). There are reasons enough, in fact, for astonishment. The presiding deity is no longer "The Everliving" of *On Baile's Strand;* it is but a heron, not indeed without ample proportions and considerable powers, yet indisputably no more than a heron. This singular deity's priestess, Attracta, is rather singular too, capable as she is of mistaking her rape by seven men for a visitation of the supernatural. The numerous other oddities include the fight between King Congal and King Aedh, their weapons not lances or swords but, all too unheroically, table legs. In the end, Congal dies only to be reincarnated as a donkey. "All that trouble," Attracta's servant justifiably observes as the curtain descends, "and nothing to show for it, / Nothing but just another donkey" (VPl 1040). No effort is spared to underline the farcical situation: the stage directions for the second scene specify "a donkey on wheels like a child's toy, but life-size" (VPl 1014), while the stage directions for the final scene call for a particular kind of moon, "the moon of comic tradition, a round smiling face" (VPl 1034). It is in that final scene that Tom the Fool first appears. His advent had been foretold earlier, by Attracta's servant, in the immemorial rhythms of nonsense verse:

> 'He that a herne's egg dare steal
> Shall be changed into a fool,'
> *Said the old, old herne that had but one leg.*
>
> 'And to end his fool breath
> At a fool's hand meet his death,'
> *Said the old, old herne that had but one leg.*
>
> [VPl 1018]

Once on stage, however, the Fool is interested in his mission only because of the pennies he is to collect. He would have failed altogether had not Congal seized the initiative and, displacing the Fool as executioner, killed himself. Even so, Congal dies in accordance with the prophecy that he was to have met his death "at a Fool's hand": he has not only carried out a task assigned to the Fool, but has himself become a Fool. His cry shortly before he dies ("Fool! Am I myself a Fool?" [VPl 1038]) echoes Lear's equally rhetorical question ("Dost thou call me a fool, boy?"). Congal the Fool is a mere fool when he trespasses on the transcendental; but he is Fool when his blunder is overcome by a noble acceptance of the destiny he provoked. Overjoyed, ecstatic, "gay," he casts himself into the arms of death, one with Fools like Lear and Hamlet and Oedipus—or the two Fools who figure in Yeats's lyrical poetry, Crazy Jane and Tom the Lunatic, the one at the outset of the sequence "Words for Music Perhaps," the other near its end.

The three poems allotted to Tom the Lunatic attest to a realistic if convoluted perspective that joins time to eternity and life to death in a context ever under God's unchanging eye. But the seven poems allotted to Crazy Jane—and the additional one in *On the Boiler* ("Crazy Jane on the Mountain")—are foremost among Yeats's lyrics in their endorsement of the wisdom that informs his vision of folly. Immediately, one is overwhelmed by extremities of feeling articulated urgently, feverishly, in clipped sentences that surge and spill, tumbling forth. As the manner is, so is the person: saltatory, restless, impassioned, effusive, energetically dedicated to life at its most intense. Jane—"crazy" only so far as the world misunderstands her passionate nature—had known love with "wild Jack" (P 259), now dead; and having taken a number of lovers, she can be stunningly candid about the abuse of her body ("like a road / That men pass over" [P 259]) and, with equally uncompromising frankness, about love's more distinctly physical aspects ("Love has pitched his mansion in / The place of excrement" [P 259–60]). Her love life, censured by society and the Church as the coming together of "beast and beast" (P 256), is defended by Jane on the Blakean premise that life is compounded of interlinked contraries ("fair needs foul" [P 259]) and therefore one must be committed to the single, indivisible, "whole / Body and soul" (P 257). But she also knows that our easy generalizations are likely to be confirmed (if at all) only in a timeless dispensation. The requisite questions are raised in the final stanza of that seminal poem, "Crazy Jane on the Day of Judgment":

> "What can be shown?
> What true love be?
> All could be known or shown
> If Time were but gone."
> *'That's certainly the case,'* said he.
>
> [P 257]

The last time we see her, in "Crazy Jane on the Mountain," she is stretched out on the dirt, crying tears down in passionate execration of injustice. It is a posture entirely appropriate to Songs of Experience whether by Blake or by Yeats.

The endorsement of "the whole / Body and soul" in the Crazy Jane poems embraces a number of other poems too. The severance of the physical and the spiritual in "Sailing to Byzantium," for instance, is abolished in the subsequent, more profound "Byzantium," while the poems carefully placed immediately after the latter—"The Mother of God" and the sequence of eight lyrics entitled "Vacillation"—apply its experiential life more to the reality of the internal life than to that of the external one, to "things that seem" (P 252). However, given the ever-present awesome complexities—"complexities of mire or blood" (P 248)—tentativeness and suggestiveness necessarily displace mere clarity. Question follows question: "What images are these . . . What heads shake or nod?" (P 254); "Saw I an old man young / Or young man old?" (P 261); "What rough beast, its hour come round at last, / Slouches towards Bethlehem to be born?" (P 187); "Did she put on his knowledge with his power / Before the indifferent beak could let her drop?" (P 215). But questions are present even where the mark of interrogation is absent. A sudden insight is wont to surprise, intentionally; and, no less intentionally, the brevity of its articulation demands that we end the poem as a question. "Oil and Blood" may be quoted in its entirety:

> In tombs of gold and lapis lazuli
> Bodies of holy men and women exude
> Miraculous oil, odour of violet.
>
> But under heavy loads of trampled clay
> Lie bodies of the vampires full of blood;
> Their shrouds are bloody and their lips are wet.
>
> [P 239]

The hideous vision cannot be accepted as final. Like all major poets, Yeats prefers not to determine but to propose, nor to conclude but to imply. The ultimate reality is represented neither by the pale unsatisfied ones of "The Magi," their faces stony and their eyes fixed, nor by the bestial intelligence in "The Second Coming," its menacing movements slow and its gaze blank. Immediately following "The Second Coming," after all, Yeats placed—with premeditated care, as always—the dramatically different vision contained in "A Prayer for my Daughter":

> She can, though every face should scowl
> And every windy quarter howl
> Or every bellows burst, be happy still.
>
> [P 190]

Yeats's interrogation into a diversity of possible experiences is like his interrogation into a variety of philosophical systems, playfully tentative:

> Plato thought nature but a spume that plays
> Upon a ghostly paradigm of things;
> Solider Aristotle played the taws
> Upon the bottom of a king of kings;
> World-famous golden-thighed Pythagoras
> Fingered upon a fiddle-stick or strings
> What a star sang and careless Muses heard. . . .
>
> [P 217]

Single-mindedly to endorse one system or one experience is to be possessed of the exclusive "one purpose" that the incisively realistic political poem, "Easter 1916," regards as certain to "trouble the living stream." Whatever their natures, obsessions damage irreparably: "Too long a sacrifice / Can make a stone of the heart." Yet, for all that, the result is a "terrible beauty" because the obsession that is fanaticism is compounded of both terror as an inevitable consequence and an "excess of love" (P 181–82) as a driving force. Apparent opposites may not be opposed too categorically, for they may turn out to be intimately related. The exchange in "Ego Dominus Tuus" is apposite:

> *Ille.* ... art
> Is but a vision of reality.
> What portion in the world can the artist have
> Who has awakened from the common dream
> But dissipation and despair?
>
> *Hic.* And yet
> No one denies to Keats love of the world;
> Remember his deliberate happiness.
>
> *Ille.*
> His art is happy, but who knows his mind?
>
> [P 161]

The apparent "comedy" may be a mask for "tragedy," precisely as "Tragedy wrought to its uttermost" (P 294) converts itself into "comedy," the gaiety we have observed to transfigure all that dread. The approach parallels habits traditional among major creative writers, in each case representing a disposition after the "ultimate truth to life."

I am quoting the judgment on Yeats by another poet, Seamus Heaney: "one is awed by the achieved and masterful tones of that deliberately pitched voice, its bare classical shapes, its ability to modulate from emotional climax to wise reflection, its ultimate truth to life"[5] Such "truth" is present, Heaney argues, in spite of Yeats's addiction to fairies and gyres and Phases of the Moon. Be our conclusions about Yeats's "magic" what they may, they do not affect the essential aim of his poetry. He stated it best himself, in *The King's Threshold* (1904):

> when all falls
> In ruin, poetry calls out in joy,
> Being the scattering hand, the bursting pod,
> The victim's joy among the holy flame,
> God's laughter at the shattering of the world,
> And now that joy laughs out
> On these bare steps.
>
> [VPl 267]

"We that look on but laugh in tragic joy," Yeats was to write later, in "The Gyres" (P 293). Yet it would appear that, at its most perceptive, joy is the prerogative solely of ancient, glittering eyes.

Notes

1. *Writers at Work: The Paris Review Interviews,* Second Series, ed. George Plimpton (New York: Viking, 1963) 43.
2. *The Irish Weekly and Ulster Examiner* (12 September 1931): 9.
3. T. S. Eliot, *Collected Poems 1909–1962* (London: Faber and Faber, 1963) 55.
4. Leonard E. Nathan, *The Tragic Drama of William Butler Yeats: Figures in a Dance* (New York: Columbia University Press, 1965) 110, 128.
5. "Yeats as an Example?" *Yeats, Sligo and Ireland,* ed. A. Norman Jeffares (Totowa, N.J.: Barnes & Noble, 1980) 68.

Notes on the "Memory"-Sequence in Yeats's *The Wild Swans at Coole*

M. L. Rosenthal

Subtly controlling the exact center of Yeats's *The Wild Swans at Coole* is a sequence of eight intensely personal poems: "Memory," "Her Phoenix," "The People," "His Phoenix," "A Thought from Propertius," "Broken Dreams," "A Deep-sworn Vow," and "Presences." All these poems first appeared in 1916 or 1917 and were incorporated into the 1917 Cuala Press edition of *The Wild Swans at Coole*. The expanded 1919 Macmillan volume includes them in the same order, with "Her Phoenix" retitled "Her Praise."

The psychological moment of the sequence is the period preceding Yeats's marriage in October 1917: something not mentioned in the poems. Nor do they say "Maud Gonne"—even if the name springs inevitably to mind for obvious reasons, especially when one reads "The People." No matter. The poems, like those of Catullus and Propertius or Wordsworth's Lucy poems, hold up in their own right. One can hardly doubt their confessional immediacy, but it serves as affective energy within the sequence rather than as autobiographical documentation.

The most obvious unifying element in the "Memory"-sequence is that it consists of love poems. One must, however, immediately note that they are not the usual expressions of present rapture or anticipation or painful uncertainty or desire. Rather, their character is best indicated by the titles "Memory," "Broken Dreams," and "His Phoenix"—the last because the actual past intimacy, whatever its literal character, has vanished yet is constantly reborn as a commanding presence in the poet's emotional life. That is, the sequence is fixed on the persistent domination of his sensibility and imagination by the nature of the lost beloved. Her power is seen first in the simple and unforgettable physical image, in "Memory," of the hollow left in the mountain grass by the mountain hare. This image—although we meet it only once, and it is replaced further on by the slightly riddling "phoenix"-metaphor—remains the key image of reference of the entire sequence. It is mirrored in the more explicitly personal language of the penultimate poem, "A Deep-sworn Vow," and of the closing "Presences," which adds dimensions of supernatural awe and terror. Meanwhile, however, the reach of the beloved's force has, in successive poems, directed the poet toward unexpected moral and political apperceptions. And at the same time, the sequence plays with varied thoughts about her—a lover's thoughts, sometimes worshipful, sometimes playful, sometimes critical—as if indeed the relationship were an actual empirical reality. The pathos impicit in this dreaming gives the sequence an elegiac cast, while the larger effect is of a self-created world of passionate meanings rooted in a past that refuses to disappear.

For the length of these eight poems, we are totally within that world. It is interesting that they are preceded by "The Hawk," a poem of self-reproach in which the poet reminds himself how easily the "hawk of [his] mind" (P 149) loses its self-possession. This sharp stab of humility clears the way for poems of submission to a nobler, tutelary spirit. Similarly, the sequence is followed by "The Balloon of the Mind," which pulls the volume back into its previous orbit after immersion in the haunted realm of unrequited love and its permutations. This sequence is an anticipatory reply to the question Yeats was later to raise in "The Tower": "Does the imagination dwell the most / Upon a woman won or woman lost?" (P 197).

"Memory" (P 149–50), a masterpiece of imagist resonance, sets the emotional pitch with its compressed power. It begins in cavalier fashion, its tone that of a man totally free of romantic enslavement—

> One had a lovely face,
> And two or three had charm,
> But charm and face were in vain . . .

—and then swerves wrenchingly into an image of irrevocable possession, at once delicate and vital, of one being by another:

> Because the mountain grass
> Cannot but keep the form
> Where the mountain hare has lain.

Because it is called "Memory," and because the mountain hare is no longer lying in the mountain grass, the poem expresses loss as well as undying passionate subjection to a stronger personality and its sexual force. The language of shallow, hardly caring gallantry is dropped for that of ungenteel, animal reality, a displacement made even more emphatic by the reversal of sexual roles implicit in the imagery. The sustained enjambment presses the displacement urgently.

This tiny poem of sheer yet complex power is quickly followed by "Her Praise" (P 150), whose opening line—"She is foremost of those that I would hear praised"—becomes a refrain when repeated in line ten. (In retrospect it seems tinged with plaintive obsessiveness.) The word "praise" recurs three more times, the last time at the very end. The human situation is both homely and touching: a lover's desire to speak his beloved's name and introduce it in all conversation. Whereas "Memory" has the form of pure song and the impact of an arrow shot unerringly from a crossbow, "Her Praise" is more openly confessional, a confiding, unfolding, musing incantation. Its language is restless, impatient:

> I have gone about the house, gone up and down,
> As a man does who has published a new book,
> Or a young girl dressed out in her new gown. . . .

This tone is not *passionate*—not exactly. What it conveys, in context, is a confusion of excited awareness, rather than a sense of being helpless under the spell of another's personal magnetism. The ending moves the celebratory tone into a mood of almost commemorative adoration and prepares us for the brilliant turn in the next poem, "The People." The "mountain hare" of the first poem has left her imperishable imprint, but not only on a man who finds all other loves tame by comparison. "Her Praise" concludes:

> I will talk no more of books or the long war
> But walk by the dry thorn until I have found
> Some beggar sheltering from the wind, and there
> Manage the talk until her name comes round.
> If there be rags enough he will know her name
> And be well pleased remembering it, for in the old days,
> Though she had young men's praise and old men's blame,
> Among the poor both old and young gave her praise.

Again sustained enjambment presses home a striking emotional recognition: in this instance, of the engulfing compassion of a woman. The insight carries the poem's celebratory momentum into something like an attribution of divine grace. An irresistible surge of illumination, transcending private concerns, has reoriented the whole current of association and emphasis. The lover's feelings at the beginning (the restless excitement already noted, and the need to praise the beloved everywhere—"I have turned the talk by hook or crook / Until her praise should be the uppermost theme")—are still present, but a whole new world of social bearing now encompasses them without obliterating their private glow. The long, loosely four- or five-stress lines (almost verging on free verse) and the intricately reflexive rhyme scheme give room for the more complex development of this poem. Yet ultimately it depends on the same kind of torque in its second half that marks the much shorter "Memory"; and by its end it too focuses on "remembering."

The third poem, "The People" (P 150–51), is just over twice the length of the eighteen-line "Her Praise." Written in blank verse, it has an even higher frequency of enjambment and presents a deceptively expansive and leisurely surface in its opening verse-unit. In its rhetorical progression, "The People" is a dialogue reminiscent of "Adam's Curse," written some fourteen years earlier. It too centers on a vehement protest by the poet against the public's ingratitude, a rejoinder by a beautiful woman, and a startlingly intimate shift of feeling at the end. But it is much less of a set piece. It lacks the romantic mood-setting start, the carefully patterned rhyming couplets, and the lovely, fragile, ninetyish desolation of the passage describing the waning moon "washed by time's waters" (P 81) in "Adam's Curse." Instead, "The People" starts at once with its partly mean-spirited complaint:

> 'What have I earned for all that work,' I said,
> 'For all that I have done at my own charge?
> The daily spite of this unmannerly town. . . .'

The mountain hare ("my phoenix" in this poem) has bitter knowledge too, but refuses to let it influence her or even be made public. Her reply is sharply to the point, yet pitched on higher moral ground than the poet's combined grousing and eloquent daydreaming about the life he might have led in agreeable company and "among the images of the past— / The unperturbed and courtly images." She reminds him that she has suffered fiercer ingratitude than he without losing sight of her duty to the oppressed and ignorant. Her revolutionary faith is unshakable:

> 'The drunkards, pilferers of public funds,
> All the dishonest crowd I had driven away,
> When my luck changed and they dared meet my face,
> Crawled from obscurity, and set upon me
> Those I had served and some that I had fed;
> Yet never have I, now nor any time,
> Complained of the people.'

Her staunchness puts the poet on the defensive—to no avail, for it has compelled him to face his own self-indulgence and unconscious pettiness, reflected in the poem's opening question with its cash-metaphors: "What have I earned"; "at my own charge." The closing verse-paragraph begins with his rationalizing outward response but ends with a double stress on his inner abashment before her preternatural moral authority: a "natural force" like that of the mountain hare in "Memory." Its place in the buried sequence has enabled "The People" to build on the two previous poems. The initial poem of unresolved passionate domination by a wild life-force in another being gives a fierce, almost brute anchorage to the giddy obeisance paid the loved person and her divinely bountiful spirit in "Her Praise"—which, in turn, reveals the particular lustre of her political faithfulness and resistance to disillusionment in "The People." Suddenly we have the extraordinary experience of seeing the poet forced off his high horse of aristocratic pretentiousness with a pang of simple shame, just as he rises to sheer eloquence:

> All I could reply
> Was: 'You, that have not lived in thought but deed,
> Can have the purity of a natural force,
> But I, whose virtues are the definitions
> Of the analytic mind, can neither close
> The eye of the mind nor keep my tongue from speech.'
> And yet, because my heart leaped at her words,
> I was abashed, and now they come to mind
> After nine years, I sink my head abashed.

This is not the place to go into questions of poetic theory, but I believe we have here a magnificent instance of artistic self-transcendence. That is, the associative process has led the poet to a point beyond his ordinary expressed attitudes, a point of humble recognition of psychological self-deception and irrefutable human realities. The sequence has at this point reached a climax of introspective discovery. It has moved quickly from its opening metaphor of passionate obsession, centered on a private emotional state, through a phase of attention to the dominant other being (the beloved) and her beautiful humanity—and then back to the private self, now vulnerable and "abashed" at the core of its intellectual pride.

The ending of "The People" reminds us, too, of the double time-stream of the poems. The climactic moment described took place in the past, and the sequence derives much power from its refusal to relinquish the immediacy of what that past has embodied. Therefore the affective coloration of the sequence depends on its vibrant sense of repossession of the past, with its lost possibilities, in the *present* volatile circumstance. Memory here is by no means a tranquil recollection of emotion; it is the return of experience with all its original life, though necessarily in an added, elegiac dimension:

> And yet, because my heart leaped at her words,
> I was abashed, and now they come to mind
> After nine years, I sink my head abashed.

But the sequence must return to the primary object of its attention, must break loose from this transfixed attention to the goddess's irrevocable rebuke to her worshipper and go on to new forms of celebration and awareness. The next poem, "His Phoenix" (P 151-52), breaks loose with a vengeance. It is a piece of deliberate buffoonery, almost doggerel, with a rollicking ballad rhythm and a cleverly overlapping rhyme scheme capped by the refrain, "I knew a phoenix in my youth, so let them have their day." Yet within this happy, drinking-song frame it rings many emotional changes: something the refrain itself, with its mixed nostalgia and jollity, would suggest. The range of reference, too, is sophisticated from the start despite the colloquial air, so that the effect somewhat resembles that of Byron's *Don Juan:*

> There is a queen in China, or maybe it's in Spain,
> And birthdays and holidays such praises can be heard
> Of her unblemished lineaments, a whiteness with no stain,
> That she might be that sprightly girl trodden by a bird;
> And there's a score of duchesses, surpassing womankind,
> Or who have found a painter to make them so for pay
> And smooth out stain and blemish with the elegance of his mind:
> I knew a phoenix in my youth, so let them have their day.

"His Phoenix" is in its way a ballad of fair women of every sort: grand ladies, dancers, actresses, and beauties "who live in privacy." Until the final stanza, the phoenix of the refrain is but one among the many. There, however, the poem turns from its free and easy gaiety and exalts her unique glory in her youth. An added sharp turn comes in the closing lines, which swing the mood back into the strangely elegiac exaltation established in the previous poems:

> There'll be that crowd, that barbarous crowd, through all the centuries.
> And who can say but some young belle may walk and talk men wild
> Who is my beauty's equal, though that my heart denies,
> But not the exact likeness, the simplicity of a child,
> And that proud look as though she had gazed into the burning sun,
> And all the shapely body no tittle gone astray.
> I mourn for that most lonely thing; and yet God's will be done:
> I knew a phoenix in my youth, so let them have their day.

That final note is of bitter loss, of a vision as well as a reality. The next poem, "A Thought from Propertius" (P 153), holds cleanly up to view what is was that the would-be lover once lost: both the real woman and the vision ("that most lonely thing") of ideal womanhood surrounding her like an aureole. This is the one poem in which she alone holds the stage:

> She might, so noble from head
> To great shapely knees
> The long flowing line,
> Have walked to the altar
> Through the holy images
> At Pallas Athena's side,
> Or been fit spoil for a centaur
> Drunk with the unmixed wine.

In this single, lapidary poetic sentence, with its careful rhythmic balances and almost secret off-rhyming ($abcdb'a'd'c$), the tangible sexuality of "Memory" and the supernatural aura evoked in "Her Praise" and "The People" come together as they might in some marvelous piece of Grecian sculpture. The poem's shining isolation as an image of pure pagan divinity whose true life would have flourished in a world of mythical earthiness is enhanced by its placement between the largely boisterous "His Phoenix" and the touching, ordinarily human "Broken Dreams" (P 153–54). In the latter poem, the lover addresses his lost beloved directly for the first time, as older man to older woman:

> There is grey in your hair.
> Young men no longer suddenly catch their breath
> When you are passing. . . .

He even makes free to favor her with a denial of her perfection:

> You are more beautiful than anyone,
> And yet your body had a flaw:
> Your small hands were not beautiful. . . .

In lines like these, she is for the first time brought into the ranks of normally mortal women, and made more believable thereby as an actual person. In this poem too, memory itself is for one poetic instant reduced to average proportions:

> Your beauty can but leave among us
> Vague memories, nothing but memories.

Although all this plain realism humanizes and makes familiar the figure of the beloved, its function in "Broken Dreams" is to arouse a counter-assertion—one that, in turn, only brings into the foreground of the sequence the anguish that has been lurking offstage all the while. The deeper music of this exquisitely articulated poem is that of irrevocable frustration. Hence its insistence on renewing the past from the altered standpoint of the dream-driven present:

> Vague memories, nothing but memories,
> But in the grave all, all, shall be renewed.
> The certainty that I shall see that lady
> Leaning or standing or walking
> In the first loveliness of womanhood,
> And with the fervour of my youthful eyes,
> Has set me muttering like a fool.

The poignancy of this penultimate verse-unit, and of certain lines in the closing unit that imagine her changed to a swan and thus even further out of reach, is a corrective to any impression of reconciliation to loss. The poet sizes himself up accurately: not as a triumphant lover in his indomitable imagination, or as one who has gone beyond the follies of romantic desire, but as "the poet stubborn with his passion." At the end the mood sinks into self-dismissiveness:

> The last stroke of midnight dies.
> All day in the one chair
> From dream to dream and rhyme to rhyme I have ranged
> In rambling talk with an image of air:
> Vague memories, nothing but memories.

Yet the sequence ends with two poems that renew the power of that inescapable "image of air." The first, "A Deep-sworn Vow" (P 154), begins in bitterness: "Others because you did not keep / That deep-sworn vow have been friends of mine." The lines are a quickening of the negative or critical feelings advanced more gently in "Broken Dreams." They are an accusation and an apology, and they continue the humanizing direction of the preceding poem. Nevertheless, the image of the beloved once more takes over as powerfully as ever when the conscious mind lets down its guard. When the thought of his own death overcomes the speaker, or when he is "excited with wine" or with highly emotional dreams, then—the poem confesses—"suddenly I meet your face." The closing poem, "Presences" (P 154–55), intensifies this new emphasis on states of fierce psychic arousal and leaves the sequence in a climactic context of unmediated vision clamoring for expression. The woman-figure who has been in control so far has split up into her three major aspects—sexual, innocently childlike, and regal—in the dream-life. She has become many women, all studying *him* to find the ultimate meaning of his theme: "that monstrous thing / Returned and yet unrequited love." The sequence ends on a note of awestruck bafflement and perturbation, but still entranced by the sexually charged mystery with which it has been coping.

The buried "Memory"-sequence has its unique character, and I shall not at this point elaborate on its place in *The Wild Swans at Coole* considered as a whole. It has obvious affinities with poems like "On Woman" and "The Double Vision of Michael Robartes"; and "Solomon to Sheba" might well be called a happier alternative vision. It provides another elegiac dimension besides those for Mabel Beardsley, Major Robert Gregory, and Alfred Pollexfen. And there are other shared concerns elsewhere: weariness with oneself, changes of perspective in old age, the desire to recapture the feelings of "burning youth." Most of all, these poems at the heart of the book reveal the deeply subjective current of introspection underlying—and implicit in—"The Phases of the Moon" and related pieces.

One more point of some interest (among many that might be adduced in connection with this sequence). *At the Hawk's Well* was published in the Cuala Press edition of *The Wild Swans at Coole*. This is a play without resolution, juxtaposing its elements (the chief of which are the irresistible attraction of Cuchulain to Aoife and the Old Man's frustration) very much as the contradictory elements in the "Memory" group are juxtaposed, though less complexly or subjectively. Yeats's process of increasingly seeing aspects of his own struggles and relationships in the Cuchulain he recreated seems to begin with *At the Hawk's Well*, in fact. That identification reaches its height in *The Only Jealousy of Emer* (the closest in emotional positioning to the "Memory"-sequence) and finds its furthest, darkest discoveries—beyond those of the "Memory" poems—in *The Death of Cuchulain*. But that is another turn on our subject, to be explored in a further discussion.

Dining with Landor

R. H. Super

When Landor in 1853 remarked, in the Imaginary Conversation between himself and his friend Archdeacon (Julius) Hare, "I shall dine late; but the dining-room will be well lighted, the guests few and select," he was predicting a posthumous fame rather for his *Imaginary Conversations* than for his poetry; "Poetry was always my amusement, prose my study and business."[1] But it does him no injustice to enjoy also the well-lighted feast of his poetry, as Yeats clearly did when, in his somewhat flippant little verses "To a Young Beauty," he concluded:

> There is not a fool can call me friend,
> And I may dine at journey's end
> With Landor and with Donne.
>
> [P 140]

Donne is of the party, no doubt, both because of the obvious care with which his poems are wrought and because he too was scarcely known in his day: the poems we like best, *Songs and Sonnets*, were not published in his lifetime. As recently as 1880–81, T. Humphry Ward reflected the current taste by printing only five of Donne's poems in his four-volume anthology of *The English Poets*, though by that time Swinburne and other younger poets and critics would have disagreed with such neglect.

There's another poem of Yeats's I cannot resist quoting—a poem aimed at dull academics who shuffle and grind out editions of and commentaries upon the works of authors infinitely beyond them in experience and intelligence:

> The Scholars
>
> Bald heads forgetful of their sins,
> Old, learned, respectable bald heads
> Edit and annotate the lines
> That young men, tossing on their beds,

> Rhymed out in love's despair
> To flatter beauty's ignorant ear.
>
> All shuffle there; all cough in ink;
> All wear the carpet with their shoes;
> All think what other people think;
> All know the man their neighbour knows.
> Lord, what would they say
> Did their Catullus walk that way?
>
> [P 140-41]

Catullus was in fact Landor's favorite poet throughout the whole of a long life—a master of the epigram, the short poem often filled with passion and love, a work of exquisite craftsmanship. Such masters too were Landor and Yeats themselves. All three made use of a single female figure who no doubt had an origin in the poet's life but who came to stand for the whole range of the poet's emotional experience, sometimes intense, sometimes whimsical: the Lesbia of Catullus, Ianthe of Landor, and the "woman Homer sung" (P 89-90), the Helen figure of Yeats. Both Landor and Yeats were constantly linking this figure with the eternal feminine of the ancient poets; for both, myth and poetic craftsmanship gave not merely expression but form to their emotions.

We might illustrate the point from a poem of Catullus (*Carmen VIII*) of which Landor says, "No poet, uttering his own sentiments on his own condition in a soliloquy, has evinced such power in the expression of passion, in its sudden throbs and changes, as Catullus has done here," and of which he translates the conclusion thus:

> But you shall grieve while none complains,[2]
> None, Lesbia! None. Think, what remains
> For one so fickle, so untrue!
> Henceforth, O wretched Lesbia! who
> Shall call you dear? shall call you his?
> Whom shall you love? or who shall kiss
> Those lips again? Catullus! thou
> Be firm, be ever firm, as now.
>
> [CW 11:196-97]

(Such a poem must be read aloud, in order to make clear the reversal at the end, when the poet realizes he is getting into deep water as he lets his mind stray over his mistress's beauty.) The same ambivalence is wonderfully reproduced in one of Landor's own epigrams:

> So late removed from him she swore,
>   With clasping arms and vows and tears,
> In life and death she would adore,
>   While memory, fondness, bliss, endears . .

> Can she forswear? can she forget?
>   Strike, mighty Love! strike, Vengeance! . . soft!
> Conscience must come, and bring Regret . .
>   These let her feel! nor these too oft!
>
>   [CW 15:378]

One of Landor's best-known epigrams is in the long tradition of poems that celebrate the poet's expression above the objective reality it expresses: it is the poet alone that conveys immortality.

> Past ruin'd Ilion Helen lives,
>   Alcestis rises from the shades;
> Verse calls them forth; 'tis verse that gives
>   Immortal youth to mortal maids.
>
> Soon shall Oblivion's deepening veil
>   Hide all the peopled hills you see,
> The gay, the proud, while lovers hail
>   In distant ages you and me.
>
> The tear for fading beauty check,
>   For passing glory cease to sigh;
> One form shall rise above the wreck,
>   One name, Ianthe, shall not die.
>
>   [CW 15:376]

The union of present with past in the eternity of poetry is similarly, but more ironically, expressed in Yeats's "No Second Troy."

> Why should I blame her that she filled my days
> With misery, or that she would of late
> Have taught to ignorant men most violent ways,
> Or hurled the little streets upon the great,
> Had they but courage equal to desire?
> What could have made her peaceful with a mind
> That nobleness made simple as a fire,
> With beauty like a tightened bow, a kind
> That is not natural in an age like this,
> Being high and solitary and most stern?
> Why, what could she have done, being what she is?
> Was there another Troy for her to burn?
>
>   [P 91]

Or the even more cynical "When Helen lived," in which Yeats recalls Homer's description of the way the old men of Troy reacted when Helen mounted the walls to look out over the battlefield:

> We have cried in our despair
> That men desert,
> For some trivial affair

> Or noisy, insolent sport,
> Beauty that we have won
> From bitterest hours;
> Yet we, had we walked within
> Those topless towers
> Where Helen walked with her boy,
> Had given but as the rest
> Of the men and women of Troy
> A word and a jest.
>
> [P 111]

Landor can contrast the immortal beauty of the poet's eye with the realities of mortality in a poem to Ianthe that combines wit, tenderness, and good humor:

> When Helen first saw wrinkles in her face
> ('Twas when some fifty long had settled there
> And intermarried and brancht off awide)
> She threw herself upon her couch, and wept:
> On this side hung her head, and over that
> Listlessly she let fall the faithless brass[3]
> That made the men as faithless.
>   But when you
> Found them, or fancied them, and would not hear
> That they were only vestiges of smiles,
> Or the impression of some amorous hair
> Astray from cloistered curls and roseat band,
> Which had been lying there all night perhaps
> Upon a skin so soft . . No, no, you said,
> Sure, they are coming, yes, are come, are here . .
> Well, and what matters it . . while you are too!
>
> [CW 15:380]

Perhaps the best-known of Landor's epigrams is his lament for an early friend, Rose Aylmer—one of that multitude of English who went to India as part of the British government establishment and were annihilated by disease. (Dickens's son, Walter Landor Dickens, died in India, and Matthew Arnold's younger brother William Delafield Arnold sailed for home fatally ill and died in the Mediterranean.) Rose was of an ancient noble family that had the blood of the early Norman kings in their veins.

> Ah what avails the sceptred race,
>   Ah what the form divine!
> What every virtue, every grace!
>   Rose Aylmer, all were thine.
> Rose Aylmer, whom these wakeful eyes
>   May weep, but never see,

> A night of memories and of sighs
> I consecrate to thee.
>
> [CW 15:339]

(I once came upon a letter in which Landor said he composed that poem one night as he was washing his teeth before going to bed.[4]) And then there is the quatrain Swinburne admired above all,[5] one which uses the effective Catullan device of bringing the entire poem together with the final word:

> Dirce
>
> Stand close around, ye Stygian set,
> With Dirce in one boat conveyed!
> Or Charon, seeing, may forget
> That he is old and she a shade.
>
> [CW 16:72]

There is one splendid poem of Yeats's that is almost an echo of a Landorian epigram. Landor's is:

> Proud word you never spoke, but you will speak
> Four not exempt from pride some future day.
> Resting on one white hand a warm wet cheek
> Over my open volume, you will say,
> "This man loved *me!*" then rise and trip away.
>
> [CW 15:393]

Yeats's is:

> When you are old and grey and full of sleep,
> And nodding by the fire, take down this book,
> And slowly read, and dream of the soft look
> Your eyes had once, and of their shadows deep;
>
> How many loved your moments of glad grace,
> And loved your beauty with love false or true,
> But one man loved the pilgrim soul in you,
> And loved the sorrows of your changing face;
>
> And bending down beside the glowing bars,
> Murmur, a little sadly, how Love fled
> And paced upon the mountains overhead
> And hid his face amid a crowd of stars.
>
> [P 41]

There remains one other, very important, impact of Landor upon Yeats. It may come from the conviction both had that prose must be as polished, as finished, as verse, so that when in verse they use a prosaic idiom and cadence, it seems perfectly natural, perfectly beautiful, even exciting, while it also seems so calm and ordinary. At the end of his long life, Landor was still writing elegant verse even though in his daily life he was frequently confused, bewildered. His last volume was published when he was 88. Fully aware of his condition, he included in that volume a poem, "Memory," remarkable for its casual perfection:

> The mother of the Muses, we are taught,
> Is Memory: she has left me; they remain,
> And shake my shoulder, urging me to sing
> About the summer days, my loves of old.
> *Alas! alas!* is all I can reply.
> Memory has left me with that name alone,[6]
> Harmonious name, which other bards may sing,
> But her bright image in my darkest hour
> Comes back, in vain comes back, call'd or uncall'd.
> Forgotten are the names of visitors
> Ready to press my hand but yesterday:
> Forgotten are the names of earlier friends
> Whose genial converse and glad countenance
> Are fresh as ever to mine ear and eye;
> To these, when I have written, and besought
> Remembrance of me, the word *Dear* alone
> Hangs on the upper verge, and waits in vain.
> A blessing wert thou, O oblivion,
> If thy stream carried only weeds away,
> But vernal and autumnal flowers alike
> It hurries down to wither on the strand.[7]
>
> [CW 15:403]

Place beside that, for casual, informal perfection, the beginning of the poem Yeats in old age (though still well short of Landor's fourscore and eight) placed near the conclusion of his collected poems:

> The Circus Animals' Desertion
>
> I sought a theme, and sought for it in vain,
> I sought it daily for six weeks or so.
> Maybe at last, being but a broken man,
> I must be satisfied with my heart, although
> Winter and summer till old age began
> My circus animals were all on show,
> Those stilted boys, that burnished chariot,
> Lion and woman and the Lord knows what.
>
> [P 346–47]

As Browning said, when he heard the news of Landor's death, "He has written passages not exceeded in beauty and subtlety by any literature that I am acquainted with."[8]

Notes

1. *The Complete Works of Walter Savage Landor*, ed. T. Earle Welby and Stephen Wheeler (London: Chapman and Hall, 1927–36) 6:37. Hereafter cited in the text as CW.
    These remarks originally were delivered as part of the Robert Browning Birthday Lecture at Baylor University, 7 May 1984. More recently, Donald Davie has also dealt with the relationship between Landor and Yeats in "Attending to Landor," *Ironwood* 24 (1984): 103–11. The two essays are complementary but not duplicative; the reader of them will find, however, that Professor Davie and I are both warm admirers of the richness and intensity of the lapidary epigram.
2. That is, writes "complaints," or love-poems, to you.
3. The hand-mirror of polished brass.
4. To Henry Crabb Robinson, 2 November 1831; in Dr. Williams's Library, London.
5. *The Letters of Algernon Charles Swinburne*, ed. Edmund Gosse and Thomas James Wise (London: Heinemann, 1918) 1:134.
6. The name "Ianthe."
7. I am indebted to Robert Pinsky's very sensitive book, *Landor's Poetry* (Chicago: University of Chicago Press, 1968) 128–33, for calling my attention to this poem, which grows more meaningful year by year. In line 16 Landor records his experience of beginning a letter "Dear . . ." and then being unable to think of the name of the friend to whom he means to write.
8. *Robert Browning and Julia Wedgwood . . . Letters,* ed. Richard Curle (New York: Stokes, 1937) 78–79.

A Yeats Bibliography for 1985/1986

K. P. S. Jochum

Most items in this bibliography were published in 1985; there are some from 1981–84. To improve the flow of information I have included those publications from 1986 that I was able to see before completion of the manuscript on 1 November 1986. The appendix lists additions to previous entries. As usual, items marked ° could not be inspected personally; J refers to my 1978 bibliography; and 81–, 82–, etc. identify entries in previous compilations in this annual. Thank you this time to James Lovic Allen, Brian Arkins, George Bornstein, Birgit Bramsbäck, Alan M. Cohn, Richard J. Finneran, Richard Taylor, the Yeats Society of Japan, and Susanne Heindel, the patient book carrier.

85–1. ADAMS, HAZARD: "Byron, Yeats, and Joyce: Heroism and Technic," *Studies in Romanticism*, 24:3 (Autumn 1985), 399–412.

85–2. ———: "Constituting Yeats's Poems as a Book," *Yeats*, 4 (1986), 1–16.

85–3. ADAMS, STEVE LAMAR: "A Critical Edition of the First Two Months of W. B. Yeats's Automatic Script," °Ph.D. thesis, Florida State University, 1982. 278 pp. (*DAI*, 45:8 [Feb. 1985], 2522A; reprinted in *Yeats*, 4 [1985], 179–80)

85–4. AHRENDS, GÜNTER, and HANS ULRICH SEEBER, eds.: *Englische und amerikanische Naturdichtung im 20. Jahrhundert*. Tübingen: Narr, 1985. 456 pp.
H. U. Seeber: "Selbstdarstellung von Dichtung in moderner englischer Lyrik und die Tradition der Pastoraldichtung," 31–49; contains a note on "The Song of the Happy Shepherd" and "The Sad Shepherd," pp. 38–40.

85–5. ALBRIGHT, DANIEL: *Lyricality in English Literature*. Lincoln: University of Nebraska Press, 1985. xi, 276 pp.
Frequent references to Yeats's poetry (see index).

85-6. ALEXANDER, HARRIET SEMMES: *American and British Poetry: A Guide to Criticism 1925-1978*. Athens, Ohio: Swallow Press, 1984. xii, 486 pp.
See pp. 459-72 for about 700 items of English-language criticism of individual poems by Yeats.

85-7. ALLEN, JAMES LOVIC: "'The Red and the Black': Understanding 'The Historical Cones,'" *Yeats Annual*, 3 (1985), 209-12.
The importance of the red and black parts of the diagram in *A Vision*.

85-8. ——: "What Rough Beast? Yeats's 'The Second Coming' and *A Vision*," *REAL: The Yearbook of Research in English and American Literature*, 3 (1985), 223-63.
Discusses, among other things, the system of history underlying Yeats's thought, the origin and meaning of the "beast," and the importance of the sphinx image and its source in the tarot deck.

85-9. *Angol-amerikai filológiai-módszertani ülésszak 1980*. Edited by Miklós Trócsányi and A. C. Rouse. Pécs: Pécsi Tanárképző Főiskola, 1981. vi, 209 pp.
Csilla Bertha: "The Patriotic and Universal Concerns of W. B. Yeats as Demonstrated in His 'Dance Plays,'" 136-47. On *The Only Jealousy of Emer*, *The Dreaming of the Bones*, and *Calvary*.

85-10. ANON.: "The Yeats Summer School," *Irish Literary Supplement*, 5:1 (Spring 1986), 13.
Includes "A Student's View" by Gabriel Fitzmaurice.

85-11. ANON.: "Green Sculpture Honours Yeats," *Irish Times*, 1 Sept. 1986, 6.
On Henry Moore's Yeats sculpture in St. Stephen's Green.

85-12. APPLEWHITE, JAMES: *Seas and Inland Journeys: Landscape and Consciousness from Wordsworth to Roethke*. Athens: University of Georgia Press, 1985, ix, 236 pp.
"Romantic Duality and Unity of Being," 162-95; on *Autobiographies* and some poems.

85-13. ARKINS, BRIAN: "Yeats and Propertius," *Liverpool Classical Monthly*, 10:5 (May 1985), 72-73.
Part of a projected study of Greek and Roman themes in Yeats's works; discusses "A Thought from Propertius."

85-14. ——: "Yeats and the Prophecy of Eunapius," *Notes & Queries*, 230 / 32:3 (Sept. 1985), 378-79.
The phrase "a fabulous, formless darkness" (in "Two Songs from a Play") comes from Eunapius via E. R. Dodds.

85-15. ARMSTRONG, GORDON: "Symbols, Signs, and Language: The Brothers Yeats and Samuel Beckett's Art of the Theater," *Comparative Drama*, 20:1 (Spring 1986), 38-53.
Jack Yeats, not WBY, had the greater influence on Beckett's theater practice.

85-16. AYLING, RONALD, ed.: *O'Casey: The Dublin Trilogy. "The Shadow of a Gunman," "Juno and the Paycock," "The Plough and the Stars." A Casebook*. London: Macmillan, 1985. 207 pp.
Numerous references to Yeats in Ayling's introduction and in the reprinted pieces (see index).

85-17. BAKER, PAMELA M., and HELEN M. YOUNG: "W. B. Yeats Material in the University of London Library," *Yeats Annual*, 4 (1986), 175-80.
Especially in the Thomas Sturge Moore collection.

85-18. BALBERT, PETER, and PHILLIP L. MARCUS, eds.: *D. H. Lawrence: A Centenary Consideration*. Ithaca: Cornell University Press, 1985. 263 pp.
P. L. Marcus: "Lawrence, Yeats, and 'the Resurrection of the Body,'" 210-36. Yeats is also referred to in Sandra M. Gilbert: "Potent Griselda: 'The Ladybird' and the Great Mother," 130-61.

85-19. BANFIELD, STEPHEN: *Sensibility and English Song: Critical Studies of the Early 20th Century*. Cambridge: Cambridge University Press, 1985. 2 vols.
"The Celtic Twilight," 1:248-74, includes discussions of several musical settings of Yeats's poems. See also index, 2:619, for a select bibliography of these settings.

85-20. BARNARD, JOHN: "Dryden: History and 'The Mighty Government of the Nine,'" *English*, 32:143 (Summer 1983), 129-53.
First published in *University of Leeds Review*, 24 (1981), 13-42. Contains a short comparison between Dryden's "Absalom and Achitophel" and "Easter 1916."

85-21. BATTAGLIA, ROSEMARIE: "Yeats, Nietzsche, and the Aristocratic Ideal," *College Literature*, 13:1 (Winter 1986), 88-94.

85-22. BAX, SIR ARNOLD: *Tone Poems 2*. Bryden Thomas conducts the Ulster Orchestra. Chandos Records, ABRD 1133, 1985. 1 12" longplay record.
This includes *Into the Twilight* (1908) and *In the Faery Hills* (1909); the sleeve note by Lewis Foreman comments on Bax's interest in Yeats. The score (apparently not published) of *Into the Twilight* is prefaced by Yeats's poem of that title. *In the Faery Hills* has a middle section based to some extent on a passage from "The Wanderings of Oisin"; published London: Murdoch, 1926.

85-23. BENSKO, JOHN RICHARD: "Narrative in the Modern Short Poem," °Ph.D. thesis, Florida State University, 1985. 303 pp. (*DAI*, 46:8 [Feb. 1986], 2297A)
Chapter 3 includes a discussion of some Yeats poems.

85-24. BERMAN, DAVID: "George Berkeley: Pictures by Goldsmith, Yeats and Luce," *Hermathena*, 139 (Winter 1985), 9-23.
Yeats's view of Berkeley was indebted to Goldsmith's (although he did not know it) and was rightly criticized by A. A. Luce (see J2199).

85-25. BERTHA, CSILLA: "A mitikus-költói dráma két változata: W. B. Yeats és Tamási Aron játékai," *Egri Ho Si Minh Tanárkepzó Fóiskola tudományos közleményei*, 17 (1984), 391-403.
Includes a summary in English entitled "An Irish and a Hungarian Model of Mythic Drama: W. B. Yeats and Aron Tamási."

85-26. BILLIGHEIMER, RACHEL V.: "The Eighth Eye: Prophetic Vision in Blake's Poetry and Design," *Colby Library Quarterly*, 22:2 (June 1986), 93-110.
Includes some notes on Yeats.

85-27. ———: "'Passion and Conquest': Yeats' Swans," *College Literature*, 13:1 (Winter 1986), 55-70.
The image of the swan in various poems.

85-28. BÖKER, UWE, HORST BREUER, and ROLF BREUER: *Die Klassiker der englischen Literatur: Von Geoffrey Chaucer bis Samuel Beckett*. Düsseldorf: Econ Taschenbuch Verlag, 1985. 256 pp. (Hermes Handlexikon.)
U. Böker: "William Butler Yeats," 237-42.

85-29. BONNEFOY, YVES: "Translating Poetry." Translated by John Alexander and Clive Wilmer, *PN Review*, 46 (1985), 5-7.
English version of the essay in *Entretiens sur la poésie* (82-23).

85-30. BORNSTEIN, GEORGE, ed.: *Ezra Pound among the Poets*. Chicago: University of Chicago Press, 1985. xiii, 238 pp.
A. Walton Litz: "Pound and Yeats: The Road to Stone Cottage," 128-48.

85-31. BOTHEROYD, SYLVIA, and PAUL F. BOTHEROYD: *Irland: Kunst- und Reiseführer mit Landeskunde*. Stuttgart: Kohlhammer, 1985. 408 pp.
A Baedeker with some references to Yeats (see index).

85-32. BRADY, ANNE M., and BRIAN CLEEVE: *A Biographical Dictionary of Irish Writers*. Mullingar: Lilliput Press, 1985. xii, 388 pp.
New edition of Cleeve's *Dictionary of Irish Writers* (J385). Yeats, pp. 251-53.

85-33. BRAMSBÄCK, BIRGIT: "William Butler Yeats och Sverige," *Tvärsnitt*, 8:1 (1986), 4-13.
On Yeats's visit to Sweden, his reception, and the award of the Nobel Prize.

85-34. BRANDUARDI, ANGELO: *Branduardi canta Yeats: Dieci ballate su liriche di William Butler Yeats*. Ariola Eurodisc, 207783. 1986. 1 12" longplay record.
Recording of Italian versions of "The Wild Swans at Coole," "The Cap and Bells," "The Song of Wandering Aengus," "The Cloak, the Boat and the Shoes," "To a Child Dancing in the Wind," "The Fiddler of Dooney," "When You Are Old," "An Irish Airman Foresees His Death," "Down by the Salley Gardens," and "The Lake Isle of Innisfree." The translations/adaptations by Luisa Zappa Branduardi are printed on the inside of the jacket. The music is by Branduardi, except for "The Song of Wandering Aengus," which is by Donovan Leitch.

85-35. BRENNAN, GENEVIEVE: "Yeats, Clodd, *Scatological Rites* and the Clonmel Witch Burning," *Yeats Annual*, 4 (1986), 207-15.
Yeats's reaction to one of the least palatable instances of Irish folk superstition and his contacts with the folklorist Edward Clodd.

85-36. BURTON, RICHARD EDMUND: "The Spiring Treadmill and the Preposterous Pig: The Accommodation of Science in the Political, Occult, and Poetic Development of W. B. Yeats, 1885-1905," Ph.D. thesis, University of London, 1985. 294 pp.
The chapter on politics is mainly concerned with Yeats's proto-fascist leanings, that on occultism with the importance of theosophy. Extended discussions of *Mosada, The Seeker, Time and the Witch Vivien*, "The Two Trees," and *Where There Is Nothing*. Science is represented among others by Darwin, Haeckel, Huxley, and Tyndall.

85-37. BUSH, RONALD: "Yeats, Spooks, Nursery Rhymes, and the Vicissitudes of Later Modernism," *Yeats*, 3 (1985), 17-33.
Reincarnation in Yeats's works and thought.

85-38. BYRNE, CYRIL J., and MARGARET HARRY, eds.: *Talamh an Eisc: Canadian and Irish Essays*. Halifax, N.S.: Nimbus, 1986. viii, 255 pp.
Identical with *Canadian Journal of Irish Studies*, 12:2 (June 1986). See Robert O'Driscoll: "Foundations of the Literary and Musical Revival," 48-70, which contains a note on *Deirdre*.

85-39. CAHILL, KEVIN M., ed.: *The American Irish Revival: A Decade of "The Recorder"—1974-1983*. Port Washington, N.Y.: Associated Faculty Press, 1984. xxiii, 807 pp.
Pieces reprinted from *The Recorder* (published by the American Irish Historical Society, New York). Contains: Kevin Sullivan:

"James Joyce and Anglo-Ireland," 81–91 (reprint of 82–182); Narayan Hegde: "Yeats, India and Long Island," 145–52, reprinted from 41 (1980), 86–93 (on Yeats's interest in India and on the Yeats archives at SUNY, Stony Brook).

85–40. CARDULLO, BERT: "Notes toward a Production of W. B. Yeats's *The Countess Cathleen*," *Canadian Journal of Irish Studies*, 11:2 (Dec. 1985), 49–67.

85–41. CARPENTER, CHARLES A.: *Modern Drama Scholarship and Criticism 1966–1980: An International Bibliography.* Toronto: University of Toronto Press, 1986. xxxv, 587 pp.
Yeats, pp. 147–50 (ca. 250 items).

85–42. CAVANAUGH, CATHERINE: *Love and Forgiveness in Yeats's Poetry.* Ann Arbor: UMI Research Press, 1986. xi, 174 pp. (Studies in Modern Literature, 57.)
Incorporates 84–24. Mainly on "The Three Bushes," "A Man Young and Old," the Crazy Jane poems, the Ribh poems in "Supernatural Songs," and "The Wild Old Wicked Man."

85–43. CAWS, MARY ANN: "Winging It, or Catching Up with Kierkegaard and Some Swans," *Yale French Studies*, 66 (1984), 83–90.
Compares "Leda and the Swan" with its French translation by Yves Bonnefoy.

85–44. CECI, LOUIS G.: "The Case for Syntactic Imagery," *College English*, 45:5 (Sept. 1983), 431–49.
Contains notes on the syntax of "Byzantium" and "Two Songs from a Play."

85–45. CENTRE D'ÉTUDE DU THEATRE ANGLO-SAXON. GROUPE D'ÉTUDE THEORIQUE DU ROMAN DE LANGUE ANGLAISE: *De William Shakespeare à William Golding: Mélanges dédiés à la mémoire de Jean-Pierre Vernier.* Préface de Sylvère Monod. Rouen: Université de Rouen, 1984. 157 pp. (Publications de l'Université de Rouen, 84.)
Jacqueline Genet: "W. B. Yeats: La poétique du visible et de l'invisible," 11–25; on various manifestations of the supernatural in Yeats's works.

85–46. CHIBA, YOKO: "Ezra Pound's Versions of Fenollosa's Noh Manuscripts and Yeats's Unpublished 'Suggestions & Corrections,'" *Yeats Annual*, 4 (1986), 121–44.

85–47. CHRISTIE, MANSON & WOODS INTERNATIONAL: *Modern Literature from the Library of James Gilvarry.* Sale of 7 February 1986. New York: Christie's, 1986.

For Yeats material see items 321–23, 339, 348, 350, 351 (postcard from Lionel Johnson to Yeats, reproduced), 370, 393 (Joyce's copy of *John Sherman and Dhoya*), 403 (a comment by Valery Larbaud on Yeats), 418, 462 (pen and ink drawing of WBY by his brother Jack), 463–565 (first editions with and without inscriptions, letters to May Whitty, Mrs. F. R. Benson, D. J. O'Donoghue, John O'Leary, Ernest Rhys, Violet Hunt, Wilfrid Scawen Blunt, "Michael Field," John Butler Yeats, Arthur Symons, Karel Musek, Ellen Duncan, Lady Gregory, Herman Radin, Joseph M. Hone, Frank Harris, Patrick McCartan, Alice Milligan, John Cournos, A. K. Coomaraswamy, the Duchess of Sutherland, and others, and other material). See report by H. R. Woudhuysen: "Sale of Books and MSS," *TLS*, 14 Feb. 1986, 175.

85–48. CLARK, ROSALIND ELIZABETH: "Goddess, Fairy Mistress, and Sovereignty: Women of the Irish Supernatural," Ph.D. thesis, University of Massachusetts, 1985. xiii, 558 pp. (*DAI*, 46:3 [Sept. 1985], 704A)

Yeats's use of Irish mythological material is discussed passim, especially on pp. 218–33, 296–310 (*The Death of Cuchulain*), 320–28 ("The Wanderings of Oisin"), 364–73 (*The Only Jealousy of Emer*), and 394–420 (*Cathleen ni Houlihan*).

85–49. CLARK, TOM: "The Gang of Eight," *Exquisite Corpse*, 2:5–7 (May–July 1984), 12–13.

A short prose sketch (if this is the word) of a robbery featuring characters called Yeats, Hemingway, Pound, Joyce, Ford, Hulme, Wyndham Lewis, and Dillinger. Yeats drives the getaway car.

85–50. CLEARFIELD, ANDREW MARK: *These Fragments I Have Shored: Collage and Montage in Early Modernist Poetry.* Ann Arbor: UMI Research Press, 1984. xii, 150 pp. (Studies in Modern Literature, 36.)

Note on the "modernism" of Yeats's poetry, pp. 47–50.

85–51. COLEMAN, ANTONY: "The Big House, Yeats, and the Irish Context," *Yeats Annual*, 3 (1985), 33–52.

Yeats's treatment of the big houses reveals that he wasn't rooted in Irish soil. He used his access to the Irish tradition for his own purposes.

85–52. COLLEGE LITERATURE: "Yeats Issue," *College Literature*, 13:1 (Winter 1986).

See 85–21, 27, 68, 116, 135, 150, 168, 177, 197, 200, 211, 308.

85–53. COLLINS, ROBERT A., and HOWARD D. PEARCE, eds.: *The Scope of the Fantastic: Culture, Biography, Themes, Children's Literature. Selected Essays from the First International Conference on the Fantastic in*

Literature and Film. Westport, Ct.: Greenwood Press, 1985. xii, 284 pp. (Contributions to the Study of Science Fiction and Fantasy, 11.)
Bradford Crain: "Masks, Mirrors, and Magic: Fantasy as Autobiography in the Works of Hesse and Yeats," 91–97.

85–54. COLLS, ROBERT, and PHILIP DODD, eds.: *Englishness: Politics and Culture 1880–1920.* London: Croom Helm, 1986. vi, 378 pp.
Peter Brooker and Peter Widdowson: "A Literature for England," 116–63, contains some notes on Yeats.

85–55. CONRAD, PETER: *The Everyman History of English Literature.* London: Dent, 1985. xi, 740 pp.
"The Last Romantic?" 546–59, and passim (see index).

85–56. COULTER, CAROL: "An Irishwoman's Diary," *Irish Times*, 8 Sept. 1986, 11.
On James W. Flannery and his interest in Yeats's plays.

85–57. CRANDALL, DAVID: *Crazy Jane: A Dance-Drama in One Act.* Tokyo: Clearwater, 1983. i, 14 pp.
In English, together with a Japanese translation by Noriko Komatsu; title on cover. A play on motifs derived from Yeats, first performed in September 1983 at the Tokyo Union Church.

85–58. CRONIN, ANTHONY: *An Irish Eye.* Dingle, Co. Kerry: Brandon, 1985. 141 pp.
"Farewell Kiltartan," 32–36. Yeats's hatred of the middle class will not do these days.

85–59. CULLINGFORD, ELIZABETH: "Yeats and Women: Michael Robartes and the Dancer," *Yeats Annual*, 4 (1986), 29–52.
Discusses Yeats's treatment of Maud and Iseult Gonne, Constance Markievicz, and his own marriage in "Michael Robartes and the Dancer," "Easter 1916," "Solomon and the Witch," "A Prayer for My Daughter," and other poems.

85–60. D'AMICO, MASOLINO: *Dieci secoli di teatro inglese 970–1980.* Milano: Mondadori, 1981. x, 462 pp.
Some notes on Yeats's theatrical activities, pp. 318–21, 346–48.

85–61. DASENBROCK, REED WAY: *The Literary Vorticism of Ezra Pound & Wyndham Lewis: Towards the Condition of Painting.* Baltimore: Johns Hopkins University Press, 1985. xii, 271 pp.
See index for some notes on Yeats.

85–62. DAVENPORT, GUY: "Claiming Kin: Artist, Critic and Scholar as Family," *Shenandoah*, 36:1 (1985–86), 35–86.
Contains a note on the Crazy Jane poems and their indebtedness to Meredith's poem "Jump-to-Glory Jane," pp. 42–46.

85-63. DAVIS, KAY: *Fugue and Fresco: Structures in Pound's "Cantos."* Orono, Maine: National Poetry Foundation, 1984. 125 pp.

Incorporates 83-43. Discusses Yeats's view of Pound in *A Packet for Ezra Pound*, particularly in connection with the fugue structure of the *Cantos* (pp. 76-81) and the Schifanoia Frescoes in the Schifanoia Palace, Ferrara (pp. 94-97).

85-64. DAWE, GERALD, and EDNA LONGLEY, eds.: *Across a Roaring Hill: The Protestant Imagination in Modern Ireland. Essays in Honour of John Hewitt*. Belfast: Blackstaff Press, 1985. xix, 242 pp.

John Kelly: "Choosing and Inventing: Yeats and Ireland," 1-24.
W. J. McCormack: "'The Protestant Strain': Or, a Short History of Anglo-Irish Literature from S. T. Coleridge to Thomas Mann," 48-78. Edna Longley: "Louis MacNeice: 'The Walls Are Flowing,'" 99-123 (contains notes on MacNeice's view of Yeats).
Short references to Yeats in some of the other contributions and in the editors' introduction.

85-65. DEANE, SEAMUS: *Celtic Revivals: Essays in Modern Irish Literature 1880-1980*. London: Faber & Faber, 1985. 199 pp.

"The Literary Myths of the Revival," 28-37; reprinted from Joseph Ronsley, ed., *Myth and Reality in Irish Literature* (1977); on Yeats's myth of the ascendancy.
"Yeats and the Idea of Revolution," 38-50; revised version of "Yeats, Ireland and Revolution," *Crane Bag*, 1:2 (1977), 56-64; also in 83-90.
"O'Casey and Yeats: Exemplary Dramatists," 108-22; revised from *Threshold*, 30 (Spring 1979), 21-28; incorporates J7113a.
Also passim (see index).
Reviews:
Denis Donoghue: "A Myth and Its Unmasking," *TLS*, 1 Nov. 1985, 1239-40.
Peter Sirr: "The Burden of History," *Irish Times*, 28 Sept. 1985, 13.

85-66. ———: *A Short History of Irish Literature*. London: Hutchinson, 1986. 282 pp.

See "Irish Modernism: Poetry and Drama," 141-67, and the index for numerous other references.

85-67. DELANEY, J. G. P.: "'Heirs of the Great Generation': Yeats's Friendship with Charles Ricketts and Charles Shannon," *Yeats Annual*, 4 (1986), 53-73.

85-68. DETTMAR, KEVIN J. H.: "'Evil Gathers Head': Yeats' Poetics of Evil," *College Literature*, 13:1 (Winter 1986), 71-87.

85-69. DIGGORY, TERENCE: "American Responses to Yeats's Prose: Marianne Moore and Allen Ginsberg," *Yeats*, 3 (1985), 34-59.

85-70. *Dizionario Motta della letteratura contemporanea.* Milano: Motta, 1982. 4 vols.
L. A.: "Yeats," 4:1814–15; a summary of T. S. Eliot's article (J2512).

85-71. DONALD, ANDREW: "Yeats," *Poetry Australia,* 100 (March 1985), 86.
A poem.

85-72. DONOGHUE, DENIS: "On 'Gerontion,'" *Southern Review,* 21:4 (Oct. 1985), 934–46.
Comments on the Eliot-Yeats relationship.

85-73. DRABBLE, MARGARET, ed.: *The Oxford Companion to English Literature.* Fifth edition. Oxford: Oxford University Press, 1985. xii, 1155 pp.
See pp. 1093–94.

85-74. DRAPER, R. P.: *Lyric Tragedy.* London: Macmillan, 1985. vii, 231 pp.
See index for some notes on *Deirdre* and on Yeats's views on lyric tragedy.

85-75. DYSON, A. E., ed.: *Poetry Criticism & Practice: Developments since the Symbolists. A Casebook.* London: Macmillan, 1986. 217 pp.
Reprinted pieces; numerous references to Yeats (see index).

85-76. EAGLETON, TERRY: "Politics and Sexuality in W. B. Yeats," *Crane Bag,* 9:2 (1985), 138–42.

85-77. ———: *Against the Grain: Essays 1975–1985.* London: Verso, 1986. ix, 199 pp.
"Poetry, Pleasure and Politics," 173–80; a reprint of 83–63.

85-78. EARLE, RALPH HARDING: "Yeats's Passionate Syntax," °Ph.D. thesis, University of North Carolina at Chapel Hill, 1985. 197 pp. (*DAI*, 47:2 [Aug. 1986], 535A)
The syntax of some poems, among them "Sailing to Byzantium," "Ancestral Houses," "A Prayer for My Daughter," "A Dialogue of Self and Soul," "Among School Children," "Leda and the Swan," and the sonnets.

85-79. EDDY, MICHAEL MAX: "The Grotesque in the Art of William Butler Yeats," Ph.D. thesis, Purdue University, 1984. vi, 169 pp. (*DAI*, 45:7 [Jan. 1985], 2109A–10A; reprinted in *Yeats,* 4 [1986], 178–79)

85-80. ELIOT, T. S.: "Tradition and the Practice of Poetry." Introduction and afterword by A. Walton Litz, *Southern Review,* 21:4 (Oct. 1985), 873–88.
A lecture delivered at University College Dublin on 24 January

1936. Both the introduction and the afterword discuss the Eliot-Yeats relationship.

85–81. ELLMANN, RICHARD: *W. B. Yeats's Second Puberty*. A lecture delivered at the Library of Congress on April 2, 1984. Washington, D.C.: Library of Congress, 1985. 29 pp.
Also published, without the photographs, in *New York Review of Books*, 9 May 1985, 10, 12, 14–16, 18. The importance of the Steinach operation for Yeats's later work, especially for its treatment of sex; also on the revisions of *A Vision*.

85–82. ———: *Samuel Beckett: Nayman of Noland*. A lecture delivered at the Library of Congress on April 16, 1985. Washington, D.C.: Library of Congress, 1986. 31 pp.
First published in *New York Review of Books*, 24 April 1986, 27–28, 34–37. Includes notes on Yeats.

85–83. FARAG, FAHMY: "Forcing Reading and Writing on Those Who Want Neither: W. B. Yeats and the Irish Oral Tradition," *Canadian Journal of Irish Studies*, 11:2 (Dec. 1985), 7–15.

85–84. FIELD DAY THEATRE COMPANY: *Ireland's Field Day*. London: Hutchinson, 1985. viii, 120 pp.
Seamus Deane: "Heroic Styles: The Tradition of an Idea," 43–58; reprint of 84–39.
Richard Kearney: "Myth and Motherland," 59–80; reprint of 84–100.
Declan Kiberd: "Anglo-Irish Attitudes," 81–105; reprint of 84–103.
Denis Donoghue: "Afterword," 107–20; comments on the Yeats interpretations offered in the above contributions.

85–85. FINNEY, BRIAN: *The Inner I: British Literary Autobiography of the Twentieth Century*. London: Faber & Faber, 1985. 286 pp.
"W. B. Yeats: *Reveries over Childhood and Youth*," 150–57, and passim (see index). See also review by P. N. Furbank: "Early Lives," *London Review of Books*, 5 June 1986, 11–12.

85–86. FISCH, HAROLD: *A Remembered Future: A Study in Literary Mythology*. Bloomington: Indiana University Press, 1984. xi, 194 pp.
Note on "The Second Coming," pp. 146–47.

85–87. FITE, DAVID: *Harold Bloom: The Rhetoric of Romantic Vision*. Amherst: University of Massachusetts Press, 1985. xiv, 230 pp.
Bloom's treatment of Yeats is discussed at length in "Yeats and the Spectre of Modernism," 35–54, and "Vision's Revision: The Anxiety of Influence," 55–90.

85–88. FLEMING, DEBORAH DIANE: "The Irish Peasant in the Work of W. B. Yeats and J. M. Synge," °Ph.D. thesis, Ohio State University, 1985. 239 pp. (*DAI*, 46:12 [June 1986], 3724A–25A)

85-89. FLEMING, NOEL: "Berkeley and Idealism," *Philosophy*, 60:233 (July 1985), 309-25.
Contains a note on "Blood and the Moon."

85-90. FOLEY, BRIAN: "Yeats's 'King Goll': Sources, Revision, and Revisions," *Yeats*, 4 (1986), 17-32.

85-91. FOSTER, JOHN WILSON: "Yeats and the Easter Rising," *Canadian Journal of Irish Studies*, 11:1 (June 1985), 21-34.
On "Easter 1916" and related poems and on Yeats's borrowings from Pearse.

85-92. FOWLER, ROGER: *Linguistic Criticism*. Oxford: Oxford University Press, 1986. vii, 190 pp.
Note on "An Irish Airman Foresees His Death" and "Among School Children," pp. 90-93.

85-93. FRANCHI, FLORENCE: "Les *Four Plays for Dancers* de W. B. Yeats et l'influence du No japonais," thesis, Doctorat de spécialité de 3ème cycle, Université Paul Valéry, Montpellier III, 1982. vii, 392 pp.

85-94. FRASER, ROBERT HUGH: "George Barker and the English Poets: 'The Minor Bird on the Bough,'" Ph.D. thesis, University of London, 1984. 526 pp.
"'The Pilgrimage along the Drogheda Road': George Barker, W. B. Yeats and the Idea of Ireland," 282-309. See also Fraser's article with the same title in *Yeats Annual*, 3 (1985), 133-47.

85-95. GARDINER, BRUCE: "Decadence: Its Construction and Contexts," *Southern Review* [Adelaide], 18:1 (March 1985) 22-43.
Contains some notes on Yeats.

85-96. GARDNER, JOANN: "The Rhymers' Club Reviews and Yeats's Myth of Failure," *Yeats*, 4 (1986), 33-54.
The influence of the reviews of the first *Book of the Rhymers' Club* on Yeats's views of the Rhymers'. Includes a complete list of the reviews.

85-97. GARTON, JANET, ed.: *Facets of European Modernism: Essays in Honour of James McFarlane Presented to Him on His 65th Birthday, 12 December 1985*. Norwich: University of East Anglia, 1985. 372 pp.
Simon Williams: "John Millington Synge: Transforming Myths of Ireland," 79-98; includes comments on Yeats.

85-98. GENIUSHENE, IZOL'DA-GABRIELE LIAONO: *Pozdniaia poeziia U. B. Ieĭtsa: Problema metoda*. Avtoreferat dissertatsii . . . kandidata filologicheskikh nauk. Moskva: Moskovskiĭ . . . gosudarstvennyĭ universitet im. M. V. Lomonosova, 1984. 26 pp.
"Yeats's late poetry: The problem of method"; a dissertation abstract.

85-99. GHAURI, H. R.: "Yeats, Pound, Eliot, Joyce: Lawrence's Secret Sharers," *Ariel* [University of Sind], 7 (1981-82), 54-74.
There is very little on Yeats in this article, and his share in Lawrence's work (or vice verse) is not made clear.

85-100. GIANNOTTI, THOMAS JOHN: "A Language of Silence: Writing the Self in Yeats and Synge, Joyce and Beckett," °Ph.D. thesis, University of California, Riverside, 1985. 233 pp. (*DAI*, 46:12 [June 1986], 3725A)
Discusses *Memoirs* and *Autobiographies*.

85-101. GIFFORD, HENRY: *Poetry in a Divided World*. The Clark Lectures 1985. Cambridge: Cambridge University Press, 1986. ix, 111 pp.
Discusses Yeats's "position in Irish life" as reflected in his poetry and the "affinities and opposition" between Yeats and Blok, pp. 38-44. See also pp. 60-61 for a Yeats-Eliot comparison.

85-102. GILBERT, R. A.: "'The One Deep Student': Yeats and A. E. Waite," *Yeats Annual*, 3 (1985), 3-13.
"Utterly opposed to each other as they were in all things occult, each man evidently respected the other." Quotes from Waite's unpublished diaries.

85-103. GONZALES, DEBORAH MARTIN, comp.: "Dissertation Abstracts, 1984," *Yeats*, 3 (1985), 206-16.
Reprints the abstracts of Boyd (84-14), Holdsworth (84-86), Gardner (84-61), Farrell (84-51), Helmling (84-80), Oppel (84-160), Suleri (84-195), Weinraub (84-213), Chadwick (84-26), Cavanaugh (84-24), and Martinich (84-137).

85-104. ———: "Dissertation Abstracts, 1985," *Yeats*, 4 (1986), 177-86.
Reprints the abstracts of Keane (85-154), Eddy (85-79), Adams (85-3), Greene (85-112), Laity (85-173), Stanfield (85-286), McMahan (85-196), Jacobs (85-142), Good (84-64), and McVeigh (84-129).

85-105. GOSE, ELLIOTT B.: *The World of the Irish Wonder Tale: An Introduction to the Study of Fairy Tales*. Dingle, Co. Kerry: Brandon, 1985. xxiv, 228 pp.
Short note on Yeats, pp. xvii-xviii.

85-106. GOULD, WARWICK.: "Two Omissions from *The Secret Rose, Stories by W. B. Yeats: A Variorum Edition*," *Yeats Annual*, 3 (1985), 198.

85-107. ———: "How Ferencz Renyi Spoke Up, Part Two," *Yeats Annual*, 3 (1985), 199-205.
Variants in the later reprintings of the poem "How Ferencz Renyi Kept Silent."

85-108. ———, and OLYMPIA SITWELL: "'Gasping on the Strand': A Yeats Bibliography, 1981-1983," *Yeats Annual*, 3 (1985), 304-23.

85–109. ———: "A Recent Yeats Bibliography, 1983–84," *Yeats Annual*, 4 (1986), 323–25.

85–110. GRAMM, CHRISTIE DIANE: "The Development of Prophecy in the Poetry of W. B. Yeats," °Ph.D. thesis, University of Oregon, 1985. 131 pp. (*DAI*, 46:7 [Jan. 1986], 1948A)

85–111. GREENBERG, MARTIN: *The Hamlet Vocation of Coleridge and Wordsworth*. Iowa City: University of Iowa Press, 1986. xiv, 209 pp.

The Coleridge chapter contains a note on Yeats's "Hamletism," pp. 87–89.

85–112. GREENE, ROLAND ARTHUR: "Origins and Innovations of the Western Lyric Sequence," °Ph.D. thesis, Princeton University, 1985. 459 pp. (*DAI*, 45:12 [June 1985], 3631A; reprinted in *Yeats*, 4 [1986], 180–81)

Includes a discussion of "two short series by Yeats."

85–113. GRENE, NICHOLAS: "Shaw in Ireland: Visitor or Returning Exile?" *Shaw*, 5 (1985), 45–62.

Contains a few notes on Yeats and Shaw.

85–114. GRIFFIN, CHRISTOPHER: "Visions and Revisions," *Theatre Ireland*, 9/10 (Spring/Summer 1985), 145–51.

Interview with Eric Bentley who comments on Yeats's plays.

85–115. GRIFFIN, JASPER: *The Mirror of Myth: Classical Themes & Variations*. London: Faber & Faber, 1986. 144 pp. (T. S. Eliot Memorial Lectures 1984.)

Chapter 1, "Myth and Paradigm," 9–42, contains some notes on the use of Classical myth in Yeats's poetry.

85–116. GRIFFIN, JON: "Profane Perfection: 'The Statues,'" *College Literature*, 13:1 (Winter 1986), 21–28.

85–117. GUTIERREZ, DONALD: *The Maze in the Mind and the World: Labyrinths in Modern Literature*. Troy, N.Y.: Whitston, 1985. xv, 197 pp.

"Yeats and the Noh Theatre," 38–54; discusses *At the Hawk's Well*, *The Dreaming of the Bones*, and *Purgatory*.

85–118. HANEY-PERITZ, JANICE: "Refraining from the Romantic Image: Yeats and the Deformation of Metaphysical Aestheticism," *Studies in Romanticism*, 25:1 (Spring 1986), 3–37.

Discusses, among others, the Crazy Jane poems, "I Am of Ireland," "Long-legged Fly," and "What Then."

85–119. HANSON, CLARE: *Short Stories and Short Fictions, 1880–1980*. London: Macmillan, 1985. viii, 189 pp.

Contains some notes on the importance of Yeats's theory of the imagination, especially on pp. 83–85. Does not discuss Yeats's own fiction.

85-120. HARPER, GEORGE MILLS, and SANDRA L. SPRAYBERRY: "Complementary Creation: Notes on 'Another Song of a Fool' and 'Towards Break of Day,'" *Yeats*, 4 (1986), 69-85.

The role of Mrs. Yeats's automatic writing in the drafting of the two poems; reproduces the drafts of "Towards Break of Day."

85-121. HARTNETT, MICHAEL: *Collected Poems: Volume 1.* Dublin: Raven Arts Press / Manchester: Carcanet Press, 1985. 168 pp.

"A Farewell to English," 157-59, contains a section on "Chef Yeats"; first published in *A Farewell to English and Other Poems.* Dublin: Gallery Press, 1975.

85-122. HARWOOD, JOHN: "Olivia Shakespear and W. B. Yeats," *Yeats Annual*, 4 (1986), 75-98.

See also Deirdre Toomey: "An Afterword on *Rupert Armstrong*," *Yeats Annual*, 4 (1986), 99-102.

85-123. HASAN, MASSODUL: "Yeats's Theory of Drama," *Indian Journal of English Studies*, 24 (1984), 43-52.

85-124. HASSETT, JOSEPH M.: "Yeats and the Chief Consolation of Genius," *Yeats*, 4 (1986), 55-67.

Yeats's relations with Dorothy Wellesley, Margot Ruddock, Ethel Mannin, and Edith Shackleton Heald, and their reflections in his poetry.

85-125. ———: *Yeats and the Poetics of Hate.* Dublin: Gill & Macmillan / New York: St. Martin's Press, 1986. ix, 189 pp.

On hate in Yeats's thinking and poetry, particularly the Crazy Jane and Ribh poems. Discusses the relationship to Blake, T. H. Huxley, Locke, Swift, and John Butler Yeats; includes a chapter on *Per Amica Silentia Lunae.*

Reviews:

Tom Clyde: "Bananas and the Oozalum Bird," *Books Ireland,* 106 (Sept. 1986), 167-68.

Sean Dunne: "A Healthy Hate," *Irish Literary Supplement,* 5:2 (Fall 1986), 24-25.

Peter Sirr: "Yeatsian Love and Hate," *Irish Times,* 30 Aug. 1986, 14.

85-126. HEANEY, SEAMUS: *Among School Children.* A lecture dedicated to the memory of John Malone. Belfast: John Malone Memorial Committee, [1985?]. 16 pp.

Contains notes on Yeats's poem.

85-127. ———: "Envies and Identifications: Dante and the Modern Poet," *Irish University Review,* 15:1 (Spring 1985), 5-19.

Contains a note on "Ego Dominus Tuus."

85-128. HECHLER, DAVID: "Opening Yeats Trove to Academe," *New York Times*, 19 Jan. 1986, section 21, 10.
The cataloging of the Yeats Archives at SUNY Stony Brook.

85-129. HEMINGWAY, ERNEST: *Dateline: Toronto. The Complete "Toronto Star" Dispatches, 1920-1924*. Edited by William White. New York: Scribner's, 1985. xxxi, 478 pp.
"'Nobelman's Yeats," 384-86; reprint of J1386. "W. B. Yeats a Nighthawk," 427-28; reprint of J686.

85-130. HEPBURN, JAMES: *Critic into Anti-Critic*. Columbia, S.C.: Camden House, 1984. xi, 238 pp. (Studies in English and American Literature, Linguistics, and Culture, 3.)
"Leda and the Dumbledore," 115-24; reprinted from *Sewanee Review*, 88:1 (Winter 1980), 52-66; compares Yeats and Hardy, particularly "Leda and the Swan" and "An August Midnight."

85-131. HESSE, EVA, MICHAEL KNIGHT, and MANFRED PFISTER: *Der Aufstand der Musen: Die "Neue Frau" in der englischen Moderne*. Passau: Haller, 1984. 153 pp.
"The revolt of the muses: The 'new woman' in modern English literature"; contains numerous references to Yeats's alleged anti-emancipatory view of women. See especially pp. 18-19, 56-57 (on Florence Farr), 64-74 (on Maud Gonne), 83-96 (on Lady Gregory).

85-132. HILLS, S. J.: "Frieda Lawrence," *TLS*, 6 Sept. 1985, 975.
Letter to the editor asking for information about Frieda Weekley, the co-translator of *Das Land der Sehnsucht* (Wade, p. 406). See also letter by John Worthen, 11 Oct. 1985, 1139.

85-133. HÖLTGEN, KARL JOSEF, LOTHAR HÖNNIGHAUSEN, EBERHARD KREUTZER, and GÖTZ SCHMITZ, eds.: *Tradition und Innovation in der englischen und amerikanischen Lyrik des 20. Jahrhunderts: Arno Esch zum 75. Geburtstag*. Tübingen: Niemeyer, 1986. xii, 271 pp.
E. Kreutzer: "W. B. Yeats und sein testamentarisches Credo in 'Under Ben Bulben,'" 95-110.

85-134. HOPE, A. D.: "Coming to Grips with Proteus," *Yeats Annual*, 4 (1986), 161-71.
Hope discusses his relationship to Yeats, particularly in the five poems which he has written about him (here reprinted). One of the poems is on the mistreatment of Yeats by Robert Graves.

85-135. HOPENWASSER, NANDA: "Crazy Jane: Writer of Her Own Justification," *College Literature*, 13:1 (Winter 1986), 9-20.

85-136. HOŠEK, CHAVIVA, and PATRICIA PARKER, eds.: *Lyric Poetry: Beyond New Criticism*. Ithaca: Cornell University Press, 1985. 375 pp.
Jonathan Culler: "Changes in the Study of the Lyric," 38-54, dis-

cusses Cleanth Brooks's reading of "Among School Children" (J2948), pp. 44-46.

85-137. HOUGH, GRAHAM: "*A Vision:* Some Notes and Queries," *Yeats Annual,* 3 (1985), 213-21.
Incorporated in 84-89.

85-138. HUNTER, CHARLES: "*Calvary* and *Resurrection* at the Peacock," *Irish Times,* 17 Sept. 1986, 12.
Review of a performance.

85-139. *Index of Manuscripts in the British Library.* Cambridge: Chadwyck-Healey, 1984-86. 10 vols.
See 10:545 for the Yeats MSS.

85-140. *Interpretatsiia khudozhestvennogo teksta v iazykovom vuze: Sbornik nauchnykh trudov.* Leningrad: Leningradskiĭ ordena trudovogo krasnogo znameni gosudarstvennyĭ pedagogicheskiĭ institut imeni A. I. Gertsena, 1981. 156 pp.
T. I. Sil'man: "Lingvisticheskaia interpretatsiia liriki poetov 'Irlandskogo Vozrozhdeniia,'" 82-95; analyses "The Lake Isle of Innisfree."

85-141. JACKSON, THOMAS H.: "Herder, Pound, and the Concept of Expressionism," *Modern Language Quarterly,* 44:4 (Dec. 1983), 374-93.
Includes comments on Yeats's symbolist theories.

85-142. JACOBS, MARGARET ELIZABETH GUERNSEY: "Swordsman, Saint, or Prophet—'Is That, Perhaps, the Sole Theme?': Yeats's Shaping of Autobiography into Prophecy through Creation of a Personal Myth," Ph.D. thesis, Emory University, 1985. xi, 403 pp. (*DAI,* 46:6 [Dec. 1985], 1634A; reprinted in *Yeats,* 4 [1986], 183-84)
On Yeats's "conception of the poet's role in society and its foundation in his belief in the importance of poetry as a metaphysical force" (p. 1).

85-143. JAKOBSON, ROMAN: *Verbal Art, Verbal Sign, Verbal Time.* Edited by Krystyna Pomorska and Stephen Rudy. Oxford: Blackwell, 1985. xiv, 209 pp.
"On Poetic Intentions and Linguistic Devices in Poetry: A Discussion with Professors and Students at the University of Cologne," 69-78; "Yeats' 'Sorrow of Love' through the Years," 79-107; both reprinted from 81-72.

85-144. JAMES, ELIZABETH INGLI: "The University of Reading Collections," *Yeats Annual,* 3 (1985), 167-72.
Of Yeatsiana and related material.

85-145. JARRELL, RANDALL: *Randall Jarrell's Letters: An Autobiographical and Literary Selection.* Edited by Mary Jarrell. Boston: Houghton

Mifflin, 1985. xix, 540 pp.
Several references to Yeats (see index).

85-146. JEFFARES, A. NORMAN: "Yeats's Birthplace," *Yeats Annual*, 3 (1985), 175-78.

85-147. JOHNSON, WENDELL STACY: *Sons and Fathers: The Generation Link in Literature 1780-1980*. New York: Lang, 1985. vii, 237 pp. (Studies in Romantic and Modern Literature, 1.)
"Sons and Fathers: Yeats, Joyce, and Faulkner," 153-202; discusses the Cuchulain plays, "Sailing to Byzantium," "A Prayer for My Daughter," and "A Prayer for My Son."

85-148. JOHNSTON, DILLON: *Irish Poetry after Joyce*. Notre Dame: University of Notre Dame Press / Mountrath: Dolmen Press, 1985. xv, 336 pp.
"Yeats's Legacy: An Antithetical Art," 13-28, and passim on Yeats's "troubling presence" in Irish poetry after 1941.

85-149. JORDAN, CARMEL PATRICIA: "A Terrible Beauty: The Mask of Cuchulain in 'Easter 1916,'" Ph.D. thesis, Fordham University, 1984. iii, 198 pp. (*DAI*, 46:4 [Oct. 1985], 989A)

85-150. ———: "The Stone Symbol in 'Easter 1916' and the Cuchulain Plays," *College Literature*, 13:1 (Winter 1986), 36-43.

85-151. KALINA DE PISZK, ROSA: "La paradoja como elemento unificador en *El tigre luminoso* de Alfonso Chase," *Káñina: Revista de Artes y Letras de la Universidad de Costa Rica*, 7:2 (July-Dec. 1983), 39-42.
Notes the influence of Yeats.

85-152. KAMP, PETER G. W. VAN DE: "Some Notes on the Literary Estate of Pamela Hinkson," *Yeats Annual*, 4 (1986), 181-86.
Discusses the relationship between Yeats and Katharine Tynan (Pamela Hinkson's mother) on the basis of unpublished material.

85-153. ———: "Yeats's Noh-Noh Drama," *Irish Literary Supplement*, 5:1 (Spring 1986), 16.
A review of Masaru Sekine: *Ze-Ami and His Theories of Noh Drama* (1985); the book itself contains only a passing reference to Yeats.

85-154. KEANE, MICHAEL JAMES: "Private and Public Voices in Irish Poetry: W. B. Yeats, Patrick Kavanagh, and Seamus Heaney," Ph.D. thesis, University of Michigan, 1984. iii, 268 pp. (*DAI*, 45:7 [Jan. 1985], 2097A-98A; reprinted in *Yeats*, 4 [1986], 177-78)
Discusses Yeats's public and political poetry, his version of the Anglo-Irish tradition, and the theme of violence.

85-155. KEANE, PATRICK J.: "Yeats's Counter-Enlightenment," *Salmagundi*, 68-69 (Autumn 1985), 125-45.

With a drawing of Yeats by Lowell Boyers. On Yeats's romantic battle with mechanistic materialism, particularly in "Fragments," and the influence of Blake.

85-156. KEARNEY, RICHARD, ed.: *The Irish Mind: Exploring Intellectual Traditions.* Dublin: Wolfhound Press, 1985. 365 pp.
R. Kearney: "An Irish Intellectual Tradition? Philosophical and Cultural Contexts," 7-38, 311-18.
John Jordan: "Shaw, Wilde, Synge and Yeats: Ideas, Epigrams, Blackberries, and Chassis," 209-25, 340-42. Despite the title, very little is said about Yeats.
Elizabeth Cullingford: "The Unknown Thought of W. B. Yeats," 226-43, 343-45. A survey of Yeats's "beliefs."

85-157. KELLY, JOHN S.: "'Song of Spanish Insurgents': A Newly Discovered Poem by Yeats," *Yeats Annual,* 3 (1985), 179-81.
First published in the Dublin weekly *North & South,* 5 March 1887. See also James Loughlin: "A Long-Lost Poem by W. B. Yeats," *Irish Times,* 22 July 1986, 10.

85-158. ———: "Yeatsian Magic and Rational Magic: An Uncollected Review of W. B. Yeats," *Yeats Annual,* 3 (1985), 182-89.
An anonymous review of G. C. Leland's *Gypsy Sorcery* in the *National Observer,* 18 April 1891.

85-159. KENNEDY, DENNIS: *Granville Barker and the Dream of Theatre.* Cambridge: Cambridge University Press. 1985. xiv, 231 pp.
See index for a few notes on Yeats.

85-160. KENNER, HUGH: "A Possible Source in Coleridge for 'The Phases of the Moon,'" *Yeats,* 3 (1985), 174-75.

85-161. KERMODE, FRANK: *Forms of Attention.* Chicago: University of Chicago Press, 1985. xv, 93 pp.
"Botticelli Recovered," 2-31, contains some remarks on Herbert Horne and Yeats.

85-162. KHOROL'SKIĬ, V. V.: "Simbolizm A. Bloka i U. B. Ĭitsa (Nekotorye problemy tipologii evropeĭskogo simbolizma)," *Voprosy russkoĭ literatury,* 45 (1985), 90-96.
"The symbolism of Blok and WBY: Some problems of the typology of European symbolism."

85-163. KIASASHVILI, NICO, ed.: [in Georgian] *Three Essays on John Donne, W. B. Yeats and T. S. Eliot.* Tbilisi: Tbilisi University Press, 1984. v, 144 pp.
The Russian bibliographical description is as follows: KARUMIDZE, ZURAB LEVANOVICH, and others: *Dzhon Donn . . . Uil'iam Batler Ĭits . . . Tomas Sternz Eliot. . . .* Pod red. Niko Kiasashvili. Tbilisi: Izdfatel'stvo Tbilisskogo universiteta, 1984.

Paata Eduardovich Shevardnadze: "W. B. Yeats: Impersonal Emotion," 62–96; in Georgian, with summaries in Russian and English. Relates the "impersonality" of Yeats's later poetry to the influence of Bergson's "élan vital." See also 85–273.

85–164. KIBERD, DECLAN: *Men and Feminism in Modern Literature.* London: Macmillan, 1985. xii, 250 pp.

"W. B. Yeats: Robartes' Quarrel with the Dancer," 103–35, and passim (see index). On Yeats's view of woman in his life and poetry, particularly the New Woman, the dancer, and the *anima* figure.

85–165. KINAHAN, FRANK: "A Source Note on 'The Madness of King Goll,'" *Yeats Annual*, 4 (1986), 189–94.

85–166. KING, MARY C.: *The Drama of J. M. Synge.* London: Fourth Estate, 1985. ix, 229 pp.

Some remarks on Yeats (see index).

85–167. KINSELLA, THOMAS, ed.: *The New Oxford Book of Irish Verse.* Oxford: Oxford University Press, 1986. xxx, 423 pp.

The "Introduction," xxiii–xxx, includes some comments on Yeats. A selection of seven poems appears on pp. 309–16.

85–168. KLUG, M. A.: "Pursuit of Confusion in 'The Tower,'" *College Literature*, 13:1 (Winter 1986), 29–35.

85–169. KNAPP, BETTINA LIEBOWITZ: *A Jungian Approach to Literature.* Carbondale: Southern Illinois University Press, 1984. xvi, 403 pp.

"4. Yeats (1865–1939): At the Hawk's Well—An Unintegrated Anima Shapes a Hero's Destiny," 227–64; reprint of 83–116. Reviewed by Barbara J. Frieling, *Yeats*, 4 (1986), 204–6.

85–170. KOHFELDT, MARY LOU: *Lady Gregory: The Woman behind the Irish Renaissance.* London: Deutsch, 1985. xiii, 367 pp.

Based on Mary Lou Kohfeldt Stevenson: "Lady Gregory: A Character Study," Ph.D. thesis, University of North Carolina at Chapel Hill, 1977. xiv, 295 pp. (*DAI*, 38:6 [Dec. 1977], 3490A–3491A), incorporates Mary Lou Stevenson: "Lady Gregory and Yeats: Symbiotic Creativity," *Journal of the Rutgers University Libraries*, 40:2 (Dec. 1978), 63–77. Yeats figures prominently in a book remarkable for its rather gushy style.

Reviews:

Roy Foster: "Sacrifice and Inspiration," *TLS*, 12 July 1985, 778.

David Krause: "No Justice to Lady Gregory," *Irish Literary Supplement*, 4:2 (Fall 1985), 28–29.

85–171. KOSOK, HEINZ: *O'Casey the Dramatist.* Translated by the author and Joseph T. Swann. Gerrards Cross: Colin Smythe / Totowa,

N.J.: Barnes & Noble, 1985. xiv, 409 pp. (Irish Literary Studies, 19.) Revised and translated version of J7147. Numerous references to Yeats, see particularly pp. 354–57.

85–172. KUCH, PETER: *Yeats and A. E.: "The Antagonism That Unites Dear Friends."* Gerrards Cross: Colin Smythe / Totowa, N.J.: Barnes & Noble, 1986. xiii, 291 pp.

Discusses the period 1884–1907, with particular reference to both poets' interest in theosophy and spiritism, Irish literature and tradition, and the revival of the theater. Numerous quotations from AE's unpublished letters to Yeats and from some unpublished Yeats letters. See review by Derek Mahon: "The Hare and the Tortoise," *Irish Times*, 26 July 1986, 11.

85–173. LAITY, CASSANDRA: "From Fatal Woman to New Woman: Yeats' Changing Image of Woman in His Art and Aesthetic," Ph.D. thesis, University of Michigan, 1984. iii, 209 pp. (*DAI*, 45:12 [June 1985], 3646A; reprinted in *Yeats*, 4 [1986], 181)

Discusses relevant poems and plays, particularly *The Shadowy Waters*, *Deirdre*, and *The Player Queen*.

85–174. ———: "W. B. Yeats and Florence Farr: The Influence of the 'New Woman' Actress on Yeats's Changing Images of Women," *Modern Drama*, 28:4 (Dec. 1985), 620–37.

85–175. LEAMON, WARREN: "Yeats: Skeptic on Stage," *Éire-Ireland*, 21:1 (Spring 1986), 129–35.

On the realistic elements in the plays.

85–176. LEHNER, THOMAS ed.: *Keltisches Bewusstsein*. München: Dianus-Trikont, 1985. 344 pp.

Contains "Aengus' Wanderlied," a German translation of "The Song of Wandering Aengus" by Gisela H. Malter, p. 253.

85–177. LENSING, GEORGE S.: "'Among School Children': Questions as Conclusions," *College Literature*, 13:1 (Winter 1986), 1–8.

85–178. LEWIS, WYNDHAM: *Rude Assignment: An Intellectual Autobiography*. Illustrated by the author, edited by Toby Foshay. With six letters by Ezra Pound, edited and annotated by Bryant Knox. Santa Barbara: Black Sparrow Press, 1984. 315 pp.

New edition of J1448. See pp. 13, 17, 55–56, 108, 111, 136–37, 141, 215–16.

85–179. LOMAS, HERBERT: "The Critic as Anti-Hero: War Poetry," *Hudson Review*, 38:3 (Autumn 1985), 376–89.

Includes notes on Yeats's view of war poetry.

85–180. LONGENBACH, JAMES BURTON: "A Sense of the Past: Pound, Eliot, and Modernist Poetics of History," Ph.D. thesis, Princeton

University, 1985. xi, 325 pp. (*DAI*, 46:5 [Nov. 1985], 1277A–78A)
Discusses Yeats's influence on Pound. The following two items have been extracted from the thesis:
"The Order of the Brothers Minor: Pound and Yeats at Stone Cottage 1913–1916," *Paideuma*, 14:2–3 (Fall–Winter 1985), 395–403.
"The Secret Society of Modernism: Pound, Yeats, Olivia Shakespear, and the Abbé de Montfaucon de Villars," *Yeats Annual*, 4 (1986), 103–20. Mainly on Pound's interest in *Le Comte de Gabalis* by Montfaucon de Villars, which was translated by Olivia Shakespear. Yeats seems to have played a minor role in this matter by rekindling Pound's interest in occult literature.

85–181. LONGLEY, EDNA: "Poetry and Politics in Northern Ireland," *Crane Bag*, 9:1 (1985), 26–40.
Includes comments on Yeats.

85–182. LOWERY, ROBERT G., ed.: *A Whirlwind in Dublin: "The Plough and the Stars" Riots*. Westport, Ct.: Greenwood Press, 1984. xiii, 122 pp. (Contributions in Drama and Theatre Studies, 11.)
An annotated anthology of contemporary reactions to the first performance in 1926; see index for references to Yeats.

85–183. MCCARTHY, PATRICK A.: "Joyce's *Finnegans Wake*, 3.18–21," *Explicator*, 43:3 (Spring 1985), 26–28.
The reference is to Yeats's advice to Synge to visit the Aran Islands.

85–184. MCCASLIN, SUSAN ELIZABETH: "Vernon Watkins, Metaphysical Poet," °Ph.D. thesis, University of British Columbia, 1984. (*DAI*, 45:12 [June 1985], 3635A)
Discusses the influence of Yeats.

85–185. MCCORMACK, W. J.: *Ascendancy and Tradition in Anglo-Irish Literary History from 1789 to 1939*. Oxford: Clarendon Press, 1985. xi, 423 pp.
The Yeats chapters are revised versions of articles previously published in *The Crane Bag*, in 83–90 and in 84–193.
"W. B. Yeats: Two Approaches," 293–331; a historical approach to "Nineteen Hundred and Nineteen" and a discussion of the father-son conflict in *On Baile's Strand*.
"The Invention of Tradition," 332–67; i.e., Yeats's particular Anglo-Irish tradition.
"On *Purgatory*," 368–99.
Reviewed by Denis Donoghue: "A Myth and Its Unmasking," *TLS*, 1 Nov. 1985, 1239–40.

85–186. MCDOUGAL, STUART Y., ed.: *Dante among the Moderns*. Chapel Hill: University of North Carolina Press, 1985. xiii, 175 pp.

George Bornstein: "Yeats's Romantic Dante," 11–38; reprinted from *Colby Library Quarterly*, 15:2 (June 1979), 93–113.

85–187. McDowell, Colin: "The 'Opening of the *Tinctures*' in Yeats's *A Vision*," *Éire-Ireland*, 20:3 (Fall 1985), 71–92.

85–188. ———: "The Six Discarnate States of *A Vision* (1937)," *Yeats*, 4 (1986), 87–98.

85–189. ———: "To 'Beat upon the Wall': Reading *A Vision*," *Yeats Annual*, 4 (1986), 219–27.

85–190. ———, and Timothy Materer: "Gyre and Vortex: W. B. Yeats and Ezra Pound," *Twentieth Century Literature*, 31:4 (Winter 1985), 343–67.

"Pound worked in the same esoteric tradition that Yeats developed."

85–191. McGowan, John P.: *Representation and Revelation: Victorian Realism from Carlyle to Yeats*. Columbia: University of Missouri Press, 1986. vii, 206 pp.

"Yeats: Poverty and the Tragic Vision," 175–202.

85–192. McGowan, Moray: "Pale Mother, Pale Daughter? Some Reflections on Böll's Leni Gruyten and Katharina Blum," *German Life & Letters*, 37:3 (April 1984), 218–28.

Comments on Böll's use of Yeats in his *Gruppenbild mit Dame* and *Die verlorene Ehre der Katharina Blum*.

85–193. McGuinness, Nora Mahoney: "The Creative Universe of Jack B. Yeats," Ph.D. thesis, University of California, Davis, 1984. viii, 435 pp. (*DAI*, 46:2 [Aug. 1985], 421A)

Discusses "the familial events which contributed to making him [Jack Yeats] the distanced outsider" (abstract), including WBY's contribution.

85–194. MacKenzie, Norman H.: "Anglo-Irish Enrichments to Queen's University Libraries," *Canadian Journal of Irish Studies*, 11:1 (June 1985), 49–52.

Queen's University, Kingston, Ontario. The collection includes several Yeats items.

85–195. MacKillop, James: *Fionn Mac Cumhaill: Celtic Myth in English Literature*. Syracuse: Syracuse University Press, 1986. xvii, 227 pp. (Irish Studies.)

See index for notes on Yeats's use of the myth, especially in *Diarmuid and Grania* and "The Wanderings of Oisin."

85–196. McMahan, Noreen Dee: "Tragedy or Eternal Return: Yeats's and Nietzsche's Reversal of Aristotle," °Ph.D. thesis, University of Texas at Austin, 1984. 338 pp. (*DAI*, 46:4 [Oct. 1985], 990A; reprinted in *Yeats*, 4 [1986], 182–83)

Includes interpretations of *Where There Is Nothing* and *Purgatory*.

85–197. McWHIRTER, DAVID B.: "The Rhythm of the Body in Yeats's 'Nineteen Hundred and Nineteen,'" *College Literature*, 13:1 (Winter 1986), 44–54.

85–198. MARTIN, AUGUSTINE, ed.: *The Genius of Irish Prose*. Dublin: Mercier Press, 1985. 174 pp. (Thomas Davis Lectures.)

Terence Brown: "Literary Autobiography in Twentieth-Century Ireland," 89–98; on Yeats's autobiography and his presence in other writers' autobiographies.

A. Martin: "Fable and Fantasy," 110–20; contains a note on the stores in *The Secret Rose*.

Maurice Harmon: "Literary Biography in Twentieth Century Ireland," 155–64; on Hone's Yeats biography (J561).

A few short references to Yeats in some of the other contributions.

85–199. MARTIN, STODDARD: *Art, Messianism and Crime: A Study of Antinomianism in Modern Literature and Lives*. London: Macmillan, 1986. vi, 218 pp.

Discusses Nietzsche's influence on Yeats, pp. 65–72. See also index for further references.

85–200. MARVEL, LAURA: "Blake and Yeats: Visions of Apocalypse," *College Literature*, 13:1 (Winter 1986), 95–105.

85–201. MASTERSON, DONALD, and EDWARD O'SHEA: "Code Breaking and Myth Making: The Ellis-Yeats Edition of Blake's *Works*," *Yeats Annual*, 3 (1985), 53–80.

The preparation undertaken by the editors, including their work on Swedenborg and Boehme. Includes a discussion of "The Two Trees" as a by-product of the edition.

85–202. METSCHER, PRISCILLA: *Republicanism and Socialism in Ireland: A Study in the Relationship of Politics and Ideology from the United Irishmen to James Connolly*. Frankfurt / M.: Lang, 1986. vii, 617 pp. (Bremer Beiträge zur Literatur- und Ideologiegeschichte, 2.)

Contains a section on the "Irish language and literary renaissance," pp. 260–68, which includes some comments on Yeats.

85–203. MEYERS, JEFFREY, ed.: *The Craft of Literary Biography*. London: Macmillan, 1985. x, 253 pp.

William M. Murphy: "John Butler Yeats," 33–54; on the genesis of Murphy's JBY biography, *Prodigal Father* (1978).

85–204. MIKHAIL, EDWARD HALIM: *Sean O'Casey and His Critics: An Annotated Bibliography 1916–1982*. Metuchen: Scarecrow, 1985. x, 348 pp. (Scarecrow Author Bibliographies, 67.)

Contains some Yeats material.

85-205. MILLER, JOSEPH HILLIS: *The Linguistic Moment: From Wordsworth to Stevens*. Princeton: Princeton University Press, 1985. xxi, 446 pp.
"Yeats," 316-48, and passim (see index). Mainly on "Nineteen Hundred and Nineteen."

85-206. MILLER, KARL: *Doubles: Studies in Literary History*. Oxford: Oxford University Press, 1985. xiii, 468 pp.
See index for several notes on Yeats.

85-207. MILLER, SUSAN FISHER: "Hopes and Fears for the Tower: William Morris's Spirit at Yeats's Ballylee," *Éire-Ireland*, 21:2 (Summer 1986), 43-56.
Morris's influence extends beyond Yeats's early works to the Tower years, i.e., the time when Yeats acquired Thoor Ballylee and wrote about it.

85-208. MOORE, THOMAS STURGE: "'Do We or Do We Not, Know It?': An Unpublished Essay on W. B. Yeats," *Yeats Annual*, 4 (1986), 145-56.
Followed by Warwick Gould: "Thomas Sturge Moore and W. B. Yeats—An Afterword," 157-60. Moore's essay was probably written in 1929 and discusses Yeats's poetry.

85-209. MORRIS, BRUCE: "Elaborate Forms: Symons, Yeats, and Mallarmé," *Yeats*, 4 (1986), 99-119.
Yeats's reaction to Symons's Mallarmé translations.

85-210. MORRIS, HELEN: *The New Where's That Poem: An Index of Poems for Children*. Arranged by subject, with a bibliography of books of poetry. Oxford: Blackwell, 1985. vii, 264 pp.
See index for some Yeats references under such headings as cats, changelings, dancing, fiddlers, ghosts, etc.

85-211. MURPHY, RUSSELL: "Josef Strzygowski and Yeats' 'A Starlit or a Moonlit Dome,'" *College Literature*, 13:1 (Winter 1986), 106-11.
Strzygowski's influence on *A Vision* and "Byzantium."

85-212. MURRAY, CHRISTOPHER: "Three Sketches by Jack B. Yeats of the Camden Theatre, 1902," *Yeats Annual*, 3 (1985), 125-32.
Revised version of 83-151.

85-213. NASH, NANCY RUTKOWSKI: "Yeats and Heffernan the Blind," *Yeats Annual*, 4 (1986), 201-6.

85-214. NEVO, RUTH: "Yeats and Schopenhauer," *Yeats Annual*, 3 (1985), 15-32.
Discusses the influence on several poems, especially "Meru," and on *A Vision*.

85-215. ———: "Yeats's Passage to India," *Yeats Annual*, 4 (1986), 13–28.

Discusses *The Herne's Egg* and the indebtedness of the play to Yeats's reading of the Upanishads.

85-216. NIMS, JOHN FREDERICK: *A Local Habitation: Essays on Poetry*. Ann Arbor: University of Michigan Press, 1985. xi, 306 pp.

"Yeats and the Careless Muse," 145–69, reprinted from J2682.

85-217. NORTH, MICHAEL: *The Final Sculpture: Public Monuments and Modern Poets*. Ithaca: Cornell University Press, 1985. 263 pp.

Incorporates 82-146 and 83-153. The treatment of public monuments in modern poetry reveals one of its major concerns, "the contradiction between hermeticism and public ambition." Yeats is one of the "preeminent modern examples of the kind of imaginative writer who hopes to build a culture to receive his own work partly by calling attention to other works of art" (p. 9). See "W. B. Yeats," 41–99, on statues in the poetry and particularly in "The Statues." Reviewed by Terence Diggory, *Yeats*, 4 (1986), 213–18.

85-218. Ó BROIN, LEÓN: *Protestant Nationalists in Revolutionary Ireland: The Stopford Connection*. Dublin: Gill & Macmillan / Totowa, N.J.: Barnes & Noble, 1985. vi, 234 pp.

Several references to Yeats (see index).

85-219. O'CONNOR, FRANK: "Two Friends: Yeats and AE," *Yale Review*, 75:1 (Autumn 1985), 40–62.

Reprint of J2256.

85-220. O'DONNELL, WILLIAM H.: "Portraits of W. B. Yeats: This Picture in the Mind's Eye," *Yeats Annual*, 3 (1985), 81–103.

Yeats's opinions of portraits and studio photographs, especially of himself. Includes a "Preliminary Checklist of Portraits of W. B. Yeats."

85-221. O'GRADY, THOMAS BRENDAN: "'A Certain Fascination': Parnell in the Irish Literary Imagination," Ph.D. thesis, University of Notre Dame, 1985. v, 239 pp. (*DAI*, 45:12 [June 1985], 3647A)

Frequent references to Yeats's view of Parnell, especially on pp. 157–75.

85-222. O'HARA, DANIEL T.: *The Romance of Interpretation: Visionary Criticism from Pater to de Man*. New York: Columbia University Press, 1985. xi, 255 pp.

Discusses Geoffrey H. Hartman's reading, in *Criticism in the Wilderness* (1980), of "Leda and the Swan," pp. 125–29.

85-223. Ó HÓGAIN, DÁITHÍ: *The Hero in Irish Folk History*. Dublin: Gill & Macmillan, 1985. x, 354 pp.

See pp. 314–21 for some notes on Yeats's indebtedness to Irish folklore.

85-224. OMIDSALAR, MAHMOUD: "W. B. Yeats' 'Cuchulainn's [sic] Fight with the Sea,'" *American Imago*, 42:3 (Autumn 1985), 315–34.
Notes the curious fact that in the revised version of the poem Cuchulain's son is also called Cuchulain, and develops this into a psychoanalytical interpretation of the oedipal motifs.

85-225. O'NEILL, PATRICK: *Ireland and Germany: A Study in Literary Relations.* New York: Lang, 1985. 358 pp. (Canadian Studies in German Language and Literature, 33.)
See index for several inadequate notes on the Yeats reception in Germany and his relationship to German literature.

85-226. OPITZ, MICHAEL J.: "Poetry as Appropriate Epistemology: Gregory Bateson and W. B. Yeats," °Ph.D. thesis, University of Minnesota, 1985. 250 pp. (*DAI*, 46:10 [April 1986], 3042A)
An approach to Yeats's poetry through the epistemological theories of scientist Gregory Bateson.

85-227. ORR, LEONARD: "Yeats's Theories of Fiction," *Éire-Ireland*, 21:2 (Summer 1986), 152–58.

85-228. O'SHEA, EDWARD: *A Descriptive Catalog of W. B. Yeats's Library.* New York: Garland, 1985. xxiii, 390 pp. (Garland Reference Library of the Humanities, 470).
Reproduces annotations and inscriptions; includes a subject index and an autograph index.
Reviews:
George Bornstein, *Yeats*, 4 (1986), 219–21.
Robert E. Ward, *Éire-Ireland*, 20:4 (Winter 1985), 154–56.

85-229. ———: "The 1920s Catalogue of W. B. Yeats's Library," *Yeats Annual*, 4 (1986), 279–90.
A catalog made after 1920 by an unknown compiler; O'Shea lists the 521 (out of 1159) items that have disappeared.

85-230. ———: "'An Old Bullet Imbedded in the Flesh': The Migration of Yeats's 'Three Songs to the Same Tune,'" *Yeats*, 4 (1986), 121–42.
Yeats's politics as reflected in the revisions of this poem.

85-231. O'TOOLE, FINTAN: "Going West: The Country versus the City in Irish Writing," *Crane Bag*, 9:2 (1985), 111–16.
Contains some notes on Yeats's view of the Irish peasant.

85-232. OUSBY, IAN: *Blue Guide: Literary Britain and Ireland.* London: Black / New York: Norton, 1985. 424 pp. and maps.
"William Butler Yeats," 405–9.

85-233. PACK, ROBERT: *Affirming Limits: Essays on Mortality, Choice, and Poetic Form.* Amherst: University of Massachusetts Press, 1985. viii, 264 pp.

"Lyric Narration: The Chameleon Poet," 23–40; a reprint of 84–163.

"Yeats as Spectator to Death," 151–73; reprinted from *Denver Quarterly*, 19:4 (Spring 1985), 93–110. On death in Yeats's poetry, especially in "A Dialogue of Self and Soul," "Lapis Lazuli," and "John Kinsella's Lament for Mrs. Mary Moore."

"The Tears of Art," 236–59; reprinted from *Kenyon Review*, 7:1 (Winter 1985), 15–32; contains a note on "Coole Park, 1929."

85–234. PADEL, RUTH: "Homer's Reader: A Reading of George Seferis," *Proceedings of the Cambridge Philological Society*, os 211 / ns 31 (1985), 74–132.

Contains notes on Seferis's knowledge and use of Yeats, pp. 79, 123, 126.

85–235. PARKINSON, THOMAS: "Yeats and the Limits of Modernity," *Yeats*, 3 (1985), 60–71.

"Yeats was a modern poet but not a modernist."

85–236. PAVLOVIĆ, MIODRAG: *Poetika modernog.* Beograd: "Vuk karadžić," 1981. 334 pp. (Izbrana dela Miodraga Pavlovića, 4.)

"O poeziji V. B. Jejtsa," 47–67; reprint of J2604.

85–237. PEARCE, DONALD R.: "The Systematic Rose," *Yeats Annual*, 4 (1986), 195–200.

The "alchemical rose of the Nineties . . . was reborn first as the visionary moon of the middle years, then as the privileged 'antithetical' phases of the System. . . . "

85–238. PERLOFF, MARJORIE: *The Dance of the Intellect: Studies in the Poetry of the Pound Tradition.* Cambridge: Cambridge University Press, 1985. xii, 243 pp.

Passim (see index).

85–239. PONNUSWAMY, KRISHNA: "Yeats and Tagore: A Comparative Study of Their Plays," °Ph.D. thesis, Madurai Kamaraj University (India), 1984. 437 pp. (*DAI*, 46:7 [Jan. 1986], 1933A–34A)

85–240. POUPARD, DENNIS, ed.: *Twentieth-Century Literary Criticism: Excerpts from Criticism of the Works of Novelists, Poets, Playwrights, Short Story Writers, and Other Creative Writers Who Lived between 1900 and 1960, from the First Published Critical Appraisals to Current Evaluations.* Volume 11. Detroit: Gale Research Co., 1983. 590 pp.

"William Butler Yeats," 504–42; a short introduction and 21 excerpts from previously published criticism.

85-241. PRITCHARD, WILLIAM H.: *Frost: A Literary Life Reconsidered.*
New York: Oxford University Press, 1984. xix, 286 pp.
See index for some notes on Yeats and Frost.

85-242. *Problemy realizma v zarubezhnoĭ literature XIX–XX vekov: Mezhvuzovskiĭ sbornik nauchnykh trudov.* Moskva: Moskovskiĭ ordena trudovogo krasnogo znameni oblastnoĭ pedagogicheskiĭ institut imeni N.K. Krupskoĭ, 1983. 136 pp.

I. K. Eremina: "Irlandskie poety-uchastniki vosstaniia 1916 g. v Dubline i U. B. Ĭits," 128–34. "Irish poets as participants of the 1916 rising in Dublin and WBY."

85-243. PRUITT, VIRGINIA D.: "W. B. Yeats: Rage, Order, and the Mask," *Éire-Ireland*, 21:2 (Summer 1986), 141–46.

The "psychodynamics of the Mask" as related to "order-inducing rage" in some of Yeats's poems.

85-244. PUHALO, DUŠAN: *Engleska književnost XIX–XX veka (1832– 1950): Istorijsko-kritički pregled.* Beograd: Naučna knjiga, 1983. 324 pp.
"Vilijem B. Jejts (William Butler Yeats), 1865–1939," 247–64.

85-245. PUTZEL, STEVEN DANIEL: *Reconstructing Yeats: "The Secret Rose" and "The Wind among the Reeds."* Dublin: Gill & Macmillan / Totowa, N.J.: Barnes & Noble, 1986. xi, 242 pp.

Based on "Yeats's Use of Irish Folklore and Mythology in the 1890's," Ph.D. thesis, University of Toronto, 1980. v, 375 pp. (*DAI*, 41:6 [Dec. 1980], 2601A; reprinted in *Yeats Annual*, 1 [1982], 218–19). Discusses Yeats's construction of a symbolic system in the two early collections. Reviewed by Terence Brown: "A Book Hard to Warm To," *Irish Literary Supplement*, 5:2 (Fall 1986), 23.

85-246. PYLE, HILARY: *Jack B. Yeats in the National Gallery of Ireland.* Dublin: National Gallery of Ireland, 1986. xviii, 94 pp.

A design for a mountain backcloth for *The King's Threshold* is reproduced and discussed on pp. 34–35. A few other references to WBY, passim.

85-247. QUILLIGAN, PATRICK: "*The Herne's Egg* at the Damer," *Irish Times*, 10 July 1986, 10.

Review of a performance by the Renaissance Theatre Company at Damer Hall.

85-248. RADCLIFFE, EVAN: "Yeats and the Quest for Unity: 'Among School Children' and Unity of Being," *Colby Library Quarterly*, 21:3 (Sept. 1985), 109–21.

85-249. RAINE, KATHLEEN: *Yeats the Initiate: Essays on Certain Themes in the Work of W. B. Yeats.* Mountrath: Dolmen Press / London: Allen & Unwin, 1986. xxiv, 449 pp. (Illustrated)

Most of the essays in this book are rewritten and republished pieces and are concerned with Neoplatonic themes and influences and with the Perennial Philosophy. Contents:
"Hades Wrapped in Cloud," 1–31; from *Yeats and the Occult* (1976).
"Fairy and Folk Tales of Ireland," 33–43; the introduction to Yeats's collection, published in 1973.
"Ben Bulben Sets the Scene," 45–64; see 81–56.
"AE," 65–81; contains some references to Yeats.
"Yeats's Debt to Blake," 82–105; see J1966.
"From Blake to *A Vision*," 106–76; published separately in 1979.
"Yeats, the Tarot and the Golden Dawn," 177–246; published separately in 1972 and 1976.
"Death-in-Life and Life-in-Death," 247–94; published separately in 1974.
"Blake, Yeats and Pythagoras," 295–330; first published in °*Lindisfarne Letter*, 1982.
"Yeats and Kabir," 331–58; first published in °*Temenos*, 5 (1984); on Yeats's interest in India and on echoes of Kabir in his poetry, especially in "Among School Children."
"Purgatory," 359–78; written as an introduction to a projected French version of the play by Pierre Leyris.
"Yeats and the Creed of St. Patrick," 379–407; on Yeats's attitude towards Christianity.
"Giraldus," 408–30; on the probable identity or model of Yeats's fictitious character.
"Yeats's Singing School: A Personal Acknowledgment," 431–49; Kathleen Raine traces her own interest in Yeats and the influence he exerted on her.

85-250. RAJAN, BALACHANDRA: *The Form of the Unfinished: English Poetics from Spenser to Pound*. Princeton: Princeton University Press, 1985. viii, 319 pp.
See index for some notes on Yeats's poems.

85-251. ———: "Its Own Executioner: Yeats and the Fragment," *Yeats*, 3 (1985), 72–87.
Unlike Pound and Eliot, "who seek the whole in parts," Yeats holds that completeness is a "delusion."

85-252. REED, JOHN ROBERT: *Decadent Style*. Athens: Ohio University Press, 1985. xiv, 274 pp.
Note on "The Wanderings of Oisin" as decadent poem, pp. 92–94.

85-253. REISING, RUSSELL J.: "Yeats, the Rhymers' Club, and Pound's *Hugh Selwyn Mauberly*," *Journal of Modern Literature*, 12:1 (March 1985), 179–82.

Pound's treatment of the members of the Rhymers' Club reflects his reaction to two Yeats lectures.

85-254. RHEE, YOUNG SUCK: "The Poetics of Etherealization: Female Imagery in the Work of W. B. Yeats," °Ph.D. thesis, University of Nebraska, 1985. 269 pp. (*DAI*, 46:10 [April 1986], 3043A)

85-255. RIAPOLOVA, VERA ALEKSANDROVNA: *U. B. Ieĭts i irlandskaia khudozhestvennaia kul'tura: 1890-e—1930-e gody.* Moskva: "Nauka," 1985. 272 pp.

"WBY and artistic culture from the 1890s to the 1930s." The first Russian monograph on Yeats, mainly concerned with the plays and the theatrical activities. Surprisingly enough, the author does not mention recent Russian Yeats criticism.

85-256. RICHARDSON, MALCOLM: "AE's *Deirdre* and Yeats's Dramatic Development," *Éire-Ireland*, 20:4 (Winter 1985), 89-105.

AE's play showed Yeats "that a heroic, familiar, Irish theme could be presented in a way both non-naturalistic and stylized without sacrificing the heroic energy to which he sought to make the audience respond."

85-257. RIDGEWAY, JAQUELINE: *Louise Bogan.* Boston: Twayne, 1984. xii, 146 pp. (Twayne's United States Authors Series, 461.)

See index for a few notes on Yeats's influence.

85-258. ROBERTS, MARIE: *British Poets and Secret Societies.* London: Croom Helm, 1986. xv, 181 pp.

"William Butler Yeats," 126-58; on Yeats's preoccupation with the Golden Dawn and with Rosicrucianism.

85-259. ROBINSON, ALAN DAVID: *Poetry, Painting and Ideas, 1885-1914.* London: Macmillan, 1985. xv, 280 pp.

American edition published as °*Symbol to Vortex: Poetry, Painting and Ideas, 1885-1914.* New York: St. Martin's Press, 1985. Numerous remarks on Yeats (see index), especially on his indebtedness to Symbolism and on the relationships with F. S. Flint, T. E. Hulme, and Ezra Pound.

85-260. ROBSON, WILLIAM W.: *A Prologue to English Literature.* London: Batsford, 1986. 254 pp.

On Yeats, pp. 203-6 and passim (see index).

85-261. RODWAY, ALLAN: *The Craft of Criticism.* Cambridge: Cambridge University Press, 1982. x, 192 pp.

"W. B. Yeats: 'An Irish Airman Foresees His Death,'" 134-37.

85-262. ROLLINS, RONALD GENE: *Divided Ireland: Bifocal Vision in Modern Irish Drama.* Lanham, Md.: University Press of America, 1985.

xi, 104 pp.

See pp. 25–34 on Yeats and Beckett and on *Purgatory.*

85–263. SACKS, PETER M.: *The English Elegy: Studies in the Genre from Spenser to Yeats.* Baltimore: Johns Hopkins University Press, 1985. xv, 376 pp.

"Yeats: 'In Memory of Major Robert Gregory,'" 260–98; "Epilogue: The English Elegy after Yeats; a Note on the American Elegy," 299–328.

85–264. SALMON, ERIC, ed.: *Bernhardt and the Theatre of Her Time.* Westport, Ct.: Greenwood Press, 1984. xi, 289 pp. (Contributions in Drama and Theatre Studies, 6.)

S. Beynon John: "Actor as Puppet: Variations on a Nineteenth-Century Theatrical Idea," 243–68; comments on Yeats's view of the actor as puppet and on the influence of Gordon Craig.

85–265. SCHLEIFER, RONALD: "The Pathway of *The Rose:* Yeats, the Lyric, and the Syntax of Symbolism," *Genre,* 18:4 (Winter 1985), 375–96.

Examines the relationship between "Yeats's early poetry and the symbolist movement in literature" and discusses "his conception of lyric poetry at the beginning of his career." Uses syntactic models derived from Derrida and concentrates on "When You Are Old" and "The Rose of Battle."

85–266. SCHUCHARD, RONALD: "The Lady Gregory—Yeats Collection at Emory University," *Yeats Annual,* 3 (1985), 153–66.

85–267. ———: "Yeats, Arnold, and the Morbidity of Modernism," *Yeats,* 3 (1985), 88–106.

85–268. ———: "Yeats's 'On a Child's Death': A Critical Note," *Yeats Annual,* 3 (1985), 190–92.

The relationship with Maud Gonne and her two children.

85–269. SCRASE, DAVID: *Wilhelm Lehmann: A Critical Biography. Volume I: The Years of Trial (1880–1918).* Columbia, S.C.: Camden House, 1984. xiii, 191 pp. (Studies in German Literature, Linguistics and Culture, 13:1.)

See index for several references to Lehmann's interest in Yeats.

85–270. SEKINE, MASARU, ed.: *Irish Writers and Society at Large.* Gerrards Cross: Colin Smythe / Totowa, N.J.: Barnes & Noble, 1985. x, 251 pp. (Irish Literary Studies, 22. / IASAIL—Japan Series, 1.)

Joan Coldwell: "The Bodkin and the Rocky Voice: Images of Weaving and Stone in the Poetry of W. B. Yeats," 16–30.

Maurice Harmon: "The Era of Inhibitions: Irish Literature 1920–60," 31–41.

A. Norman Jeffares: "Anglo-Irish Literature: Treatment for Radio," 42–95; four lectures prepared for the Australian Broadcasting Commission (see especially pp. 78–85).

Augustine Martin: "Prose Fiction in the Irish Literary Renaissance," 139–62 (includes a discussion of Yeats's early fiction).

Robert Welch: "Some Thoughts on Writing a Companion to Irish Literature," 225–36 (includes notes on Yeats's "Irishness").

85–271. SEYMOUR-SMITH, MARTIN: *Macmillan Guide to Modern World Literature*. London: Macmillan, 1985. xxviii, 1396 pp.

See pp. 240–43 for a short critical assessment of Yeats, who is said to lack intellect and sophistication.

85–272. SHAW, GEORGE BERNARD: *Collected Letters 1911–1925*. Edited by Dan H. Laurence. London: Reinhardt, 1985. xxiv, 989 pp.

Contains a letter to Yeats, pp. 190–91, reprinted from *The Times*, 15 July 1913. Yeats is also referred to on p. 235.

85–273. SHEVARDNADZE, PAATA EDUARDOVICH: *Problema "impersonal'nosti" v tvorchestve U. B. Ĭitsa*. Avtoreferat dissertatsiĭ kandidata filologicheskikh nauk. Tbilisi: Tbilisskiĭ ordena trudovogo krasnogo znameni gosudarstvennyĭ universitet, 1984. 16 pp.

A dissertation abstract. "The problem of 'impersonality' in the work of WBY"; see also 85–163.

85–274. SHIMA, HIROYUKI: "Yeats's Janus-Faced Sincerity in Last Poems," *Studies in English Literature* [Tokyo], 62:2 (Dec. 1985), 293–308.

85–275. SHIRES, LINDA M.: *British Poetry of the Second World War*. London: Macmillan, 1985. xv, 174 pp.

See index for some notes on Yeats's influence.

85–276. SIDNELL, MICHAEL J.: "'Tara Uprooted': Yeats's *In the Seven Woods* in Relation to Modernism," *Yeats*, 3 (1985), 107–20.

85–277. ———: "Yeats, Synge and the Georgians," *Yeats Annual*, 3 (1985), 105–23.

Yeats's middle poetry as related to that of the Georgian poets (who were very much influenced by Synge).

85–278. SIEGMUND-SCHULTZE, DOROTHEA, ed.: *Irland: Gesellschaft und Kultur IV*. Halle: Martin Luther Universität Halle-Wittenberg, 1985. viii, 231 pp. (Wissenschaftliche Beiträge, 1985/34 [F56].)

Thomas Metscher: "Reality and the Dream: On the Poetry of W. B. Yeats," 221–31; mainly on "The Fiddler of Dooney," "Among School Children," and "Easter 1916."

85–279. SIRR, PETER: "Some Distinction: Padraic Fallon's *Athenry*," *Éire-Ireland*, 20:3 (Fall 1985), 93–108.

Discusses Fallon's view of Yeats.

85-280. SMITH, SUSAN VALERIA HARRIS: *Masks in Modern Drama*. Berkeley: University of California Press, 1984. xi, 237 pp.
   On masks in Yeats's plays, pp. 53-60, 160-64, and passim (see index).

85-281. SMYTHE, COLIN: "*The Countess Cathleen*: A Note," *Yeats Annual*, 3 (1985), 193-97.
   A bibliographical note.

85-282. SOTHEBY PARKE BERNET: *English Literature and History Comprising Books, Autograph Letters and Manuscripts*. Sale of 22 & 23 July 1985. London: Sotheby, 1985.
   See items 351 (Broadsides) and 352 (the Great Vellum Notebook, with a two-page description and three reproductions). Press notices by Michael Foley: "£ 275,000 for Yeats Notes," *Irish Times*, 23 July 1985, 1; Warwick Gould: "Yeats's Great Vellum Notebook," *TLS*, 26 July 1985, 824.

85-283. ———: *English Literature and History Comprising Printed Books, Autograph Letters and Manuscripts*. Sale of 18 December 1985. London: Sotheby, 1985.
   Includes an unpublished essay by Basil Bunting on Yeats (written in 1930) as well as letters by Yeats to Stopford Brooke, one W. Stevens, Richard Le Gallienne, Lady Genary, D. J. O'Donoghue, one Miss Murphy, John Drinkwater, and John Lane; also the corrected galley proofs for *The King's Threshold*. See also next item.

85-284. ———: *English Literature and History Comprising Printed Books, Autograph Letters and Manuscripts*. Sale of 10-11 July 1986. London: Sotheby, 1986.
   Includes letters to Gwen John and the James F. Gallagher collection of Yeatsiana; i.e., autograph MSS., first editions as well as items from the previous sale: the O'Donoghue, Drinkwater, Murphy, and Le Gallienne letters and the galley proofs.

85-285. SPENDER, STEPHEN: *Journals 1939-1983*. Edited by John Goldsmith. London: Faber & Faber, 1985. 510 pp.
   Contains a few short notes on Yeats (see index) and a reminiscence of Mrs. Yeats (pp. 104-5).

85-286. STANFIELD, PAUL SCOTT: "W. B. Yeats and Politics in the 1930s," °Ph.D. thesis, Northwestern University, 1984. 469 pp. (*DAI*, 45:12 [June 1985], 3648A-49A; reprinted in *Yeats*, 4 [1986], 181-82)
   Discusses Yeats's views of de Valera, fascism, socialism, Balzac as a counterweight to Shelley, and eugenics.

85-287. STEAD, CHRISTIAN KARLSON: *Pound, Yeats, Eliot and the Modernist Movement*. London: Macmillan, 1986. vii, 393 pp.

A complementary book to Stead's earlier *The New Poetic* (J1632). Yeats's poetry is discussed in "Part I: The Rise of Modernism," 9–83, and in "Some Reflections on the Poetry of Hardy and Yeats," 131–59.

85–288. STEIN, RITA, and FRIEDHELM RICKERT, eds.: *Major Modern Dramatists. Volume 1: American, British, Irish, German, Austrian, and Swiss Dramatists*. New York: Ungar, 1984. xv, 570 pp.
See pp. 315–33 for 24 reprinted pieces (short extracts from longer works of criticism).

85–289. STOVEL, NORA FOSTER: "The Aerial View of Modern Britain: The Airplane as a Vehicle for Idealism and Satire," *Ariel*, 15:3 (July 1984), 17–32.
Contains a note on "An Irish Airman Foresees His Death."

85–290. SULLIVAN, ALVIN, ed.: *British Literary Magazines: The Victorian and Edwardian Age, 1837–1913*. Westport, Ct.: Greenwood Press, 1984. xxvi, 561 pp.
See index for discussions of Yeats's association with literary magazines, such as *Green Sheaf*, *Dome*, *Samhain*, *Savoy*, *Scots Observer*, and *Arrow*.

85–291. SUTTON, DAVID C.: "Location Register of Twentieth-Century Literary Manuscripts and Letters: Current Yeats Listings," *Yeats Annual*, 3 (1985), 295–303.

85–292. ———: "Location Register of Twentieth-Century Literary Manuscripts and Letters: A Supplementary Listing of Yeats Holdings," *Yeats Annual*, 4 (1986), 291–96.

85–293. THIESMEYER, LYNN: "Meditations against Chaos: Yeats's War of Irish Independence," *Perspectives on Contemporary Literature*, 10 (1984), 23–32.
The war poetry, especially "Nineteen Hundred and Nineteen" and "Meditations in Time of Civil War."

85–294. THOMAS, C. T., and others, eds.: *Focus on Literature: Essays in Memory of C. A. Sheppard*. Madras: Macmillan India, 1982. xvi, 313 pp.
Nissim Ezekiel: "The Writing of Poetry," 135–42; comments on Yeats's laborious process of writing poetry.

85–295. THOMPSON, EDWARD JOHN: "Memories of Tagore: E. P. Thompson Introduces His Father E. J. Thompson's Account of a Stay with the Bengali Poet," *London Review of Books*, 22 May 1986, 18–19.
Thompson and Tagore comment adversely on Yeats's introduction to *Gitanjali*.

85–296. THORNBURY, CHARLES: "John Berryman and the 'Majestic Shade' of Yeats," *Yeats*, 3 (1985), 121–72.

With numerous quotations from unpublished Berryman papers, including unpublished poems on Yeats.

85-297. TOLLEY, A. T.: "Philip Larkin's Unpublished Book *In the Grip of Light,*" *Agenda,* 22:2 (Summer 1984), 76-86.
Notes the influence of Yeats.

85-298. ———: *The Poetry of the Forties.* Manchester: Manchester University Press, 1985. xi, 394 pp.
Several short references to Yeats (see index).

85-299. TORCHIANA, DONALD T.: *Backgrounds for Joyce's Dubliners.* Boston: Allen & Unwin, 1986. xiv, 283 pp.
See index for numerous references to Yeats.

85-300. ———: "Yeats and Croce," *Yeats Annual,* 4 (1986), 3-11.

85-301. UDDIN, QAZI NASIR: "Horizon of Expectations: The Reception of Rabindranath Tagore in the United States and Britain (1913-41)," Ph.D. thesis, State University of New York at Binghamton, 1985. viii, 237 pp. (*DAI,* 46:5 [Nov. 1985], 1272A-73A)
See especially chapter 3, "Tagore and Britain," 57-95, for a discussion of the Yeats-Tagore relationship.

85-302. USANDIZAGA, ARANZAZU: *Teatro y política: El movimiento dramático irlandés.* Bellaterra: Universidad autónoma de Barcelona, 1985. 182 pp.
On Yeats passim, especially in "Formación del movimiento dramático," 57-71; "El teatro de Yeats," 73-115.

85-303. *A Vitalist Seminar: Studies in the Poetry of Peter Russell, Anthony L. Johnson and William Oxley.* Salzburg: Institut für Anglistik und Amerikanistik, Universität Salzburg, 1984. 313 pp. (Salzburg Studies in English Literature. Poetic Drama & Poetic Theory, 77.)
Anthony L. Johnson: "A Glance at Yeats, Eliot, Pound," 5-21. In his poetry, "Yeats was the only one of the three who was capable of displaying past, present and future as a single range of interconnected, interacting consciousness."
———: "Signifier and Signified in Verbal Art," 22-53; includes comments on the prosody of "The Wild Swans at Coole" and "After Long Silence."

85-304. WADE, ALLAN: *Memories of the London Theatre 1900-1914.* Edited by Alan Andrews. London: Society for Theatre Research, 1983. ix, 54 pp.
Numerous references to Yeats (see index).

85-305. WALL, RICHARD: "Yeats and the Folk Tradition," *Canadian Journal of Irish Studies,* 11:2 (Dec. 1985), 47-48.
"Down by the Salley Gardens" has moved "from the literary to the folk domain."

85-306. WASWO, RICHARD, ed.: *On Poetry and Poetics.* Tübingen: Narr, 1985. 212 pp. (SPELL: Swiss Papers in English Language and Literature, 2.)

Gregory T. Polletta: "Hopkins and Modern Poetics," 63-91; includes some notes comparing the poetry of Hopkins and Yeats.

85-307. WATKINS, GWEN: *Portrait of a Friend.* Llandysul: Gomer Press, 1983. xv, 226 pp.

On the Vernon Watkins—Dylan Thomas relationship with several references to Yeats (see index).

85-308. WEATHERLY, JOAN: "Yeats, the Tarot, and the Fool," *College Literature,* 13:1 (Winter 1986), 112-21.

85-309. WEINER, ALAN R., and SPENCER MEANS: *Literary Criticism Index.* Metuchen, N.J.: Scarecrow Press, 1984. xvii, 686 pp.

An index to selected bibliographies. See pp. 675-80.

85-310. WEISSMAN, JUDITH: "'Somewhere in Ear-Shot': Yeats's Admonitory Gods," *Pequod,* 14 (1982), 16-31.

Yeats's truly visionary poetry can be found in his elegies.

85-311. WELLEK, RENÉ: *A History of Modern Criticism: 1750-1950. Volume 5: English Criticism, 1900-1950.* New Haven: Yale University Press, 1986. xxiv, 343 pp.

"W. B. Yeats," 1-13 (part of a chapter "Symbolism in English") and passim (see index). For further Yeats references see index to *Volume 6: American Criticism, 1900-1950.* New Haven: Yale University Press, 1986. viii, 345 pp.

85-312. WOOD, ANDELYS: "Yeats and Measurement," *South Atlantic Review,* 50:4 (Nov. 1985), 65-80.

The idea of measurement in the poetry, particularly in "Under Ben Bulben" and "The Statues."

85-313. WOODHEAD, CHRIS, ed.: *Nineteenth and Twentieth Century Verse: An Anthology of Sixteen Poets.* Oxford: Oxford University Press, 1984. 239 pp.

Notes on Yeats's poetry, pp. 82-83, 204-7.

85-314. WRIGHT, DAVID G.: "Yeats as a Novelist," *Journal of Modern Literature,* 12:2 (July 1985), 261-76.

Discusses *John Sherman* and *The Speckled Bird.*

85-315. WRIGHT, JAMES: "The Music of Poetry," *American Poetry Review,* 15:2 (March-April 1986), 43-47.

Posthumously published version of a talk given in 1967; comments on Yeats's "traditional" poetry, especially on "Adam's Curse."

85-316. YAMASAKI, HIROYUKI: [in Japanese] "Yeats and Allegory,"

Hiroshima Studies in English Language and Literature, 29: Special number (1984), 51–62; English summary, 70–71.

85-317. YEATS, W. B.: *The Collected Letters of W. B. Yeats. Volume One: 1865–1895.* Edited by John Kelly, associate editor Eric Domville. Oxford: Clarendon Press, 1986. xlii, 548 pp.

Contains a chronological table, a general introduction, and a biographical and historical appendix (extended notes on the most important persons and places), as well as copious annotations. The major recipients in this volume are Douglas Hyde, John O'Leary, Ernest Rhys, Father Mathew Russell, Katharine Tynan, T. Fisher Unwin, and Lily (Susan Mary) Yeats.

Reviews:

Mark Abley: "A Magician of Verse," *Maclean's,* 9 June 1986, 58.

Anon.: "Poets Off Parade," *Economist,* 15 March 1986, 104.

John Carey: "Every Last Scrawl," *Sunday Times,* 9 Feb. 1986, 43.

Anthony Curtis: "Irish Poet's Eyes," *Financial Times,* 15 Feb. 1986, Weekend FT section, XIV.

Seamus Deane: "The Poet's Dream of an Audience," *TLS,* 7 March 1986, 235–36.

Denis Donoghue: "The Young Yeats," *New York Review of Books,* 14 Aug. 1986, 14–16.

Richard Ellmann: "Yeats in Love," *New Republic,* 12 May 1986, 33–35.

James Fenton: "Irish Bard Head and Mumbo-Jumbo," *Times,* 6 Feb. 1986, 11.

John Hanratty: "The Reality of Fairies," *Books Ireland,* 103 (May 1986), 99–100.

Barbara Hardy: "Cry of the Heart," *Books and Bookmen,* 365 (March 1986), 18.

Maurice Harmon, *Irish University Review,* 16:1 (Spring 1986), 101–2.

Seamus Heaney: "Genius on Stilts," *Observer,* 23 Feb. 1986, 28.

Brendan Kennelly: "Passions of a Shy Warrior," *New York Times Book Review,* 29 June 1986, 14.

John Montague: "Full of Mysticism and Magic," *Guardian,* 30 Jan. 1986, 20.

Julian Moynahan: "The Letters of W. B. Yeats," *Irish Literary Supplement,* 5:2 (Fall 1986), 24.

Conor Cruise O'Brien: "Yeats's Letters: 'Was Irish National Feeling Not Noble and Enlightened by Definition, Then?'" *Listener,* 20 March 1986, 24–25.

Richard Ormrod: "A Flight into Faeryland," *Spectator,* 8 Feb. 1986, 27.

Tom Paulin: "Dreadful Sentiments," *London Review of Books*, 3 April 1986, 9–10; discusses Yeats's early nationalist politics.

Terence de Vere White: "Yeats in His Letters," *Irish Times*, 1 Feb. 1986, 12.

85–318. ———: [in Hebrew] *Collected Poems*. Translated by Eliezra Eig-Zakov. S.l.: Cana Publishing House, 1985. 207 pp.
Contains an introduction on pp. 9–18.

85–319. ———: *El crepúsculo celta*. Translated by Javier Marías. Madrid: Ediciones Alfaguara, 1985. 195 pp. (Literature Alfaguara, 162.) "Nota sobre el texto," 13–14; "Notas," 189–91.

85–320. ———: "Horoscope of Conal O'Riordan," *Journal of Irish Literature*, 14:3 (Sept. 1985), 106.
Source not given. This issue of *JIL* is devoted to O'Riordan (pen name: Norreys Connell) with references to Yeats in Judith O'Riordan's introduction (including a reprint of Yeats's speech preceding the performance of *The Piper*; see J1002) and in the chronology (pp. 107–13).

85–321. ———: "Méditations en temps de guerre civile," *Études irlandaises*, 10 (Dec. 1985), 13–18.
Translated by René Fréchet.

85–322. °———: *A Poet to His Beloved: The Early Love Poems of W. B. Yeats*. Introduction by Richard Eberhart. New York: St. Martin's Press, 1985. xi, 65 pp.

85–323. ———: *Purgatory: Manuscript Materials Including the Author's Final Text*. Edited by Sandra F. Siegel. Ithaca: Cornell University Press, 1986. xi, 222 pp. (The Cornell Yeats.)
The "Introduction," 3–26, discusses the manuscripts, the "Patterns of Revision" of the play, the publication of *On the Boiler*, and the arguments advanced in both the play and the essay. This is followed by facsimile reprints and transcriptions of various versions of the play.

85–324. ———: "Rymdens härskara," *Lyrikvännen*, 32:2 (1985), 87–88.
Swedish translation of "The Host of the Air" by Jan Östergren.

85–325. ———: "Stare baśnie irlandzkie: Teig O'Kane (Tadh O Cathan) i trup." Translated by Małgorzata Grabowska, *Literatura na świecie*, 5 (May 1984), 215–39.
A translation of "Teig O'Kane (Tadhg O Cáthán) and the Corpse" from *Fairy and Folk Tales of the Irish Peasantry*.

85–326. *Yeats: An Annual of Textual and Critical Studies*. Volume 3: A Special Issue on Yeats and Modern Poetry. Edited by George Bornstein and Richard J. Finneran. Ithaca: Cornell University Press, 1985. 274 pp.

Contains the following items: 85-37, 69, 103, 160, 235, 251, 267, 276, 296, reviews, brief notices by Mary FitzGerald, and this compiler's 1983 bibliography (pp. 175-205).

85-327. ———: Volume IV, 1986. Edited by Richard J. Finneran. Ann Arbor: UMI Research Press, 1986. xvi, 231 pp. (Studies in Modern Literature, 61.)

Contains the following items: 85-2, 90, 96, 104, 120, 124, 188, 209, 230, reviews, brief notices by Mary FitzGerald, and this compiler's 1984 bibliography (pp. 143-76).

85-328. *Yeats Annual No. 3*. Edited by Warwick Gould. London: Macmillan, 1985. xix, 323 pp.

Contains the following items: 85-7, 51, 94, 102, 106-8, 137, 144, 146, 157-58, 201, 212, 214, 220, 266, 268, 277, 281, 291, reviews, and an "Editorial Miscellany," 285-94 (short reviews of recent publications). Reviewed by Charles O'Neill: "Macmillan's Yeats Annuals," *Irish Literary Supplement,* 5:2 (Fall 1986), 23.

85-329. *Yeats Annual No. 4.* Edited by Warwick Gould. London: Macmillan, 1986. xxi, 335 pp.

Contains the following items: 85-17, 35, 46, 59, 67, 109, 122, 134, 152, 165, 180, 189, 208, 213, 215, 229, 237, 292, 300, reviews, an "Editorial Miscellany," 269-76 (on recent publications), "Recent Postgraduate Research," compiled by K. P. S. Jochum, Olympia Sitwell and Warwick Gould (pp. 297-322). The last item consists of the following parts: "Preliminary Checklist of Unpublished European Doctoral Dissertations on Yeats, 1969-1980," "Recent UK Dissertations," and "Dissertation Abstracts, 1982-83"—the abstracts of Bell (82-13), Boyd (84-14), Bronson (82-29), Davies (82-50), Farrell (84-51), Finkelstein (82-60), Foster (81-49), Gardiner (83-72), Gardner (84-61), Gerety (83-76), Gore (82-76), Helmling (84-80), Holdsworth (84-86), Hood (83-97), Islam (82-94), Kappler (83-106), Krogfus (83-121), Manning (82-134), Oppel (84-160), Salvati (82-167), Sarwar (83-182), Sherman (83-189), So (83-195), Suleri (84-195), Sutton (82-183), Wang (82-193). Reviewed by Alison Armstrong Jensen: "Macmillan's Yeats Annuals," *Irish Literary Supplement,* 5:2 (Fall 1986), 23.

85-330. *Yeats Society of Japan: Bulletin,* 16 (Oct. 1985).

Contains: Ann Saddlemyer: "Yeats's Voices in the Theatre: *The Words upon the Window-Pane,*" 125-110; and the following articles (all in Japanese, some with English summaries):

Mitsuko Ohno: "The Woman in the Mirror: Yeats's Idea of Woman," 1-10, 108.

Masami Nakao: "The People, the Land, and the Art: On 'In Memory of Major Robert Gregory,'" 11-20, 104-103.

Iwao Mizuta, Ken'ichi Matsumara, Mark S. Suzuki, and Hiroshi Shimizu: Symposium on "The Man and the Echo," 21-47, 107-104.

"Commemoration Essays," 48-76; news, reviews, and a bibliography, 77-102.

85-331. YORK, R. A.: *The Poem as Utterance.* London: Methuen, 1986. viii, 214 pp.

"Yeats," 109-27; discusses the poetry as "imitated utterance," with particular reference to "Leda and the Swan."

85-332. YOSHINO, MASAAKI: "Yeats's Logic of Death: The Fairy Poems and the Gregory Poems," *Studies in English Literature* [Tokyo], English number 1985, 37-51.

Mainly a discussion of "Upon a House Shaken by the Land Agitation," *On Baile's Strand,* and "An Irish Airman Foresees His Death."

85-333. YOUNG, VERNON: "The Music of What Happens," *Parnassus: Poetry in Review,* 11:2 (Fall/Winter 1983-Spring/Summer 1984), 323-35.

Contains a few notes on Yeats's part in the Irish literary revival.

Additions to Entries in Previous Bibliographies

81-56. GENET: *William Butler Yeats*
Reviews:
Nicholas Grene, *Études anglaises,* 38:2 (April-June 1985), 240-41.

81-77. KRIMM: *W. B. Yeats and the Emergence of the Irish Free State*
Reviews:
Seamus Deane, *Yearbook of English Studies,* 15 (1985), 330-31.

81-100. O'HARA: *Tragic Knowledge*
Reviews:
Seamus Deane, *Yearbook of English Studies,* 15 (1985), 330-31.

82-4. ALLEN: *Yeats's Epitaph*
Reviews:
Karen Dorn, *Yeats Annual,* 3 (1985), 255-57.

82-20. BOHLMANN: *Yeats and Nietzsche*
Reviews:
G. K. Blank, *Comparative Literature Studies,* 22:4 (Winter 1985), 549-51.

82-30. BUCHTA: *Rezeption und ästhetische Verarbeitung*
Reviews:
K. P. S. Jochum, *Yeats Annual,* 4 (1986), 249-51.

82–45. CRAIG: *Yeats, Eliot, Pound, and the Politics of Poetry*
Reviews:
Richard Burton, *Yeats Annual*, 3 (1985), 264–70.
F. Farag, *Canadian Journal of Irish Studies*, 11:2 (Dec. 1985), 87–88.

82–168. SCHRICKER: *A New Species of Man*
Reviews:
Jo Russell, *Yeats Annual*, 4 (1986), 261–62.

82–184. SYNGE: *Theatre Business*
Reviews:
Richard Allen Cave, *Yeats Annual*, 3 (1985), 249–54.
Brian Tyson, *English Studies in Canada*, 11:1 (March 1985), 99–102.

82–206. YEATS: *The Death of Cuchulain*
Reviews:
Richard Allen Cave, *Yeats Annual*, 3 (1985), 244–48.

82–214. *Yeats Annual No. 1*
Reviews:
Craig Wallace Barrow, *Éire-Ireland*, 20:2 (Summer 1985), 147–49.

83–2. ADAMS: *Philosophy of the Literary Symbolic*
Reviews:
Edward Engelberg, *Yeats*, 3 (1985), 217–24.

83–7. ARCHIBALD: *Yeats*
Reviews:
Richard Taylor, *Yeats Annual*, 3 (1985), 282–84.
Wolfgang Wicht, *Zeitschrift für Anglistik und Amerikanistik*, 33:3 (1985), 277–78.

83–38. CLARK: *Yeats at Songs and Choruses*
Reviews:
George Bornstein: "Yeats's Texts and Contexts," *Modern Language Studies*, 16:2 (Spring 1986), 82–87.
Ian Fletcher, *Yeats Annual*, 3 (1985), 258–63.
J. P. Frayne, *Journal of English and Germanic Philology*, 84:2 (April 1985), 284–86.

83–44. DIGGORY: *Yeats & American Poetry*
Reviews:
Robert Belflower, *Review of English Studies*, 37:145 (Feb. 1986), 133–34.
Vivian Mercier: "Putting Himself in His Place," *TLS*, 25 Jan. 1985, 80.
Marjorie Perloff, *Yeats Annual*, 3 (1985), 271–75.
Joseph Ronsley, *Queen's Quarterly*, 92:1 (Spring 1985), 173–75.

83-55. FINNERAN: *Editing Yeats's Poems*
Reviews:
Daniel Albright: "The Magician," *New York Review of Books*, 31 Jan. 1985, 29–32.
Seamus Heaney, *Yeats*, 3 (1985), 260–66; reprint of the review in *New York Times Book Review* (see 84–229).
Michael J. Sidnell: "Unacceptable Hypotheses: The New Edition of Yeats's Poems and Its Making," *Yeats Annual*, 3 (1985), 225–43.

83-108. KENNER: *A Colder Eye*
Reviews:
Rüdiger Imhof, *Literatur in Wissenschaft und Unterricht*, 18:4 (1985), 361–63.
K. Marre, *Modern Fiction Studies*, 31:2 (Summer 1985), 377–80.
Stanley Reynolds: "Fool's Erin," *Punch*, 24 Aug. 1983, 48–49.

83-114. KLINE: *The Last Courtly Lover*
Reviews:
Karen Dorn, *Yeats Annual*, 4 (1986), 258–60.
Peter van de Kamp, *Irish University Review*, 15:1 (Spring 1985), 108–11.

83-117. KNOWLAND: *W. B. Yeats: Dramatist of Vision*
Reviews:
Richard Allen Cave, *Yeats Annual*, 4 (1986), 239–41.
James W. Flannery: "Yeats on the Aisle," *Irish Literary Supplement*, 4:2 (Fall 1985), 34.
Katharine Worth, *Review of English Studies*, 37:145 (Feb. 1986), 139–40.

83-142. MARTIN: *W. B. Yeats*
Reviews:
Terence Diggory, *Yeats*, 3 (1985), 244–49.

83-156. O'DONNELL: *A Guide to the Prose Fiction of W. B. Yeats*
Reviews:
Peter van de Kamp, *Irish University Review*, 15:1 (Spring 1985), 108–11.

83-170. QUINN: *The Letters of John Quinn to William Butler Yeats*
Reviews:
Susan Fisher Miller: "Yeats between the Letters," *Irish Literary Supplement*, 4:1 (Spring 1985), 33.
William M. Murphy, *Yeats*, 3 (1985), 238–44.
James Pethica, *Yeats Annual*, 4 (1986), 252–54.

83-171. RAI: *W. B. Yeats: Poetic Theory and Practice*
Reviews:
E. P. Bollier, *Yeats*, 3 (1985), 249–52.

83-187. SHAH: *Yeats and Eliot*
Reviews:
E. P. Bollier, *Yeats*, 3 (1985), 249-52.

83-200. STEINMAN: *Yeats's Heroic Figures*
Reviews:
Douglas Archibald, *Yeats*, 3 (1985), 252-54.
Richard Burton, *Yeats Annual*, 4 (1986), 263-64.
Daniel T. O'Hara: "The Specialty of Self-Victimization in Recent Yeats Studies," *Contemporary Literature*, 27:2 (Summer 1986), 285-89.
George J. Watson: "Heroic Examples," *Times Higher Education Supplement*, 24 Feb. 1984, 18.

83-208. THURLEY: *The Turbulent Dream*
Reviews:
K. P. S. Jochum, *Yeats*, 3 (1985), 254-57.

83-212. VLASOPOLOS: *The Symbolic Method of Coleridge, Baudelaire, and Yeats*
Reviews:
Michael André Bernstein, *Yeats*, 3 (1985), 257-60.
R. Bienvenu, *Revue de littérature comparée*, 59:4 (Oct.-Dec. 1985), 472-73.

84-2. ADAM: *Yeats and the Masks of Syntax*
Reviews:
Jacqueline Genet, *Études irlandaises*, 10 (Dec 1985), 308-9.

84-4. BAKER: *The Echoing Green*
Reviews:
Hugh Witemeyer, *Yeats*, 4 (1986), 187-89.

84-15. BRAMSBÄCK: *Folklore and W. B. Yeats*
Reviews:
Genevieve Brennan, *Yeats Annual*, 4 (1986), 247-48.
G. Lernout, *Revue belge de philologie et d'histoire*, 63:3 (1985), 629-33.
Janet Madden-Simpson: "All Arts and Parts," *Books Ireland*, 91 (March 1985), 36-37.
Dáithí Ó hÓgáin, *Irish University Review*, 16:1 (Spring 1986), 93-94.
Mary Helen Thuente, *Yeats*, 4 (1986), 189-92.

84-27. CHRIST: *Victorian and Modern Poetics*
Reviews:
Daniel A. Harris, *Yeats*, 4 (1986), 192-99.

84-34. CULLINGFORD: *Yeats: Poems*
Reviews:
Jacqueline Genet, *Études anglaises*, 39:2 (April-June 1986), 236-37.

Peter van de Kamp, *Irish University Review*, 15:1 (Spring 1985), 108–11.
James Simmons, *Notes & Queries*, 231 / 33:2 (June 1986), 267.

84-42. DORN: *Players and Painted Stage*
Reviews:
David R. Clark, *Yeats Annual*, 4 (1986), 231–35.
Mari Kathleen Fielder, *Theatre Journal*, 37:3 (Sept. 1985), 394–95.
James W. Flannery: "Yeats on the Aisle," *Irish Literary Supplement*, 4:2 (Fall 1985), 34.
Nicholas Grene, *Theatre Research International*, 10:2 (Summer 1985), 185–86.
Peter van de Kamp, *Irish University Review*, 15:1 (Spring 1985), 108–11.
David Krause, *Yeats*, 3 (1985), 225–29.

84-89. HOUGH: *The Mystery Religion of W. B. Yeats*
Reviews:
James Lovic Allen, *Yeats Annual*, 4 (1986), 265–67.
George Mills Harper, *Yeats*, 4 (1986), 199–202.
Peter van de Kamp, *Irish University Review*, 15:1 (Spring 1985), 108–11.
Johannes Kleinstück, *Anglia*, 104:1 / 2 (1986), 262–63.

84-93. JACK: *The Poet and His Audience*
Reviews:
Andrew Carpenter, *Yeats*, 4 (1986), 202–4.

84-96. JEFFARES: *A New Commentary on the Poems of W. B. Yeats*
Reviews:
Daniel Albright: "The Magician," *New York Review of Books*, 31 Jan. 1985, 29–32.
Richard J. Finneran: "W. B. Yeats: A Commentary on the *New Commentary*," *Review*, 7 (1985), 163–89.
James Olney, *Yeats*, 3 (1985), 229–38.
Michael J. Sidnell: "Unacceptable Hypotheses: The New Edition of Yeats's Poems and Its Making," *Yeats Annual*, 3 (1985), 225–43.

84-106. KOMESU: *The Double Perspective of Yeats's Aesthetic*
Reviews:
Hazard Adams, *Yeats*, 4 (1986), 206–9.
Justine Johnstone, *Hermathena*, 138 (Summer 1985), 82–83.
Peter van de Kamp, *Irish University Review*, 15:1 (Spring 1985), 108–11.
Janet Madden-Simpson: "All Arts and Parts," *Books Ireland*, 91 (March 1985), 36–37.

84-125. McDiarmid: *Saving Civilization*
Reviews:
F. Farag, *Canadian Journal of Irish Studies*, 11:2 (Dec. 1985), 87-88.
Vincent Fitzpatrick: "Art and Politics in Yeats, Auden, and Eliot," *Virginia Quarterly Review*, 62:2 (Spring 1986), 360-65.
Nicholas Grene, *Notes & Queries*, 231 / 33:3 (Sept. 1986), 423-24.
Steven Helmling, *Kritikon Litterarum*, 13:1-4 (1984), 108-10.
Sidney Poger, *Éire-Ireland*, 20:3 (Fall 1985), 150-52.

84-132. De Man: *The Rhetoric of Romanticism*
Reviews:
Northrop Frye: "In the Earth, or in the Air?" *TLS*, 17 Jan. 1986, 51-52.
Daniel T. O'Hara: "The Specialty of Self-Victimization in Recent Yeats Studies," *Contemporary Literature*, 27:2 (Summer 1986), 285-89.

84-138. Maxwell: *A Critical History of Modern Irish Drama*
Reviews:
James F. Kilroy, *Yeats*, 4 (1986), 209-13.

84-153. "4 Yeats Plays"
Reviews:
Richard Allen Cave, *Yeats Annual*, 4 (1986), 242-46.
David Krause, *Yeats*, 3 (1985), 225-29.

84-198. Taylor: *A Guide to the Plays of W. B. Yeats*
Reviews:
E. J. Dumay, *Études irlandaises*, 10 (December 1985), 307-8.
James W. Flannery: "Yeats on the Aisle," *Irish Literary Supplement*, 4:2 (Fall 1985), 34.
Rory Ryan, *Unisa English Studies*, 23:1 (April 1985), 52-53.
Katharine Worth, *Yeats Annual*, 4 (1986), 238.

84-225. Yeats: *Les histoires de la rose secrète*
Reviews:
René Fréchet, *Études anglaises*, 38:4 (Oct.-Dec. 1985), 486.
Jean-Luc Gautier, *Nouvelle revue française*, 390-91 (July-Aug. 1985), 171-72.

84-229. Yeats: *The Poems: A New Edition*
Reviews:
Daniel Albright: "The Magician," *New York Review of Books*, 31 Jan. 1985, 29-32.
George Bornstein: "Yeats's Texts and Contexts," *Modern Language Studies*, 16:2 (Spring 1986), 82-87.
Seamus Heaney, *Yeats*, 3 (1985), 260-66; reprint of the review in

New York Times Book Review (see 84-229).
Daniel T. O'Hara: "The Specialty of Self-Victimization in Recent Yeats Studies," *Contemporary Literature*, 27:2 (Summer 1986), 285-89.
Michael J. Sidnell: "Unacceptable Hypotheses: The New Edition of Yeats's Poems and Its Making," *Yeats Annual*, 3 (1985), 225-43.

84-230. YEATS: *Poems of W. B. Yeats*
Reviews:
René Fréchet, *Études anglaises*, 39:2 (April-June 1986), 235-36.
James Simmons, *Notes & Queries*, 231/33:2 (June 1986), 267-68.
Katharine Worth, *Review of English Studies*, 37:146 (May 1986), 287-88.

84-240. *Yeats: An Annual of Critical and Textual Studies.* No. 2
Reviews:
Daniel T. O'Hara: "The Specialty of Self-Victimization in Recent Yeats Studies," *Contemporary Literature*, 27:2 (Summer 1986), 285-89.
Sidney Poger, *Éire-Ireland*, 21:1 (Spring 1986), 151-52.

Dissertation Abstracts, 1986

Compiled by *Gwenn de Mauriac*

The dissertations abstracts included here are reprinted with permission of University Microfilms, Inc., publisher of *Dissertation Abstracts International* (copyright © 1986 by University Microfilms International), and may not be reproduced without their prior permission.* Full-text copies of the dissertations are available upon request, for a fee, from University Microfilms, Inc., 300 North Zeeb Road, Ann Arbor, Michigan 48106.

The Development of Prophecy in the Poetry of W. B. Yeats.
Christie Diane Gramm, Ph.D. University of Oregon, 1985. 131 pp. Adviser: A. Kingsley Weatherhead. Order No. DA8520714.

In tracing the development of Yeats's prophetic poetry, this dissertation beings with an examination of the transcendent principles of mysticism which inform the early poems. Because the transcendent impulse of mysticism implies a transcendence of language, Yeats eventually discovered the inadequacy of mystic premises for the purposes of the poet, who relies on language for his art. In re-examining his premises, Yeats reconsidered the purpose of his poetry, a re-evaluation which included a significant change in the way he conceived of the role of audience in his poetry. While mysticism tends to limit linguistic expression, prophecy is based on the power of language to affect an audience. In determining that audience response would play a much greater role in his poetic purpose, he evolved a prophetic poetic which is analogous to the style and purpose of Biblical prophecy. In its final form, Yeats's prophetic poetry establishes a vision which retains the concrete particular within the universal, in contrast to the transcendent vision of the earlier poems.

(*DAI* 46.7 [January 1986] 1948A)

---

*Minor corrections have been made.

Yeats and Tagore: A Comparative Study of Their Plays.
Krishna Ponnuswamy, Ph.D. Madurai Kamaraj University (India), 1984. 437 pp. Supervisor: K. Chellappan. Order No. DA8518890.

The dissertation makes a thematic comparison of the plays of W. B. Yeats and Rabindranath Tagore, who were contemporaries and friends for a considerable period of time. It attempts to substantiate how these two internationally reputed poets were also good playwrights. The two playwrights, living under similar political and socio-economic conditions, adopted the dramatic form to give expression to their national problems and to work out a national regeneration through literary renascence.

The study traces the ancient connections between the peoples of Ireland and India and the similarities in certain racial and national traits. These two playwrights had a wide concept of patriotism and aimed at national identity and revival of the cultural and spiritual values of the past, fighting internal differences and social evils. The second chapter discusses how these playwrights paved the way for national freedom through the *Bodhisattva* principles by delineating suitable heroic characters. The third chapter deals with the tragic sense of life of these two writers and analyses the conflicting forces of good and evil, sin and expiation in their tragic plays. The next two chapters examine how the playwrights lay emphasis on the humanistic creed of love and sympathy, mainly engendered in women characters, who overcome not only personal tragedy but also the tragic elements in the national and cosmic life. There is a new interpretation of some of Yeats's women characters who rise to the height of mother-goddesses. The sixth chapter discusses in detail how the playwrights make use of various myths and symbols to bring out the national identity and the cultural and spiritual renascence of their respective countries.

The last chapter sums up the findings. Though these playwrights were activated by their milieu, their mythic themes and symbols effectively inculcate cultural and ethical values which are universal. The similarities in themes, treatment and technique as well as the differences between the dramatists are pointed out. As a study of drama is not complete without a discussion of the aesthetic pleasure derived from it, there is a brief reference to *rasa* and how it is reflected in the structure of the plays of Yeats and Tagore, working out emotional balance and *Santi*.

(*DAI* 46.7 [January 1986] 1933–34A)

Poetry as Appropriate Epistemology: Gregory Bateson and W. B. Yeats.
Michael J. Opitz, Ph.D. University of Minnesota, 1985. 250 pp. Chair:
C. G. Anderson. Order No. DA8528829.

Gregory Bateson was a senior figure in fields as diverse as anthropology, biology, cybernetics, information theory and psychology. Near the end of his life, he became increasingly critical of reductionist thinking and of the scientific-industrial paradigm which occupy central places in contemporary epistemology. Bateson argued that the scientific-industrial paradigm presents an inaccurate map of the living world. For Bateson, aesthetic perception and poetic expression are important cornerstones of a new world view.

This study uses Bateson's last work as a starting point and argues that poetic thought is an important step in the process of recognizing "mind" in nature. The levels of complexity inherent in the living world are more appropriately described by paradox, metaphor and poetry than by any other aspect of current epistemology. The first part of this study develops Bateson's critique of the role of conscious purpose in human adaptation, and forms a critical theory based upon his commentary on the epistemologically appropriate aspects of metaphor, poetry and aesthetics. Bateson's argument implies that poetry should be considered important epistemology.

The second part of this study applies this critical theory to the poetry of W. B. Yeats. Yeats is universally regarded as one of the great modern poets. His systemic poetry provides appropriate ways of thinking about the complex variety of the living world—the world of "mind in nature." By interpreting Yeats's poetry in Batesonian terms, this study seeks to establish the epistemological importance of his poetry.

Thus, on one level, Bateson's scientific, psychological, and epistemological writings are extended into a critical theory which can provide a fundamental method of reading Yeats's poetry. At a higher level, this poetry recurs as a much more effective and beautiful way of expressing many of Bateson's epistemological insights. The comparison of these two significant bodies of work creates a metaphor, and argues that this kind of metaphor is an appropriate method for understanding the world.

(*DAI* 46.10 [April 1986] 3042A)

The Poetics of Etherealization: Female Imagery in the Work of W. B. Yeats.
Young Suck Rhee, Ph.D. The University of Nebraska—Lincoln, 1985. 269 pp. Adviser: Linda Ray Pratt. Order No. DA8526631.

W. B. Yeats used images of women throughout his work, beginning with pre-Raphaelite beauty which he later associated with Maud Gonne and ending some fifty years later with the "Olympians" in *Last Poems*. Many of his poetic images are drawn from three women who played important roles in his life: Maud Gonne, Lady Gregory, and his wife, George. Through his long, complicated relationships with these and other women, Yeats's knowledge of women resulted in a change in the imagery of women from the abstract beauty of youthful idealized "fairy brides" to the earthy passions of Crazy Jane and the independent character of women who become "beautiful lofty things" because of their own courage, will, and talent. The change in the images of women mirrors Yeats's deepening sense of a poetry of human reality and the abandonment of his earlier idealizing, symbolic work.

Chapter 1 introduces the method and format of the dissertation, and chapter 2 surveys the women who became important in Yeats's poetry. Chapter 3 defines pre-Raphaelite beauty in "The Wanderings of Oisin." Chapter 4 examines poems about Maud Gonne, whose pre-Raphaelite beauty and extreme personality were inharmonious. Study includes "The Cap and Bells," "The Sorrow of Love," "No Second Troy," and *The Shadowy Waters* and *The Countess Cathleen*. Chapter 5 emphasizes Lady Gregory as the embodiment of an aristocratic world at Coole. Chapter 6 focuses on women as sexual force after Yeats's marriage and includes "Leda and the Swan," the "Solomon" poems, "The Gift of Harun Al-Rashid," and the Crazy Jane and Ribh poems. Chapter 7 examines the women in *Last Poems* who have become mythic through their place in history, and who now symbolize only themselves and Yeats's friendships with them.

The study concludes that the images of women are the key to Yeats's blending of his life, artistic theory, and poetic symbolism in that they help to structure the poems in form and content.

(*DAI* 46.10 [April 1986] 3043A)

The Irish Peasant in the Work of W. B. Yeats and J. M. Synge
   Deborah Diane Fleming, Ph.D. The Ohio State University, 1985. 239 pp. Adviser: Morris Beja. Order No. DA8602994.

The literary treatment of the peasant played a crucial and controversial role in the emerging Irish national consciousness in the early twentieth century. The belief that in past ages people were nobler, stronger, more virtuous and more civilized than the present is an important literary theme often associated with ideas about the desirability of country people's way of life. W. B. Yeats and J. M. Synge, the two key figures in the Irish Literary Revival, believed that the Irish peasants' culture perpetuated that virtue and beauty which had been lost to the modern world.

Yeats's and Synge's different but complementary ways of looking at Irish peasants helped to establish a new cultural and linguistic identity in Ireland by transforming Irish folklore into art and by capturing the rhythms of the Anglo-Irish dialect. Synge was concerned with the peasants of his own time, while Yeats saw them primarily as inheritors of Celtic tradition.

The first two chapters discuss the social and political situation of Irish peasants at that time and Yeats's and Synge's use of the literary convention of the Noble Savage. The author then examines their literary treatment of the peasants—their relationship to nature, the peasant and love, the peasant as outcast, the peasant as artist.

Yeats and Synge remind us that if the peasants' culture has represented a mystical and virtuous tradition, that culture too has suffered from the degradation of modern times. And yet, even though their way of life is threatened by the outside world, the country people display courage and the ability to endure.

While not indulging in sentimental pastoral, both Yeats and Synge were romantics, both transformed the peasants into ideal figures. They were interested in whatever provided images for art; thus, the peasant became a wanderer, a mystic, a man of nature. Such artistic recreation characterized the Irish Renaissance as a whole—Irish culture and history were idealized in order to create a traditional inheritance.

(*DAI* 46.12 [June 1986] 3724–25A)

A Language of Silence: Writing the Self in Yeats and Synge, Joyce and Beckett.
Thomas John Giannotti, Jr., Ph.D. University of California, Riverside, 1985. 233 pp. Chair: John B. Vickery. Order No. DA8604129.

The metaphor of silence, one frequently invoked in the tropes and themes of the Romantics, hovers behind and within the discourse of self in modern literature, and the concept of a language of silence engages and answers questions of form and discourse in the tradition of modern Irish autobiography. The binary structure of the concept, devised and delimited by a transformation of Romantic concerns with self-consciousness and self-transcendence into postromantic, modernist, and postmodernist versions, betrays the forms of concealment and revelation that are inscribed in the structures and discourses of a series of textual mise-en-scènes, which includes Synge's fragmentary *Autobiography*, Yeats's *Memoirs* and *Autobiographies*, Joyce's *Stephen Hero* and *Portrait*, Beckett's *Krapp's Last Tape* and *Company*, along with peripheral attention to more marginal self-regarding texts.

The organizing metaphor of silence, along with its corresponding formal categories and discursive traits, is founded in phenomenological conceptions of fragmentary awareness. Thus, the underlying tension between a rhetoric of self-proliferation and narrative inexhaustibility and one of self-annihilation, between speech and stillness, public access and private hieraticism, recovery of self for public presentation and loss of self in solipsistic isolation, address to an identifiable audience and a self-address that can yield only a private language, is a conflict described by a triad of bipolarities in the language of silence that opposes silence and utterance, fragmentation and closure, self and other.

In Synge and Yeats, the opposed poles of silence are represented in the first by a movement toward annulment of language, toward fragmentation of text and failed closure, while in the second the movement is toward an overcoming of the anxieties imposed by silence through a textual revision and proliferation of selves. In Joyce, silence assumes the form of a rhetoric of omission and authorial abdication of the text; finally, in Beckett, a similar but more radically modulated authorial absence occurs in conjunction with a fragmentation of voices within the text into disparate grammatical locations of the writing self.

(*DAI* 46.12 [June 1986] 3725A)

Yeats's Passionate Syntax.
Ralph Harding Earle, Ph.D. The University of North Carolina at Chapel Hill, 1985. 197 pp. Supervisor: William Harmon. Order No. DA8605590.

An important feature of poetics that often goes overlooked is that of syntax. In the cast of Yeats, syntax is particularly consequential. Some of the most significant effects of his lyric poetry can be attributed to syntax, including a capacity to foreground material in such a way to draw attention to it, or to subtly jar the reader's perceptions of the poem, and a capacity to balance the effects of logic and association. A close look at two alternative openings to "Sailing to Byzantium" illustrates these effects.

A number of deliberate strategies are apparent in Yeatsian syntax, including the long matrix sentence, parallelism with variation, compression, enjambment, deliberate ambiguity, transposition and the nominative absolute. Stanzas from "Ancestral Houses" and "A Prayer for My Daughter" provide detailed illustrations.

The question and the rhetorical question are so prevalent that chapter 3 is entirely devoted to them. "A Dialogue of Self and Soul" illustrates Yeats's many ways of using questions. Some of his most memorable syntactic effects arise from his embedding structures like the nominative absolute within his questions.

In chapter 4, a close examination of "Among School Children" reveals the full spectrum of Yeats's syntactic strategies, and reveals the extent to which syntax can influence the meaning and effect of a poem. Yeats's most masterful effects are achieved not through a rote application of devices, but through a complex texture of syntax.

Some of Yeats's syntactic tendencies are evident in his earliest published poems, but mastery was a gradual process that only reached fruition after 1914. Chapter 5 examines Yeats's early syntax. Chapter 6 traces the development of syntax in several sonnets and sonnet-like poems, showing how Yeats perfected the ability to work with form and syntax simultaneously in "Leda and the Swan."

The power of syntax is so subtle that it is easily overlooked. By insisting on its importance in both theory and practice, Yeats has extended the range of syntactic possibilities in poetry and asserted the place of syntax among the most important of poetic techniques.

(*DAI* 47.2 [August 1986] 535A)

Blest: Cohesion and Ironic Deflation in Six Short Poem Sequences of W. B. Yeats.
   Edward William Goggin, Ph.D. Fordham University, 1985. 305 pp. Director: Philip Sicker. Order No. DA8612857.

This dissertation examines the six short sequences that appear in the later poetry of W. B. Yeats: "Upon a Dying Lady," "A Man Young and Old," "Meditations in Time of Civil War," "A Woman Young and Old," "Supernatural Songs," and "The Three Bushes" series. The specific aim of the dissertation is to examine the cohesiveness of the short sequences and to offer as an explanation for their structure a reading that finds the sequences moving towards ironic deflation through apparently inadequate ending. The paper provides close readings of each series in order to argue that the inadequate closes of the sequences and the ironic deflation they create serve as foils to the exuberance of individuals who have expressed their affirmation or their hope. In "A Man

Young and Old" and "A Woman Young and Old" the inadequacy is in the form of tagged on, proverbial wisdom; in "Meditations in Time of Civil War" it is the questionable analysis of one caught in the whorl; in "Three Bushes" the flawed analysis of those trapped in a sexual tangle; in "Supernatural Songs" the flaccidity of disembodied, arcane wisdom; and in "Upon a Dying Lady" the lameness of an unnecessary intercession. These ostensibly inappropriate endings act as tactical measures to return the reader to the words and exaltations that have seemingly been superseded, and also serve to display affirmation and hope in the face of negation rather than merely explain them.

The treatment of the six sequences stresses their cohesiveness. The introductory chapter presents a general discussion of the sequences, considering why they can be fruitfully viewed together and how similar methods are used to advance similar effects. This initial chapter also introduces the topic of inadequate endings and considers the presence of similarly flawed endings in several poems throughout the corpus. Each subsequent chapter focuses upon a sequence and finds that, when the sequences peter out in vapid remarks, apparent misdirection or fatuous analysis, the strong characters drawn throughout the sequence rise above the final words.

(*DAI* 47.3 [September 1986] 910A)

W. B. Yeats: Poetry as Meditation.
Vara Sue Tamminga Barker, Ph.D. The University of Texas at Austin, 1984. 318 pp. Supervisor: Joseph F. Malof. Order No. DA8621750.

Throughout his lifetime, Yeats claimed that poetry was a form of meditation. As his early poetry suggests, he first approached meditation as a window into an ethereal, supernatural dimension. However, his extensive studies in Hermetic and Eastern meditative traditions encouraged him to use meditation as a way of embracing nature. This deeper view of meditation actually helped him fill his later poetry with a joyous exaltation of natural, human experience.

Yeats spent a lifetime struggling with and finally breaking through our traditional Western preconceptions about mysticism. Most critics, however, judge his work with those same preconceptions. While they acknowledge Yeats's early focus on mystical vision, they see his eventual disdain for "disembodied essences" as a rejection of meditation. In fact, Yeats dismissed the saint's otherworldly approach to meditation and began to use meditation instead as a path to wholeness, to the fully integrated life which he portrayed in the cosmic wheel of *A Vi-*

sion. In the middle poetry, he tried to create that integration through mediation, using poetry and meditation as ways of vacillating between two separate levels of reality, the natural and the supernatural. However, Yeats finally moved beyond a dualistic world view and found in philosophies such as Zen Buddhism a way of retaining the power of polarity while plunging into the eternal oneness inherent in natural experience. Most critics see the focus on nature in Yeats's late poetry as a final rejection of his metaphysics or as evidence of an endless and frustrating vacillation between "Self" and "Soul." This study of Yeats's meditative search aims at helping to illumine the motivation behind his early and middle poetry, and at encouraging appreciation of the intimate power of Yeats's late poetry as the final achievement of his meditative and artistic life.

(*DAI* 47.6 [December 1986] 2165A)

William Butler Yeats and India: Indian Ideas of Art, Religion, and Philosophy in Yeats's Works, 1885–1939.
  Sankaran Ravindran, Ph.D. University of Kansas, 1986. 217 pp. Chairman: Harold Orel. Order No. DA8619938.

Although Yeats reacted to Indian ideas of art, religion, and philosophy in three different periods of his career, the picture of Yeats using Indian ideas with mature understanding is one of progress, development, and evolution, the culmination of which was in the last phase of his career. Among the three Indians, Mohini Chatterji, Rabindranath Tagore, and Shri Purohit Swami, whom Yeats met at three stages of his career, the Swami was the most inspiring for Yeats. That Yeats's relationship with India was progressively evolutionary and that the most productive period in the relationship was in the 1880s are established in this dissertation.

Yeats's critical thinking and ideas of art decided what he accepted from his Indian sources. Yeats's Indian friends introduced him to the philosophical and religious ideas of India. However, Yeats learned, without much help, Indian ideas of art, and he discovered a sense of harmony among art, religion, philosophy, and life in Indian tradition. Yeats tried to recapture the spirit of Indian art in some of his major works and succeeded in his efforts.

Introductory statements are made in chapter 1. What is Indian in the five early Indian poems by Yeats is discussed in chapter 2. It is argued that Yeats used Indian ideas of art in these poems. Chatterji's influence was marginal.

Yeats's relation with Tagore, the development in his understanding of Indian art, religion, and philosophy that enabled him to write a critical introduction to *Gitanjali*, and the artistic reasons for his lack of interest in Tagore's later poetry are discussed in chapter 3. *Gitanjali* introduced Yeats to the art of using the Upanishadic concept of the self in poetry.

Yeats's relationship with Shri Purohit Swami and his use of the concept of the self in his poems in the 1930s and in *The Herne's Egg* are examined in chapter 4. Nearly 115 unpublished letters of Yeats and the Swami were examined for writing this chapter. The self and the soul represent one concept in the *Upanishads*. Although Yeats knew that the self and the soul were interchangeable words for the same concept, for his dramatizations in art he made them embody two principles. In the conclusion, the fifth chapter, an Indian idea behind Yeats's concept of impersonal poetry is briefly explained.

(*DAI* 47.6 [December 1986] 2171A)

Reviews

Joseph Adams. *Yeats and the Masks of Syntax.*
New York: Columbia University Press, 1984. viii + 111 pp.
Reviewed by *Edmund L. Epstein*

This interesting book on Yeats and the syntax of English is one of a small number of critical works on poetry and language in which the author really seems to know something about linguistics. When Adams writes about syntax, he writes like someone who has actually studied syntactic analysis, unlike those critics who merely carry on an unrequited flirtation with the subject. Adams has created an important work on Yeats's language, and on poetic language in general, one that should be read by every Yeatsian interested in subtle analysis of language.

    This is not to say that the book has no flaws—it has, some serious. Adams's major thesis is not supported by his text or his examples. His analysis does not take into account Yeats's own statements on language, at least one of which destroys one of Adams's crucial points. There are many aspects of Yeats's poetic language which would yield to syntactic analysis which Adams does not explore. Again, however, I insist that Adams's book is a significant work in Yeats criticism, carp how I may.

    Adams notes examples of syntactic ambiguity in Yeats and adduces his results to prove a thesis about the nature of the Subjective as the arena where differing interpretations clash, a concept usually ascribed to Hegel, here traced to the French critic Gilles Deleuze. Yeats's ambiguities are marshalled by Adams to provide gladiators for the arena.

    To describe Adams's methods, I will first employ my own examples and then treat his.

    Consider the sentence (my example):

    a. & The gang tore up the street.[1]

This sentence could mean "the gang demolished the street," or "the gang ran quickly up the street."[2] In one interpretation the complete verb is "tear-up"; in the other it is "tear":

b. The gang tore-up/the street [= demolished]
c. The gang tore/up-the-street [= ran]

b is transitive; *c* is intransitive. If we could pronounce the sentences, we could perhaps resolve the ambiguity by pauses in crucial places, but on the page the sentence is irresolvably ambiguous. Only context (other sentences) could resolve the conflict.

Adams would not *want* to resolve the ambiguity. For him the conflict is the purpose of the language, not whatever information may be contained in the sentence(s). Adams main thesis is that the sentence wears a "mask of syntax," a mask with no face beneath it, merely a second mask. Adams (following Deleuze) sees in these masks the major purpose of language, an anti-Platonic purpose, in which the play of language is its own purpose. In a "Platonist" view of language, the information contained in the sentence, about the street and about the creator of the sentence, is the important aspect of the sentence. Therefore, a resolution of the ambiguity is urgently necessary for a Platonist:

> Stylistics is platonic in seeing language as expressive. 'The artist', Spitzer writes, 'lends to an outward phenomenon of language an inner significance'.[3] For stylistics and the platonic view in general, language is thus a vehicle for meaning. It encloses meaning in a special way and thereby enables literature to convey an author's thoughts and feelings. In this model, the palpable forms of language carry an inner core of content—ultimately, the individual personality or subject—that is both their raison d'être and the force that shapes their outward, physical qualities. [2]

The "anti-Platonist" position on language that Adams and Deleuze espouse focuses on the *fact* of syntactic ambiguity and the (endless) *process* of disambiguation. The task of producing and interpreting language is itself the purpose of the language process:

> The aim of post-structuralist analysis has generally been to show language operating in a text and, in a sense, producing the text. The emphasis has not been on connecting the operations seen in a text to any entity (such as a global meaning) different in kind from those operations themselves. This analysis is particularly opposed to the platonic tradition's hierarchical model, which has a prior and essential meaning (or even a generating subject) determining the form of language. Instead of conceiving of meaning as extrinsic to the forms of language, or as more important than those forms, the antiplatonic view sees an interrelationship, or play, between forms and meanings in the text—or rather, a play between forms and meanings as the text. Meaning and form can be discriminated as they operate in and as the text, but neither one takes priority. [3]

As the post-structuralists inform us, this process partly relies on semantic ambiguities: my "gang" is not your "gang"; the speaker's "gang" is not (yet) the listener's "gang"—if it were, there would be no need to produce the sentence. However, Adams (rightly) prefers syntactic analysis to semantic analysis: semantic ambiguity is almost totally personal, idiosyncratic, whereas the syntax of English is maximally similar in any native speaker of English to any other native speaker:

> A mask most often appears as a syntactic ambiguity, but as one having little to do with enrichening the global interpretation of the poem where it occurs. The important thing about the ambiguity of the syntactic mask is that it is more or less unresolvable, so much so that an oscillation is set up between its alternative possibilities. With neither syntactic form becoming fully possible, no final meaning can be assigned. Form and meaning thus become radically dislodged from one another. Moreover, made up as they are of competing alternative forms, the syntactic masks never become integrated as complete syntactic units. [3–4]

The listener, hearing "the gang tore up the street," oscillates between transitive and intransitive, sees images of demolition alternating with those of running men—endlessly. The Subjective keeps performing its central function—of balancing diversities—and so the language deconstructs itself. Verbal transitive ousts intransitive which ousts transitive which ousts intransitive . . . each syntax defers to, and differs from, the opposing syntax (Derrida's differance/difference), the entity-deferred-to and the entity-deferring changing places, ceaselessly.

Although Adams does not call attention to the psychological background of this alteration, this procedure—"fluctuation of attention"—is ultimately based upon a phenomenon described by Gestalt psychologists, the alternating of background and foreground, between foregrounded and automatized areas of attention. In regarding the cube below (a "Necker cube"), the eye and mind oscillate:

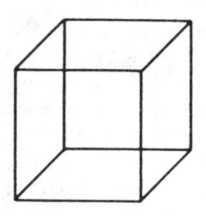

Is the cube a front-going up-to-the-right, or a front-going down-to-the-left, or a back-going-up-to-the-right, or a back-going-down-to-the-left?[4] The subjective mind can oscillate endlessly on the matter, and it rejoices in so doing, since oscillation is its function.

It is necessary for Adams's purpose that the ambiguities be unresolvable, but my example (sentence a) would certainly be resolved in context:

> a. The gang tore up the street
> 1. The laborers arrived at the excavation at dawn, and unpacked their tools. The gange tore up the street. Then they stopped and had lunch.
> 2. The robbers burst out of the bank, into Fifth Avenue, shooting at the teller. The gang tore up the street. Eventually they got away.

Adams would reject the context-disambiguation of sentence a; for the purpose of his analysis, he prefers the radically ambiguous and the unresolvable.

In the examination of Adams's analysis, two points must be considered. The first is that Adams draws only the most tenuous connection between Yeats's "masks" and the "masks" of his title. The second is that, while he leads the critic to rich fields of analysis, he overlooks subtle syntactic processes in the poetry in his search for ambiguity and "masks."

Although Adams treats as subjects for his analysis thirty-four poems by Yeats, the only suggestion by Adams that Yeats's masks are being discovered in the fluctuating syntax of the poems is, literally, just a few lines in a single paragraph:

> So the syntactic mask as a producer of subjectivity reverses the platonic view of the subject as producer of language. This reversal is also found in Yeats's own theory of the self, particularly as it was worked out in *A Vision*. For Yeats, the development of the subject as an individual is the work of a complex process. The process involves Yeats's concept of 'the Mask', one of the paired elements whirling in the system of the gyres. The subject begins to find its individuality when it pursues a Mask contrary to its 'true' self, a Mask with the likeness and character of its opposite spirit, its Daimon. But the subject is not truly an independent agent in this process. As Yeats writes: 'I am in the place where the Daimon is, but I do not think he is with me until I begin to make a new personality . . . and yet . . . not knowing when I am the finger, when the clay' [Myth 365–66]. In Yeats's model as in Deleuze's, the subject is never completely separate from the primordial field of tensions defining it ('My instructors identify consciousness with conflict' [AV-B 214]). The subject, the individual consciousness, is finally only a result within the system of gyres. It only comes about through the systematic play of oppositions, reciprocities and interdependencies among the 'Four Principles' and the 'Four Faculties' (including the Mask). [11]

Adams's first example of syntactic "masks"—his departure point for the rest of his analysis—concerns Yeats's use of the definite article *the* (as in "I walk through *the* long schoolroom questioning") and the definite demonstratives: *this, that, there, those*. These words can operate ambiguously, Adams suggests, between their "situational" use and their "anaphoric" use—that is, the use of these words to refer to external "situations" (Halliday's term) as opposed to their purely internal uses.[5] Take my sentence *The horse put its head over the fence and ate the roses*. This sentence may occur in two contexts:

A. *Situational*

Situation: in a house; one person is looking out the window; another joins the first. Both look out the window. One, pointing, says, "*The* horse put its head over *the* fence and ate *the* roses."

B. *Anaphoric*

Once upon a time there was a horse in a meadow adjoining a garden, which was separated from it by a low fence. One day the horse saw that there was a rosebush covered with roses in the garden, and it ambled over to the fence. It liked what it saw. *The* horse put its head over *the* fence and ate *the* roses.

In discourse A, the definite articles are justified because both speakers have come to understand a Situation: the use of *the* is conditional upon shared knowledge. In discourse B, the anaphoric use of *the* is purely mechanical and linguistic: *a horse, a fence, roses* become automatically and without shift of meaning *the horse, the fence, the roses*; textual antecedents lead to textual consequents. Therefore, the sentence *The horse put its head over the fence and ate the roses* is ambiguous as it stands. In context it might resolve itself into one or another meaning; however, in poetry frequently there is either no context, or inadequate context. Therefore, the mind of the reader oscillates, Adams would say.

Adams devotes his first chapter to this problem. He comments on Yeats's "I walk through *the* long schoolroom questioning," "I climb to *the* tower-top," and "In *this* altar-piece *the* knight" (P 215, 205, 175; emphasis Adams's):

. . . the ostensible mode of identification is situational. With the *the* placed near the beginning of the discourse, there is no textual antecedent so anaphora seems to be ruled out. . . . But, with no clear situational source of identification, *the* has the effect of implying that the identity of the noun is already known to or presupposed by both the narrator of the poem and the reader, a strictly fictional presupposition, which calls into play the anaphoric mode of identification—not because there is any actual antecedent, but only as a result of the unexplained presupposition. If the schoolroom is supposed to be known to us, then the illusion of a prior mention comes into play. The reader partly feels that, somewhere, a discourse has mentioned the 'long schoolroom' and hence the present mention is justifiably definite. But the presupposed knowledge simply does not exist as such. As a result, the anaphoric mode remains in an uneasy competition with the situational mode (which constantly slips back into play). The consequence is a syntactic mask. [16]

Adams here postulates a psychological process in the reader: 1) The absence of actual anaphora is initially interpreted as presupposing that the use of *the* is Situational. 2) However, there is also no real "situation," so the reader assumes actual (though absent) antecedents, which are supposed to be known Anaphorically both to the reader and the "speaker." 3) However, the reader then becomes aware that there is no real reason to assume that the poet and the reader in fact possess common knowledge, so the Situational interpretation again comes into focus. But, again, the reader knows that there is no "Situation"—and so on.

There is one main criticism of this analysis (which is the model for all the other analyses in this chapter): the dynamic process *may* in fact operate in readers, but why call it a "mask"? Yeats's masks are *in opposition* to the primary soul, not merely *different*. Situation is not the *opposite* of Anaphora. Adams has found *something*, and something that is clearly relevant to the criticism of Yeats—the role of time in the reading of literature—but he has not found Yeatsian masks. Indeed, the assumption that all syntactic ambiguity provides evidence of masks is taken for granted by Adams—any complexity, any syntactic irony, is called a "mask"; in fact, one of the flaws of the (excellent) book is precisely that it does *not* analyze what Yeats meant by "masks."

The Mask is always the sign of the creation of an Anti-Self: "I think that all happiness depends on the energy to assume the mask of some other self; that all joyous or creative life is a rebirth as something not oneself . . ." (Au 503). That the "something not oneself" is indeed an Opposite is clear from "Ego Dominus Tuus":

> I call to my own opposite, summon all
> That I have handled least, least looked upon.
> . . . .
> I call to the mysterious one who yet
> Shall walk the wet sands by the edge of the stream
> And look most like me, being indeed my double,
> And prove of all imaginable things
> The most unlike, being my anti-self. . . .
>
> [P 160, 162]

In *A Vision* the mask is always expressed as opposition: on his *Table of the Four Faculties* (AV-B 96–98) the mask appears as Illusion/Delusion: "Simplification through Intensity/Dispersal; Conviction/Domination;

Self-reliance/Isolation; Renunciation/Emulation; Oblivion/Malignity; Courage/Fear; Serenity/Self-distrust. . . ."

In general the Mask is characterized in Yeats by clear opposition, although some of these pairs seem less obviously opposite than others.

In Yeats's application of his theory to individuality his description of the root-functions of the Mask clearly defines it as Opposite: "All men are characterised upon a first analysis by the proportion in which these two characters or *Tinctures,* the objective or *primary,* the subjective or antithetical, are combined" (Au 124–25).

Yeats's oppositions have actual opposing content: *Objective–Subjective, Dark–Light, democracy–aristocracy, external morality–self-created morality, cold–tepid, golden bird–real bird.* Although Yeats seized eagerly on the abstract and subtle MacTaggart—"Yeats was in the habit of grasping at any philosophical authority that might be wrenched to support him"[6]—totally abstract polar alternatives had no interest for Yeats, who states so specifically in an important text which Adams, surprisingly, does not quote:

> I had never read Hegel [at the time of his first defining his system], but my mind had been full of Blake from boyhood up and I saw the world as a conflict—Spectre and Emanation—and could distinguish between a contrary and a negation. "Contraries are positive", wrote Blake, "a negation is not a contrary", "How great the gulph between simplicity and insipidity", and again, "There is a place at the bottom of the graves where contraries are equally true". I had never put the conflict in logical form, never thought with Hegel that the two ends of the see-saw are one another's negation, nor that the spring vegetables were refuted when over. [AV-B 72–73]

For Hegel, or for the "subtle" Hegelian MacTaggart, or for Deleuze, or for Adams, one pole is merely the negation of the other. Not for Yeats—his poles had real "contrary" content. If Adams were correct in calling "masks" the syntactic ambiguities he finds, his interpretation should be just as richly *contrary* as Yeats's oppositions, not simply *different* from each other.

Adams has found ambiguities in Yeats's syntax, but he has not found masks. What he has found is the unusual linguistic status of literature. Literature is very much a minority form of language. Astronomical numbers of casual sentences are uttered every waking minute all over the world; only a tiny amount remains as literature. Literature can be described as a set of preserved utterances—preserved beyond the (presumed) moment of utterance. Since they are preserved through time, it is possible to analyze the precise status of Adams's determiners:

1. They are *not* examples of anaphora. Anaphora is a tender blossom; remove the reference of the anaphor, and anaphora vanishes. Anaphora operates automatically. In "I walk through *the* long schoolroom questioning," there is no previous phrase "*a* long classroom," and, therefore, no anaphora.

It is possible that, if the page which we read had been torn away before the "long schoolroom" sentence, the reader might be in doubt on the matter—but it is not.

2. The *the*'s and so on *are* Situational, but since the utterance has been preserved (as it qualifies as literature) the (presumed) "Situation" has receded into the past. It is only in such preserved utterances that the rules of usual language do not apply.

Therefore, there is no mask here—either Adams's or Yeats's; there is literature.

Adams wrestles with the status of the atemporal artifact. He raises the question: "What sort of time dimension contains or explains the peculiar occurrence of the syntactic masks?" (72). The reader, as a competent reader of literature, unconsciously sees the literary text as being a "preserved" situational utterance, and the three "times" collapse into one. There is a "time dimension" (79) in the reading of the line, but it is not the abstract time of alternation from one oscillating pole to the other; it is ordinary time, through which the utterance has been preserved.

The light Adams casts on the linguistic situation of the work of art illuminates the search for the actual "situation" of poetry—on the use of preserved situationals for specifically poetic purposes. Adams's concentration on the time-situation of the poetry—see, for example, his fifth chapter, "The Grammar of Time in the Mask" (esp. 82)—leads to areas for the critic to explore with as much care as Adams devotes to his analysis.

Time, for the symbolist poet, is the enemy—Yeats describes its action as "the cracked tune that Chronos sings." Against the encroachments of time the poet has only words—but "words alone are certain good" (P 7). With words the poet constructs an utterance to be preserved through time and, therefore, to resist time. The literary text is "preserved" intact from some "moment in the past," and the reader scans the preserved moment at some unspecified time in the future. How is time to be overcome? Is it possible for the poet's "voice" to speak directly to readers as the readers scan the tokens of the text before them?

When Eliot in "Burnt Norton" produces the line "My words echo / Thus, in your mind," the "Thus" means that the line itself has echoed in the readers' minds as they read the page of their own token texts, illustrating the phenomenon known as "token-reflexivity."[7] In other words, it is the "token" page, the reader's copy, which bears the message. The words "echo" because the poet's words from the original "point of utterance" produce an echo from the reader at the point of reading. Here both the preservation of the utterance and the actual situation of reading are united. The poet overcomes the preservation of the utterances and speaks directly from the page. Whitman's "So Long!" provides an example:

> Camerado, this is no book,
> Who touches this touches a man. . . .

Eliot himself provides another one, by quoting Baudelaire in *The Waste Land*:

> You! hypocrite lecteur!—mon semblable,—mon frère!

Both Baudelaire and Eliot reach out from the reader's texts and seize the reader.

It is important for these poets to perform this art of atemporalizing the poetic text. But does Yeats ever perform this act?

He does, in an audacious and unprecedented manner. In the third section of "Nineteen Hundred and Nineteen," Yeats performs a remarkable linguistic feat:

> Some moralist or mythological poet
> Compares the solitary soul to a swan;
> I am satisfied with that,
> Satisfied if a troubled mirror show it,
> Before that brief gleam of its life be gone,
> An image of its state;
> The wings half spread for flight,
> The breast thrust out in pride
> Whether to play, or to ride
> Those winds that clamour of approaching night.
>
> A man in his own secret meditation
> Is lost amid the labyrinth that he has made
> In art or politics;
> Some Platonist affirms that in the station
> Where we should cast off body and trade
> The ancient habit sticks,
> And that if our works could
> But vanish with our breath
> That were a lucky death,
> For triumph can but mar our solitude.
>
> The swan has leaped into the desolate heaven:
> That image can bring wildness, bring a rage

218   *Reviews*

> To end all things, to end
> What my laborious life imagined, even
> The half-imagined, the half-written page;
> O but we dreamed to mend
> Whatever mischief seemed
> To afflict mankind, but now
> That winds of winter blow
> Learn that we were crack-pated when we dreamed.
>
> [P 208–9]

The first lines set up a vision:

> Some moralist or mythological poet
> Compares the solitary soul to a swan. . . .

There then follow eighteen lines of meditation on the solitary soul. Then the line occurs:

> The swan has leaped into the desolate heaven. . . .

The tense of the line—present perfect—performs a bold act of linguistic creation. Adams calls its use a mask (73). The present perfect tense traditionally presents a state of affairs that begins in the past and continues into the present: there is a present potentiality to continue the action into the future. At one point, it was possible to say "Noel Coward *has written* many skillful comedies"; after a point it was appropriate to say "Noel Coward *wrote* many skillful comedies—when he is no longer the potential creator of skillful comedies, after his death. This state of affairs may be symbolized as

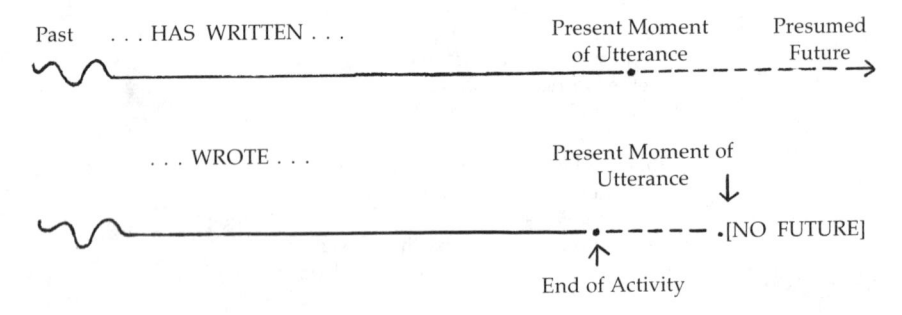

| Past | . . . HAS WRITTEN . . . | Present Moment of Utterance | Presumed Future |

∿‾‾‾‾‾‾‾‾‾‾‾‾‾‾‾‾‾‾‾‾‾‾‾‾‾‾•‐ ‐ ‐ ‐ ‐ ‐ ‐→

| | . . . WROTE . . . | Present Moment of Utterance ↓ | |

∿‾‾‾‾‾‾‾‾‾‾‾‾‾‾‾‾‾‾‾‾‾‾‾‾‾‾•‐ ‐ ‐ ‐ •[NO FUTURE]
　　　　　　　　　　　　　　　　↑
　　　　　　　　　　　　　End of Activity

Yeats's swan-statement may be symbolized as below:

```
YEATS:        Stanza (1)        Stanza (2)        Stanza (3)        type-time
                                                       ↓             of utterance
         •── ── ── ──|── ── ── ──|── •── ── ── ── →
                                                       ↑             FUTURE

                   [comparison of  [swan (presumably)  [swan has leaped
                   soul to swan]   begins to fly]      into the desolate
                                                       heaven]

READER:       Stanza (1)        Stanza (2)        Stanza (3)        token-time of
                                                                     utterance
```

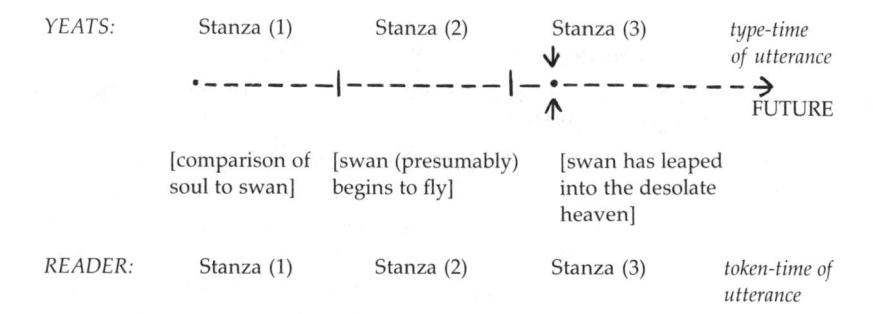

For Yeats-the-speaker, the swan began to fly during the speaker's meditation (stanza 2), and has been observed by the speaker to have flown (stanza 3).

However, since the utterance (the poem) has been preserved through time, when does the swan begin to fly for the reader also as it begins to fly for the speaker? Since preserved "type" becomes reader's "token," it can only be during Yeats's meditative intervening lines in the second stanza! In other words Yeats's conjectured swan has flown up out of the poem *while Yeats was thinking, and while the reader has been reading the intervening lines!* The present perfect tense ordinarily cannot endure "preservation" because of its link with the time of utterance in the "present." Yeats here has *preserved* his time of utterance for the reader, but fresh and active, not fossilized. The swan flies whenever the poem is read. Yeats's type-time and the readers' token-time are here fused, and Yeats reaches out from the past. A bold act!

There are many examples in Yeats of bold use of language. Readers of Yeats are always coming upon magical moments, when the readers feel "heaven blazing into the head" (P 294). These moments occur when Yeats boldly twists the rules of language—both of casual language and of literary language—to make a timeless emblem, a symbol. Adams has found many such moments and has provided a foundation for the reader or critic of Yeats.

Notes

1. The ampersand is a linguistic symbol which denotes ambiguous utterances, those which can be described structurally in at least two clearly different ways.
2. Although "tear" means something different in each interpretation, the main difference is syntactic. The semantic ambiguity in the sentences rests firmly upon syntax.

3. Adams here quotes Leo Spitzer, *Linguistics and Literary History: Essays in Stylistics* (Princeton: Princeton University Press, 1948) 28.
4. J. P. Guilford, "'Fluctuations of Attention' with Weak Visual Stimuli," *The American Journal of Psychology* 38 (1927): 534–83.
5. M. A. K. Halliday, "Notes on Transitivity and Theme in English," Part 2, *Journal of Linguistics* 3 (1967): 232, 236.
6. T. R. Henn, *The Lonely Tower: Studies in the Poetry of W. B. Yeats*. 2nd ed. (London: Methuen, 1965) 157.
7. Hans Reichenbach, *Elements of Symbolic Logic* (New York: Macmillan, 1947) 284–87. Bertrand Russell called these words "egocentric particulars," in *An Inquiry into Meaning and Truth* (New York: Norton, 1940), chap. 7, "Egocentric Particulars," 134–43.

   Reichenbach treats the present perfect tense in the same text: "in the simple past, the point of the event and the point of reference are simultaneous, and both are before the point of speech. . . . [In the present perfect tense] the past events are seen, not from a reference point situated also in the past, but from a point of reference which coincides with the point of speech" (289; see also 292–93).

Catherine Cavanaugh. *Love and Forgiveness in Yeats's Poetry.* Studies in Modern Literature, 57. Ann Arbor, Michigan: UMI Research Press, 1986. [xi] +174 pp.
Reviewed by *Thomas Parkinson*

Cavanaugh's book stirs one to meditation. Limiting herself to the love poems grants her both limits and a grand area of consideration. The poems of erotic and affectionate and sentimental and sexual relations with women comprise the majority of Yeats's lyrics. Cavanaugh has, however, restricted her subject to the poems that allow her to explore Yeats's conception (borrowed, he said, from Dryden's translation of a line from Lucretius) that "The tragedy of sexual intercourse is the perpetual virginity of the soul," or as he more lightly phrased it, "The marriage bed is the symbol of the solved antinomy, and were more than symbol could a man there lose and keep his identity, but he falls asleep." The first is from a conversation with John Sparrow recorded by Jeffares in *W. B. Yeats: Man and Poet* (London: Routledge & Kegan Paul, 1962, p. 267); the second in one of the many prefaces to *A Vision* B (52). The second tells us something about Yeats's sense of play that Cavanaugh doesn't consider important. What it recalls to me is Botticelli's Mars and Venus in the London National Gallery, which I first saw in the company of a chronic symbolizer who observed of it, "Ah yes, *discordia concors*." My tacit response was, but man falls asleep.

Cavanaugh's aim is to "delineate the evolution of Yeats's conviction about the virginity of the soul during intercourse and the ongoing process of the forgiveness of sins that this tragedy demands, and, paradoxically, redeems" (25). The limitation of the book comes from the concentrated solemnity of the treatment; the virtue comes from the suggestive and helpful insights that such concentration permits. Cavanaugh compels the reader to see familiar poems in a fresh perspective. Her arguments are especially useful for a poem like "Solomon and the Witch" but seem forced when applied to "Her Vision in the Wood." Cavanaugh gives Yeats a moral and philosophical position, but much of his work, even in his love poetry, has historical orientation, so that many of the poems lack their full dimension in Cavanaugh's analyses.

But this is no reason for being ungrateful for the book. It does bring forcibly to our attention that Yeats's world, especially the world of his love poetry, is imperfect, that failure and continual fresh starts are the mode of his poetic being. By its nature, love is condemned to incompleteness except in some remote world beyond worlds. Practically, the virginity of the soul is permanent. This confirms the lack of final resolution that most readers of Yeats have come to expect from his work; but the fact is that the variety of attack on recurring problems, the plain refusal to accept the destruction of his subject, shows the resilience and richness of his work.

I am less comfortable with Cavanaugh's stress on the "purgatorial" nature of Yeats's enterprise because I find it difficult to comprehend purgatory without purgation. Limbo might be the more appropriate term. "Forgiveness" in Yeats tends to be self-administered. He can at times forgive himself, and in Cavanaugh's primary example, "The Three Bushes" and the associated six lyrics, the priest can forgive. Cavanaugh leans heavily on "The Three Bushes" as a paradigm of sexual relations and I am not certain that it bears the weight. What she says about the set of poems is clear and enlightening, but it is difficult to place them with the Crazy Jane poems and others of unrepentant physicality, to say nothing of the poems of personal sentiment or those related to literary and historic designs.

Remorse and repentance are not the road to blessedness in Yeats's love lyrics. They must be cast out, so that the heart will not be impure. Except for some references to original sin, the concept of sin that one can expect from a Christian is not part of the drama of Yeats's most substantial body of love lyrics. Sexual life is not merely unredeemable; it justifies itself. Christian metaphors can be, as they are to Cavanaugh, useful to the critic, but Yeats was by no means a Christian.

This book compels its reader to reconsider preconceptions about Yeats and especially his love poems. It is thorough, careful, often stirring one to new perceptions. Cavanaugh makes no claim to exhausting her subject, but she has managed to bring this important body of work

222 Reviews

into an interesting and clear frame. She writes well; she presents her thought clearly; and her writing is free of the jargon of fad and fashion. For all that one must be grateful.

Paul de Man. *The Rhetoric of Romanticism.*
    New York: Columbia University Press, 1984. ix + 327 pp.
C. K. Stead. *Pound, Yeats, Eliot and the Modernist Movement.*
    New Brunswick: Rutgers University Press, 1986. vvi + 393 pp.
Reviewed by *George Bornstein*

It is illustrative of the centrality of romanticism to current criticism and theory that two such different books using such different methods can still have so much in common. Both cast wide nets in viewing modern poetry as a postromantic phenomenon growing out of (and in some ways outgrowing) nineteenth-century origins. Both see French Symbolism as a crucial link between European romanticism and modern poetry in English, with Yeats as a prime example. To be sure, their approaches differ markedly. De Man favors a rhetorical analysis which stresses images and tropes and confesses an inability to make the individual essays cohere into a patterned history, while Stead pays more attention to versecraft and argues systematically (if tendentiously) for a steadily increasing emphasis on language as language. Yet they both place their discussions firmly within postromantic frameworks. Unfortunately, neither book matches the high level of previous work by its author, and neither has much new or helpful to say about Yeats.

De Man's book reprints essays originally written 1956–1983. Their historical span reaches from Rousseau through Holderlin, Wordsworth, Shelley, Kleist, and on to Yeats. The two sections on Yeats belong to the oldest and weakest part of the book. The short comparison of "Symbolic Landscape in Wordsworth and Yeats" (published 1962) illustrates both the strengths and weaknesses of the longer "Image and Emblem in Yeats." De Man begins insightfully enough by contrasting the primacy of natural imagery in a Wordsworthian sonnet to the more symbolic use of nature in Yeats's "Coole Park and Ballylee, 1931." But de Man's awareness of the Neoplatonic aspect of Yeats's imagery quickly leads him into a bizarre misinterpretation of the poem as a critique of "his benefactor and her class" for having "made the mistake of imagining that its world of marriages, houses, and 'generations' was 'more dear than life'" (140–41). The problem here is less de Man's vigorous riding of a hobby horse than his pervasive deafness to tone, which both removes one source of poetic meaning from his analysis and robs him of one check on his own ingenuity.

That problem looms larger in the hundred-page excerpt from de Man's 1960 Harvard dissertation reprinted here as "Image and Emblem in Yeats." Columbia University Press has done a disservice to the memory of a great scholar by allowing this long section to appear unrevised and poorly edited, even while highlighting it in a blurb on the back cover as "long-fabled." Again, de Man starts from a distinction in kind of imagery: he uses "images" to designate natural figures that have a mimetic or literal sense as "natural objects" and follows one of Yeats's usages of "emblems" to mean figures that "are taken from the literary tradition and receive their meaning from traditional or personal, but not natural associations" (164–65). De Man then uses that antinomy to provide both an account of Yeats's changing style and a reading of some major poems. It works well enough on style (in de Man's special and limited sense of imagery), though the resultant account seems dated in its ignorance of—to pick only a few examples—Thomas Parkinson's second book on Yeats's development, Edward Engelberg's account of his aesthetics, or Allen Grossman's examination of *The Wind Among the Reeds,* all of which appeared as long ago as the 1960s, and which one might have expected de Man to read and absorb before republishing his dissertation.

The bizarre readings of poems adumbrated by the essay on Yeats and Wordsworth run riot in the longer section. For example, de Man nicely discriminates the emblematic nature of the tree in "Vacillation" ("A tree there is that from its topmost bough / Is half all glittering flame and half all green") but then confuses everything by asserting that "The same tree appears in the 'chestnut tree' of 'Among School Children,' in which the leaf corresponds to the green foliage, the blossom to the fire, and the bole to Attis' image" (201). But the tree at the end of "Among School Children" is an image of Unity of Being whose parts comprise a whole and merge into each other rather than bifurcate in the manner of the tree in "Vacillation." Similarly, for de Man Cuchulain's killing of his son in *On Baile's Strand* represents Yeats's killing of his own allegiance to emblems rather than to natural imagery; the "true meaning" (194) of "Adam's Curse" is that Maud is a divine emblem but her sister a natural image; and the description of the rag and bone shop of the heart in "The Circus Animals' Desertion" shows only the "bitterness" Yeats harbored toward his emblems. Such misreadings seem possible only to a critic who neglects tone as well as every other poetic device except imagery. Indeed, it would make no difference to de Man's style of criticism if Yeats's lyrics appeared in prose paragraphs rather than stanzas, or even if they were printed serially on ticker tape. He depends upon a rigorously semantic approach to linguistic images with little check from either poetic technique or the context of individual volumes.

Few scholars will turn to de Man for factual material, which is just as well. Some of his errors simply repeat now-outmoded misinformation, as when he writes that Iseult Gonne was Maud's niece or misdates the start of the Rhymers' Club as 1891. Others appear to be de Man's own invention, as in the claim that Yeats grew up "in the peripheral, eccentric atmosphere of Dublin and the J. E. Yeats family" (154). The publisher at least might have hired a competent indexer instead of one who would dutifuly repeat that mistake as "Yeats, J. E., 154" (326). This sort of disservice reaches its apotheosis in the inclusion of an annotated "Bibliography for Essay 8" at the end of the volume. It is hard to see any justification for inclusion in a book published in 1984 of such an out-of-date guide to Yeats's texts as de Man was able to assemble in the late 1950s. Due to the huge amount of Yeats textual work in the ensuing quarter-century, nearly every annotation is now wrong, sometimes ludicrously so. Thus, for example, after referring students to the unreliable first edition of *VP,* the bibliography announces that "no variorum edition of the plays is in existence" (one was first published twenty years ago). And when de Man directs students to then recondite or inaccessible periodicals for fugitive essays by Yeats, one would expect Columbia University Press to remember that such materials are much more readily available in the two-volume *Uncollected Prose by W. B. Yeats* which the Press itself published. *Blindness and Insight* and *Allegories of Reading* form far truer monuments to the memory of Paul de Man than this posthumous collection.

The New Zealand poet and critic C. K. Stead is best known in scholarly circles for his fine compressed study *The New Poetic: Yeats to Eliot* (1964). There Stead argued forcefully for a view of modernism as an extension of romanticism. His brilliant exposition of Eliot's poetry as divided against itself helped engender the contemporary, revisionist view of Eliot held by critics like Bernard Bergonzi, David Spurr, Ronald Bush, and myself, while his chapter on Yeats praised the poet's ability to mediate between public and private realms and to absorb a political event like the Easter Rising into his poetry. The new book revises the earlier one by elevating Pound and demoting Yeats in praise of a poetry of open forms which Stead sees dominating poetry in English since the 1960s. In this view, "W. B. Yeats begins as a Pre-Raphaelite, comes to think of himself as a Symbolist, and finally sheds that to make himself 'modern'; but he is never a 'Modernist', if by 'Modernism' we mean the revolution in English poetry represented by the work of Eliot and Pound" (10). So far, so good. But the argument quickly degenerates into a privileging of Pound and the early Eliot as standards of judgment to continually belabor and belittle Yeats for having written a different kind of poetry.

Stead's favorite tactic is to confuse Yeats the man with Yeats the poet, as though his subject had never written that although "A poet writes always of his personal life . . . there is always a phantasmagoria . . . he is never the bundle of accident and incoherence that sits down to breakfast" (E&I 509). For example, Stead writes of "Friends" (in which Yeats never mentions Maud Gonne by name): "Did Yeats really wake every morning and think with such passion of Maud? . . . Did he literally 'shake from head to foot'? . . . And if Yeats did indeed 'shake from head to foot' did, finally, the 'sweetness' which produced this agitation flow 'up from [his] heart's root'? Of course it did not. . . . Yeats has flashed his poet's licence and we are not supposed to ask questions" (28–29). This kind of bizarre literalism and biographical reductiveness occurs often in Stead's volume, though never in relation to Pound or the early Eliot (whom he praises) but only in regard to Yeats (whom he deprecates). In other places Stead seems to depend chiefly on mocking rhetoric, as in the attack on "In Memory of Major Robert Gregory." There Stead dismisses "the Yeats mythology machine," asks "Does Yeats know what he means by this 'measureless consumption'," and refers to "the point made (whatever it is)" (78–81). Not many readers will be persuaded by such tactics.

At a deeper level Stead's animus condemns Yeats's remaking of traditional lyric forms rather than embracing of "open form." His Yeats emerges as a recalcitrant pupil of the early Pound who never got the whole gist of Pound's teachings. According to Stead, Yeats "must plan everything, he over-plans, he thinks his poems out as statements and as rhetorical structures, until there is no room for form to discover and to create meaning" (82). This view derives from a misunderstanding of Yeats's practice of sometimes making prose drafts of his poems. The poetry Stead values "is not a product of conscious workmanship of the kind Yeats, for example, put in when, in a poem like 'Sailing to Byzantium' or 'Leda and the Swan', he laboured an idea through many drafts from a prose statement up into an arrangement of images, lines and rhymes" (336). Yet if all the textual and critical work based on Yeats's manuscript drafts has taught us anything, it is that at some point Yeats's labor always involves unforeseen leaps of imagination and genius far beyond the plodding work Stead imputes. In his recent *Yeats at Songs and Choruses* David Clark makes the point abundantly clear. Indeed, simply comparing the prose drafts and final versions of the two poems Stead cites, "Sailing to Byzantium" and "Leda and the Swan," at once reveals the folly of his account.

The slipshod method of the attack on Yeats does not carry over into the sections on Pound or the early Eliot (Stead does invoke it to attack *Four Quartets* as part of his exaltation of his favorite text, *The Pisan Cantos*). There, instead, the author brushes aside the nasty use of the Jew in "Gerontion" in favor of tonal analysis of sound patterns; at once deplores and yet prefers Pound's anti-semitism to the later Eliot's because of its "Blakean" energy (280); and judges the derisive term "Chink" as "pure . . . poetry" (240). Inconsistency of citation mirrors that of method. Stead misspells Richard Ellmann's name once (335) and that of John Ashbery twice (322, 327), and commits one of the best howlers in all Yeatsian criticism when he refers to a character called "Cathleen in Houlihan" (138). Such literary "history" as this is tendentious indeed. When Stead writes that a previous critic "is using the poem to serve the purposes of his history" (78), he provides a succinct summary of his own indulgent enterprise.

Joseph M. Hassett. *Yeats and the Poetics of Hate.*
   Dublin and New York: Gill and Macmillan and St. Martin's Press, 1986. ix + 189 pp.
   Reviewed by *Edward Engelberg*

There was much for W. B. Yeats to hate: parochialism (Catholic and Protestant), the "greasy till" associated with a boorish middle class, the "rabble of democracy" as Yeats perceived it for a time, nationalists who tried to use his name and art for propaganda, women who spurned him, realism in art, the "scientific spirit" of Huxley et al. who belittled the value of beauty. And much more. Still, while his poetry and prose, memoirs and correspondence are liberally occupied with the words *hate* or *hatred*, it would be difficult to sustain a thesis that Yeats's poetry is made of hatred (there are, of course, some few poems that are), or that like, say, Pound or even Eliot, Yeats uses hatred as a device fixed on isolating hate-objects. That is where the difficulty of this interesting volume lies, for it appears (to me at least) that the author was seduced by *words* of hate to conclude that Yeats had fashioned a "poetic" of hate as a means of sustaining the "creative process" and balancing the antinomy of love.

Show me a creative genius and more often than not you will show me someone who has fits of hatred: Dante, Milton, Swift, Pope, Goethe; Flaubert, Dostoevsky, Rimbaud, Baudelaire; Strindberg; Celine, D. H. Lawrence, Pound, Wyndham Lewis, V. Woolf. All of them have left vivid accounts of their hate and its objects. Why single out Yeats? Frankly for good reason. There can be no denying that Yeats used hate, that the word itself was not harmlessly inserted but deliberatively placed. So Hassett's volume should surprise no one who is familiar with Yeats. Someone was bound to question those references to hate and ask, "Why?" Various forms of hate or hatred occur in the concordance to the poetry some fifty times; but various forms of love occur nearly six hundred times. This does not invalidate the claim that for Yeats (as for many others) the conflict between love and hate overarches not merely the work, but—as Hassett believes is the case in Yeats—the "creative process." The obvious imbalance between the use of love and hate does, however, indicate more than the expected conventional use of "love" in poetry. There is some evidence from the imbalance itself that Yeats, while he certainly hated, was eager to overcome—not merely to balance—hatred with love. Of course, there is more to Hassett's conclusions: "Hate is Yeats's passion of preference" (vii); Yeats has a "preoccupation with hate" (vii), a poetics "based . . . heavily on [hate]" which the author considers a "dangerous . . . emotion" (ix). Despite this tilt toward hate, Hassett acknowledges throughout this study that (via Nietzsche, Jung and others) hatred served Yeats as part of the ubiquitous "antinomies," the war (in this case between love and hate) that strove toward reconciliation in the elusive Unity of Being. Since Swift and Blake were great haters, and since Yeats was deeply touched by both, they serve as original sources for Yeats's own hatred. However, what is most difficult to sort out in such an analysis is to what extent this "dangerous emotion" served, or served over and bound Yeats. Here this study becomes uncertain of itself. For unlike some of the great haters Yeats is seldom overcome by hatred; he manipulates it in doses to serve his purpose.

There was a thread that connected the various objects of Yeats's hatred: Lockean empiricism and realistic art had common denominators, and one wishes that linkages and differences were more clearly posited. What is highlighted, and in a tone of apologia, is Yeats's supernaturalism. I do not think that Yeats's beliefs in the "spiritual world" or his pursuit of "magic" are likely to "embarrass" anyone today, nor need we be cautioned any longer not to consign these numerous concerns to the "periphery of [Yeats's] life" (6). It remains fair, however, to trace Yeats's sojourn in the "spiritual" and to see how much of it gave him "metaphors" for his work, as he said of the voices or "instructors" that helped him write *A Vision*. Very early in his life he was attracted to Madame Blavatsky and The Order of the Golden Dawn, but he soon rejected the former as a partial fake and was dismissed from the latter. He fought with T. Sturge Moore about Ruskin's celebrated cat, and all his life maintained that "truth" cannot be "known," only embodied (a point Hassett makes on several occasions). In addition Yeats had interest in the Kabbalah and the Hermetics, in Bishop Berkeley and Kant—even for a time in ritual Catholicism. In the end he seemed always to return to his own sense of realities, and the older he got the less willing he was to be seduced or lured into any one else's supernatural world. Hassett invites us to survey Yeats's hatred as a function of his various "systems," and while this is perfectly true, there are other and more complex reasons which are seemingly omitted or minimized: personal events, political and artistic quarrels, and sometimes emotional strain.

One chapter is, indeed, devoted to Yeats's Oedipal problems, the hatred of his father. While sufficient evidence is produced that Yeats had fundamental disagreements with John Butler Yeats, especially with his aesthetic posture, the case remained relatively open and unrepressed. Once he reached manhood, Yeats seldom hesitated to stand up to his father and engage him as equal—even as superior; he may have suffered from some "narcissistic rage" (32), but need we invoke in addition to Nietzsche, Freud, and Jung E. Rhode, Kohut, Erickson, and Anthony Storr? I suppose I am suggesting that personal and impersonal hate are different, and sometimes I would have wished that Hassett had more clearly separated them. Instead the Blakean hatred of Lockean empiricism is treated not very differently from Yeats's rage against his father, which despite Yeats's statements to the contrary, were caused I suspect more by personal than artistic differences.

Hassett is best when he deals with a single idea—for example, the hatred and its resolution in *Per Amica Silentiae Lunae:* "Ambivalence temporarily overcome by hate: this is the road to creativity" (47). Hatred, he argues, was for Yeats a kind of purgative, something that "clears the soul" (53) and is the "wellspring of creative activity" (54). Yeats did model his hatred on Blake's frenzy and Swift's misanthropy, but there is no evidence in life or work that he ever achieved (or wanted to) their obsessive-destructive states. Yeats was a great plunderer of others, an uncanny assimilator (like Goethe), who made certain that his selective 'borrowing' from others never overpowered his own, always developing, Self.

Inevitably there are occasions in this study when the author is pulled further afield from the thesis of "hate" than perhaps intended. Hence there might be some value in isolating one chapter which keeps especially close to the subject of hate and also raises some questions. One such chapter focuses steady attention on one of Yeats's most personal poems, "A Prayer for My Daughter." Yeats, mindful of how much grief Maud Gonne has caused him, delivers an exhortation standing by his infant daughter's crib: "An intellectual hatred is the worst," she must avoid it at all costs. Hassett, seeing Yeats as a "vocal champion of hatred" (a disputable phrase) finds "more than a little irony" in this exhortation *against* hate, a "surprising indictment of hate" (73). It should surprise no one. True, marriage and children mellowed Yeats, encouraged changes in his poetry, so that Yeats schematized more, coming to see "hate as the product of a fragmentation of primal emotion occasioned by the fall" (73). But I also believe that the "sacred task of reintegrating love and hate" (73) began long before Yeats was cast into the role of husband and father. The chapter also makes much of Yeats's attacks on "abstraction" and credits "A Prayer for My Daughter" as being a kind of antidote: "By focusing on the concrete sleeping child as he paced in the 'excited reverie' of 'A Prayer for My Daughter,' Yeats managed to resolve the tension into a hope for personal salvation grounded in courtesy, the shaping power of the free mind to banish abstract hatred" (86). This is a sensible reading except that I puzzle about the distinction between such resolution and future hatred. "A Prayer for My Daughter" dates from 1919. Yeats did not stop expressing hatred, and in some late poems, in *On the Boiler*, in the correspondence, and in the Old Man's Prologue to *The Death of Cuchulain* there are expressions of a more spiteful hatred, more like Baudelaire's spleen. Hassett does not ignore these continuing occurrences of hate, but he makes little effort to distinguish them. He defends Yeats from the suggestion that he exulted in bloodletting, despite the more frequent appearances of blood imagery in poems like "The Second Coming," "The Gyres," and "Two Songs from A Play," but perhaps the defense would be unnecessary had he paid more attention to the equally increasing counterbalance of love imagery—even those of the Crazy Jane poems, which are less angry than Hassett allows. There might also have been more said about Yeats's political "hatred."

Yeats was not a poet of hate, and to join Yeats to a "poetics of hate" does not make for the best title, for it suggests far more than the use of hate to power the "creative process." It is curious that of all the generous quotations Hassett offers he omits this from the 1929 "A Dialogue of Self and Soul" (though he offers two pages of analysis of the poem):

> When such as I cast out remorse
> So great a sweetness flows into the breast
> We must laugh and we must sing,
> We are blest by everything,
> Every thing we look upon is blest.
>
> [P 234–36]

Finally to say that " . . . Yeats's philosophy installs hatred of the historical process as part of the endless struggle between love and its opposite" (133) is to tilt in a questionable direction. It is perfectly true that Yeats foresaw, in an overdetermined way, the end of a "cycle" by the year 2000; and the violence that precedes and accompanies annunciatory moments was already in his "vision." But there is ample evidence that in poems such as "A Prayer for My Daughter," "Among School Children," the Byzantium poems, "Lapis Lazuli" and others Yeats strove mightily to keep hatred in check with love—all forms of it. History at moments of crisis was to be endured; and if Yeats showed any clear feeling it was, along with rage, a fear of being dispossessed of wife, children, home, country. Most of the upheavals of history were indeed bloody; but while inevitable, the cataclysm was not welcomed but dreaded. True, he also felt a need to "intensify his hatred" as late as 1936 (134), and out of such self-conscious posturing emerged some of his angry poems, balanced nevertheless by their opposites. "Ambivalence *temporarily* overcome by hate" (47; italics mine). Hassett uses the right word—"temporarily"—but it still suggets that only hate was able to feed the creative process. Such a view of Yeats's work may not withstand even a cursory reading.

There are a number of errors by the printer: "Paonting" for painting (25), "dying int" and "described i" for dying into and described in (69), "Ellman" for Ellmann (71), "*Words Upon the Window Pane*" for *The Words Upon the Window-Pane* (81 and Index), and "Mac Niece" for MacNeice (150). In the index, entries for "E" follow rather than precede entries for "F."

John Kelly and Eric Domville, eds. *The Collected Letters of W. B. Yeats: Volume 1, 1865–1895.*
Oxford: Clarendon Press, 1986. xlii + 548 pp.
Reviewed by *Elizabeth Bergmann Loizeaux*

This first in the projected twelve-volume *Collected Letters of W. B. Yeats* is superb. Here we have the first thirty years of Yeats's life revealed in letters reprinted with all the delightful quirks of the poet's spelling and punctuation. More than 170—nearly half—are published for the first time.

There are no startling revelations here, nor any surprising finds. Most of the correspondence with Maud Gonne disappeared in raids on her house during the Irish Civil War. Irrecoverably lost, too, are letters to T. W. Rolleston, MacGregor Mathers, Annie Horniman, Lionel Johnson and others (xlii). But the new letters that the editors' exhaustive search has turned up enrich and deepen the portrait of the young poet that Allan Wade's *The Letters of W. B. Yeats* (1954) and Roger McHugh's *W. B. Yeats: Letters to Katharine Tynan* (1953) have made familiar. We are amazed anew by the number of pots Yeats had on the stove. In June 1894—to choose a month at random—the letters show him busy sending John O'Leary copies of *The Land of Heart's Desire* and *The Second Book of the Rhymers' Club;* orchestrating a favorable "reception" for A. E.'s *Homeward, Songs by the Way;* planning to "clear off" his "sheer impecuniosity" (a frequent problem) by finishing up an "Irish Anthology" (*A Book of Irish Verse*); writing a condemning article that would "only make patent the latent convictions of all the people here" concerning the "absurd" New Irish Library series of books; attending a Shaw play with his friend Dora Sigerson and her houseguest Miss Piatt; trying to coax Moina Mathers into telling Constance Gore-Booth's and Althea Gyles's fortunes (she wouldn't unless they were "at a great crisis"); and thanking Thomas Hutchinson, headmaster of a school in Northumberland, for the "pleasant verses" sent the poet on his 29th birthday (390–93). Yeats obviously delighted in all this activity. He appears often exhausted, but talkative, witty, happily combative. He emerges above all as human, not least so when he cannot manage to keep his eye on everything. Thus we get the incident of the mysterious ten shillings paid by no-one-knows-whom for two copies of *The Wanderings of Oisin* (125) or the frequent "P.S.": "I wrote enclosed letter some days ago and forgot to post it" (148).

The new letters are especially helpful in filling out details of Yeats's relationships with Douglas Hyde and T. Fisher Unwin. The more than ten new letters to Hyde—in 1888 and 1889—poignantly reveal Yeats's hopeful enthusiasm for Hyde's collection of Irish tales and his deep misunderstanding of Hyde's purposes: "I hear from O'Leary that your only reason for not printing with your long expected folklore collection, an English translation, is a question of expense. I have good reason to believe that Nutt, the publisher would be delighted to print at his expense a translation" (182). Yeats's prodding encouraged Hyde's 1890 English-language *Beside the Fire,* but this success must have made all the keener the inevitable disappointment as his hoped-for ally's commitment to a Gaelic-speaking Ireland became plain. These letters also contain one of the most comic interludes in the volume: Yeats writes from London asking Hyde to buy off an "old peasent" a suit of Irish clothes to be sent to the painter Joseph Nash who needs them as models for his illustration of John Todhunter's story "Tom Connolly and the Banshee." The letter specifies in handwriting not Yeats's but possibly Nash's, "The older the better" (112–13). When they are delivered two months later by a bemused postman, Nash pronounces the caubeen, trousers and stockings "perfection," but, Yeats reports back to Hyde, the coat is "almost to[o] 'domesticated'" (143).

In his dealings with his publisher T. Fisher Unwin, perhaps more than anywhere else in these letters, we see the young poet assuming the firmness and conviction that were to mark his later handling of the Abbey Theater's practical affairs. On 11 October 1894, Yeats wrote Unwin about what was to become *Poems* (1895):

> If you care to take the volume, I would therefore ask first that it be of a certain height & breadth, second that it be printed by either Clarke or Constable, third that I be consulted about an artist to do the title page—good "decorative" men are fairly plentiful just now & fairly cheap—I have a liking for one or two. As to the contents—It should contain a long poem "The Wanderings of Oisin" "The Countess Kathleen" (in which the copyright period of two years mentioned in agreement has just expired) & "The Land of Hearts Desire" (The copyright period on which expires next spring) & the best lyrics from the "Oisin" volume as well as from "The Countess Kathleen" one. And last I would ask you for a royalty from the first copy & that the agreement should be for a term of years as before. [402]

This is the voice of a poet up on his copyrights and confident enough to bargain over the appearance of his book and the financial settlement. The letter also reveals Yeats's current concerns. The book must not only contain his best works, but be beautiful in the William Morris tradition. Yeats requested "that the designer be asked to make the book as much a work of art as he can," and—as always, distancing himself from easy, sentimental Irishness—commanded that the cover "be not green & have no shamrocks" (434). He demanded control even over the choice of paper "(not necessarily handmade)"—a relief, undoubtedly, to Unwin—and specified the artist "Charles Shannon—of 'Rickets & Shannon' fame" (403, 434), although H. Granville Fell, another initial favorite with Yeats, designed the book in the end. Lack of funds in the family household certainly urged on Yeats the necessity for wrangling over financial terms. He is quite bold and specific in rejecting Unwin's initial offer and proposing instead

> (1) That the book be yours *for 4 years* & then return to me.
> (2) that my royalty for this period be *12½% from the first copy* insted [sic] of 10% for the first 500 as you suggest & 12½% for the next 1000 & so on.

Emboldened perhaps by his own self-assurance, he goes on to request twelve, then—as this edition of the letters allows us to see by enclosing revised material in angle brackets—crosses the number out and writes more modestly "six free copies" (403).

The new letters are also valuable for what they add to the body of Yeats's comment on his own work and aims. They expose once more the painful complexities of his life and art. From Paris—where he visited Maud Gonne, then (unknown to him) pregnant with Iseult—Yeats wrote to D. J. O'Donoghue about a bit of enclosed verse: "The wind is the vague idealisms & impossible hopes which blow in upon us to the ruin of near & common & substantial ambitions" (380). The poem became the fairy's song in *The Land of Heart's Desire*. Desolation of another but related sort surfaces in the self-criticism that, as so often, grew naturally from his thinking about the work of other writers. In October 1894 he wrote Richard LeGallienne about that author's book *The Religion of Literary Man* (1893): "The greater weight of subject helped you there I think to escape some [of] that over abundance which makes your river at times a little over spread the bank just as mind in its too great meagreness runs half dry too often & shows the rocks & half ⟨dead tree or⟩ buried ⟨tree trunks debris⟩ wreckage at the bottom" (400–401).

While Yeats holds center stage in this volume, the editors John Kelly and Eric Domville do a brilliant job supporting him. Were there no new letters, the deftly choreographed notes alone would make this book required reading for all interested in Yeats. The editors not only identify the often obscure people, places, circumstances and allusions of the letters, but vividly recreate the broader context with quotations from contemporary books and articles and from diaries and correspondence, frequently unpublished before. Snips from Yeats family journals and responses to Yeats's letters appear often, as do relevant passages from *Autobiographies* and *Memoirs*. The wit and verve of the editors' prose add to the cumulative effect of the notes: that here, more than in any of the Yeats biographies, one comes to know the characters, major and minor, in Yeats's life. It is enjoyable simply to dip in and discover, for example, Yeats's friend the "'beautiful Edmund Russell,'" a "dandy" who taught himself grace by following the nine laws of gesture set out by François Delsarte (1811–71); or to be led through the complex tangle of circumstance and motive surrounding T. W. Rolleston and Gavin Duffy's successful bid to preempt Yeats's plan for the New Irish Library. There is much impressive detective work here. When Yeats comments on the 1895 threat of war between Great Britain and the United States, "what a dusk of the nations it would be!", the editors can observe, "WBY seems to have been reading the recently published English edition of Max Nordau's *Degeneration* (2): 'In our days there have arisen in more highly-developed minds vague qualms of a Dusk of the Nations . . .'" (477).

Although the notes are extensive, Kelly and Domville have an unerring sense of what and how much a reader wants. Instead of overburdening us with information at the first mention of an annotated item, they judiciously parcel it out, giving us just what we need to understand and set a particular letter in context. A system of cross references allows the forgetful or curious reader to check back or skip forward to other related annotations. The editors supplement the detailed notes with a "Biographical and Historical Appendix" which supplies longer and more coherent accounts of the most significant people, institutions and events. The appendix, along with the introduction and a chronology of Yeats's life, offer a useful larger vista.

Although controversial, the editorial policy of reproducing Yeats's quirky spelling and punctuation, instead of silently correcting them as earlier editions of the letters have, allows the young Yeats his humanity. One cannot understand how indisputably right John Todhunter was when he said, as the job-hunting poet reported, "my bad writing and worse spelling will be much against me" (56), unless one has read, for example, Yeats's discussion of "Matthew Arnolds" "'the Scholour Gipsey'" (181). What we see here is a mind so intensely possessed of ideas and forgetful of convention that for years he addressed letters to Richard "Le Galleone" and George "Russel," who, fortunately, don't seem to have minded.

The peculiarities of spelling and punctuation further remind us of the extent to which Yeats heard what he wrote. As he explained to Robert Bridges in 1915, "I write my work so completely for the ear that I feel helpless when I have to measure pauses by stops and commas" (L 598). In addition to phonetically placed or missing punctuation, "right" nicely becomes "write," "there" "their," and we find "reccomended" (107), "renaisance" (303), "rehersals" (377) and "tecnical sence" (215). These infelicities cause no problems for the reader—although our way has perhaps been helped by the editors' questionable and inconsistent policy of silently adding periods where Yeats clearly forgot them. Nor will scholars and other writers of more conventional prose find any real difficulties using this edition. Like readers of Keats's standard letters, students of Yeats will come to expect the oddities in passages quoted from the letters. What is gained in the sense of immediacy and personality outweighs the disadvantages.

The editors' (or maybe it's the press's) thoroughness falters only in the tedious and difficult job of indexing. Because of the nature of this work, most who use it will, after an initial reading, approach it through the index which provides the only way of easily recovering discussions in notes and letters of a particular topic. For this reason, the index should be complete. The entry for the *Scots Observer*, for example, should include the note on page 123 about Yeats's anonymous review of D. R. McAnally's *Irish Wonders* published there. Such omissions in no way diminish the importance of the volume; they simply make it a bit more difficult to use.

Kelly and Domville's attentive regard for both the individual and particular nature of the letters and the larger concerns and circumstances is partly motivated by convictions about Yeats's relation to the world in which he lived. Quoting T. S. Eliot's view of Yeats as "'one of those few whose history is the history of their own time, who are a part of the consciousness of an age which cannot be understood without them,'" they argue that Yeats's "letters mediate the area between the poetry and the period; they register his reaction both to passing historical events and to the deeper movements of thought that gradually shape and reshape the consciousness of an epoch" (xxxvii). In this volume that conviction is forcefully borne out, especially in the letters that show Yeats struggling with the proper relationship among art, politics and nationalism and in those, more fantastic, that reveal his search for another world whose presence he could know. Both preoccupations echo not only through those like Douglas Hyde and MacGregor Mathers who appear in this volume, but through others who shaped the modern sensibility—Joyce and Eliot among them. The future volumes of letters—increasingly more of them new—hold the promise of showing us what happened as Yeats's first efforts for Irish literature matured into a full-fledged revival and his early ideas about poetic experimentation became, in the hands of others, Modernism.

Mary Lou Kohfeldt. *Lady Gregory: The Woman behind the Irish Renaissance.*
   New York: Atheneum, 1985. xiii +366 pp.
   Reviewed by *James F. Carens*

In 1961, when she published *Lady Gregory: A Literary Portrait* (London: Macmillan), Elizabeth Coxhead explained that her book did "not pretend to be the documented biography that must be written one day, when all the materials are available. That," Coxhead added, "is work for a scholar, preferably an Irish scholar, who can set . . . [Lady Gregory] in the whole complicated perspective of the Irish literary revival (vi). Appearing approximately a quarter of a century after those words were written, Mary Lou Kohfeldt's *Lady Gregory: The Woman behind the Irish Renaissance* (which does draw upon all the available material) reveals how much more is demanded of Lady Gregory's biographer than Elizabeth Coxhead imagined. For Lady Gregory's biographer, Irishness is not really a desideratum, though willingness both to sympathize with and view objectively the Irish literary movement that inspired her is certainly a necessity. Neither scholarship alone nor scholarly familiarity with the history of the revival can suffice for a Gregory biographer. More than a little psychological subtlety in the interpretation of character and relationships, a degree of political and cultural sophistication, some capacity for understanding the tragic crises of early modern Ireland, a certain analytic sensibility, a distinct element of critical tact in the interpretation and evaluation of literary works: all of these, a life of Lady Gregory surely demands of the biographer. Sad to say, Ms. Kohfeldt's book manifests these qualities so minimally that it demeans Lady Gregory—a great woman if not a great dramatist—and does not illuminate the real qualities of her work.

Certainly the raw material of Augusta Gregory's life has an inherent interest merely as social history, and Kohfeldt is at her best on this level. The twelfth child of sixteen, Isabella Augusta Persse was born into an Ascendancy family of West of Ireland landowners, descended patrilinearly from a late seventeenth-century Church of Ireland clergyman. But, as Kohfeldt notes, Augusta Persse also descended from almost every ethnic strand in Ireland's history, including the native Irish O'Gradys. (Both the translator and folklorist Standish Hayes O'Grady and the historian Standish James O'Grady were her cousins.) It was in her twenty-eighth year and in his sixty-third that the neighboring widower Sir William Gregory, former member of Parliament and, more recently, Governor of Ceylon, married her and took her away from her family estate, Roxborough, to his own estate, Coole Park. The house there, a stark Georgian pile considered unlovely in its exterior design by most, nevertheless reflected in its interior Sir William's cultivation and that of his forbears. Yeats praised its atmosphere: "Beloved books that famous hands have bound, / Old marble heads, old pictures everywhere; / Great rooms where travelled men and children found / Content or joy . . ." (242). In taking Augusta Persse from a life of service to and dependency on her family—at her father's death she learned that she would share £ 10,000 with eleven of her siblings—Sir William took her into a far wider world of social distinction and intellectual stimulation. Following the marriage, there were extended stays in England and Continental travels. Augusta was presented at Court and introduced to fashionable hostesses; she came to know a vast number of the most distinguished and gifted men of the age, among them such literary figures as Tennyson, Browning, and Henry James. Coole, however, which she came to love more than Roxborough, remained at the center of her emotional being.

Different as was the atmosphere at Coole from that at Roxborough, where her mother's severe Protestantism co-existed with the profligacy of the Persse men, both estates were the diminished survivals of a feudal social order that had destroyed itself through economic and political folly, not to mention personal excess. Whatever else she may or may not do, Kohfeldt gives us a dreary record of the drunken stewardship of the Persse men. Just as painful is her account of Lady

Gregory's decades of struggle to preserve Coole, following the death of Sir William, who, despite his intellectual distinction and personal probity, had further encumbered the estate with debt. Roxborough, abandoned during the Civil War to the Republican forces, was burned by a vengeful peasantry; Coole, though preserved from harm during the Troubles, was demolished by a scarcely prescient government bureau several years after Lady Gregory's death. In truth, however, the destruction of both houses had been begun by their owners several generations earlier.

When Lady Gregory undertook to involve herself in the activities of the young poet W. B. Yeats, she was, despite her allegiance to Coole and its values, casting her lot with new and revolutionary forces in the land. Only the most rigid ideologue could regard her decision as an expedient one. In a curious and rather confused passage about Lady Gregory's new friend, Mary Lou Kohfeldt makes what seems the shadow of the kind of attack on Yeats that one expects of more ideological writers. She strangely writes of Yeats (whose Anglo-Irish forbears were middle class and whose artist father had liberated him from bourgeois values) that he "had already fallen so far out of his class that his activity was not an effort to reach beyond it but eventually came to look like an effort to clamber back into its narrowness and arrogant stability" (104). Anything but consistent in the application of a theory or a metaphor, in the same context Kohfeldt tells us that the fallen-out-of-his-class Yeats had been "cut off from his roots by his father" and that his "only real identity was with himself as a poet." (When she also confides to us that Yeats "was also deep into astrology and mysticism," we may, once recovered from the tasteless sixties idiom and the midleading description of Yeats's esoteric interests, wonder how, from such deeps, Yeats could attempt to clamber back into the bourgeoisie—which Kohfeldt may be confusing with the aristocracy.) Although she once observes of Lady Gregory's plays that they were "designed to allow her to let off steam and preserve the status quo" (213), Kohfeldt does not otherwise seem tempted to apply to Lady Gregory the vaguely determinist economic notions she fleetingly applies to Yeats. Her Lady Gregory is a Cinderella figure, the least esteemed of Mrs. Persse's daughters, a plain and bookish girl headed towards spinsterhood, who, rescued by the aged prince, becomes the most distinguished member of her family. This way of seeing Lady Gregory is surely in accord with the facts. However, the psychological notion that underlies the Kohfeldt portrait is a reductive one: motivated throughout her life by a Protestant conscience—"clouds of witnesses" constantly judging her—Augusta Gregory was impelled by the need to serve others, yet she compensated for parental indifference by making herself the center of attention, whether in a game of charades or in one of the plays she wrote for the Abbey Theatre.

The notion, scarcely startling, of art as a compensation for personal frustrations, is, if simplistic, tenable. But as it is crudely applied in this book, Lady Gregory turns into a kind of monster, both grossly egoistic and hypocritical: "What did she want? What the 'little-welcomed girl' at Roxborough had learned to want without daring to think it: to be lifted above the brothers and sisters. Under cover of service, she aimed for personal glory, and she added another layer to her emotional camouflage, the primary layer of which was her widow's black, worn when she was anything but mourning" (107). Not even Lady Gregory's devotion to her son Robert, who died in the first World War, and to her grandson are exempted from this perception of egotism and hypocrisy: "She used her devotion to Richard, as she had used her devotion to his father, to protect her while she did what she wanted to do" (257).

The widow's weeds in which Lady Gregory garbed herself for forty years, the shortness and increasing plumpness of her figure, the reserve of her manner with most people, all contributed in time to her frequent identification with Queen Victoria, an identification that offended her. In Mary Lou Kohfeldt's allusions to this widow's camouflage, there is the imputation of hypocrisy. Self-protective camouflage the mourning garb doubtless was—and a considerable economy for a woman who wore Paris gowns for a brief time but, as a widow, regarded herself as in a financial bind. More important, the widow's weeds were an assertion that Augusta Gregory, who had been wife and mother, was henceforth, whatever her efforts in behalf of her son and Coole, to be herself alone. Among the revelations Kohfeldt is able to make are accounts of two love affairs that surely intensified Lady Gregory's life. Fortunately, Lady Gregory's biographer does not moralize over these as instances of late Victorian hypocrisy. Indeed, what the affairs do reveal is that, however conventional Lady Gregory's life and demeanor may have been, she was capable of boldness and of passion too, in responding to men who recognized her value and her appeal as a woman. The first of the affairs, shortly after her marriage and the birth of her son, was with the dashing, handsome, and titled poet Wilfrid Scawen Blunt, to whom Lady Gregory addressed a series of sonnets that reflected all the appropriate emotions a good Protestant wife and mother ought to feel about her infidelity but also celebrated the intensity of her delight in an accomplished lover who revealed to her, "the joys I was so late to understand" (65). One cannot help but be delighted that Lady Gregory's diary records suggestively two X's for one of the afternoons she spent with Blunt, or that she could so far forget Protestantism and propriety as to write him:

> . . . I kiss the ground
> On which the feet of him I love have trod,
> And bow before his voice whose least sweet sound
> Speaks louder to me than the voice of God.
>
> [65-68]

Mary Lou Kohfeldt observes of the end of this intense affair with Blunt, who was already off in full pursuit of other women but remained Lady Gregory's friend for life, "it is possible that at thirty-one, after three and a half years of marriage and one affair lasting eight months, her sex life was over" (69). It is a most puzzling, even misleading, statement for this biographer to make, because the second and more surprising of Kohfeldt's revelations is that at sixty, after years in the black swathings, during the course of one of her American tours, Lady Gregory began another brief love affair with a second handsome and extraordinary man who would also remain a lifelong friend. In B. L. Reid's excellent *The Man from New York: John Quinn and His Friends* (1968) we were given a far more richly textured and vivid account of the friendship of Lady Gregory and the brilliant and unconventional lawyer and collector, eighteen years her junior, who gave so much support to modern art and literature and, in particular, to Yeats, Lady Gregory, and the Abbey. But B. L. Reid left it to Ms. Kohfeldt to explore the handwritten letters Lady Gregory slipped into her typed letters to Quinn (whose own love letters to Lady Gregory were destroyed at the request of this secretive man). Once again, what Lady Gregory wrote suggests an awesome passion: "My John, my dear John, my own John, not other people's John, I love you. I care for you. I know you. I want you" (232). That there may have been an element of cynicism in the "seduction" of Lady Gregory by Blunt and Quinn—renowned celebrants of the rites of Venus—is far less important than that she responded to highly unconventional, even heroic males and that their interest paid tribute to something unconventional and heroically female in her.

To our understanding of the friendship and collaboration of Yeats and Lady Gregory, Mary Lou Kohfeldt contributes little that is new. She repeats claims respecting the authorship of various works that have been made by Elizabeth Coxhead and others but offers no substantiating evidence such as we would like to have. Instances of authorial bias against Yeats are to be found in abundance throughout the book. For example, Kohfeldt writes, "Willie had spent the last three winters in Sussex, revising, as he pompously put it, his style." What, one must ask, was pompous either in the phrasing or the fact of Yeats speaking of revising his style? (In truth, in those years, he was forging the new language of modern poetry.) "Through Ezra Pound," Kohfeldt continues—dismissing in a stroke Yeats's experimental plays and the needs of his genius that Lady Gregory herself recognized—"he had become fascinated with the Japanese Noh, and, forgetting the needs of the Abbey, had written several esoteric dramas inspired by them." Tiresome as such slanting as this may be, it does not equal for sheer silliness a remark Kohfeldt makes after she has described Yeats's pain at Lady Gregory's death. "But he did not know her well enough, he was too self-absorbed, to love her." Indeed the entire treatment of the Yeats-Gregory relationship rests on fundamental sentimental confusions about what the collaboration was and should have been: "there was . . . emptiness at the heart of their union; they were using each other. . . . Yet their association had many of the qualities of a happy, exciting and fruitful marriage" (303). Perhaps not until we have the authorized life of Yeats will we have anything like an adequate account of his friendship with Lady Gregory. Still, on the basis of the evidence we now have, it seems clear that this most fortunate association was neither an exploitation of one by the other, nor a "union," nor a "marriage," nor any love so vague as that of which Kohfeldt speaks. Indeed to speak of the association in such terms is a failure of intelligence. Troubled at times by strains and conflicts, even by an occasional pettiness, the deep and complex association of these two greatly gifted people was as productive and rewarding to both and to literature as modern history knows. To the genuineness and appropriateness of the relationship, every published line of Yeats on Lady Gregory, Lady Gregory's final, moving note to Yeats, and even Mary Lou Kohfeldt's account of Lady Gregory's final days with him attest.

For her subject's literary work, Kohfeldt seems to have very little enthusiasm. Though she is critical of Joyce and Gogarty for having ridiculed Lady Gregory, she grants that Joyce's "contempt for her folklore collections was not completely unmerited" and finds "ignorance and superstition exhibited in much of the folklore Augusta was so reverently collecting and retelling" (158). Nor does Kohfeldt find much to admire in the prose versions of the Irish epics, *Cuchulain of Muirthemne* and *Gods and Fighting Men*. In these, she tells us, Lady Gregory was "doing real women's work, making a quilt from the ragbag of Irish epic manuscripts" (140). Indeed, Kohfeldt pushes her criticism of these works to the extreme conclusion that Lady Gregory's treatment of the epics was socially destructive, an injury to "the Irish people," because the works "encouraged a kind of mindless loyalty and heroism in a people already—after centuries of oppression—severely deficient in political realism, flexibility, and a sense of social responsibility" (150). The problem with writing such as this, entirely on the level of smug and presumptuous generalization, is that it is unsupported by evidence or analysis. It seems not to have occurred to Kohfeldt that she might need to know how many of "the Irish people" were actually familiar with Lady Gregory's versions of the epics. Were "the Irish people" Augusta Gregory's audience, or only a few of them? What did certain members of the Irish, English, and American intelligentsia find in these books? What could both Yeats and Theodore Roosevelt admire in Lady Gregory's *Cuchulain?* At the same time that Kohfeldt issues sweeping moral, cultural, and political pronouncements, she offers very little in the way of a literary criticism of the books. One searches in vain for some observation on Lady Gregory's principles of selection and emphasis, for some shred of comment on her bowdlerization of the originals. We are given no real analysis of the books' mythic energy, their structure, or their dramatic force. Of Lady Gregory's medium, the "Kiltartan" style she devised, we are told not much more than that it "is the speech of the group" (131). But of its rhythms, its emotional range, its appropriateness to epic narrative, we hear nothing.

For Lady Gregory's extensive dramatic work—one-acters, comedies, tragi-comedies, tragedies, fantasies or plays of wonder—Mary Lou Kohfeldt seems to have somewhat more regard. Still, she argues that *Seven Short Plays* (1909) contained Augusta Gregory's best work and that "on this small book . . . rests most of her claim to literary fame" (212). In dealing with these "masterpieces of abbreviated complexity (213), as with those other plays to which she devotes some attention, Kohfeldt's critical method is generally to summarize the action and to quote substantial passages. Occasionally a comment of one kind or another is ventured. Here is a characteristic passage on one of Lady Gregory's greatest successes, *Spreading the News:* "Bartley's wife returns and defends her man. She goes out. (Frank Fay wrote about a successful performance, 'We got a tremendous pace into it, the pace of a hard football match'—this in a play by a woman whose most vigorous exercise was walking fast.) Bartley comes back with the fork and is greeted with the news that Jack Smith is dead" (169). One is not sure which is the least relevant, the glancing and undeveloped reference to the pace of the Abbey production or the utterly frivolous allusion to the dramatist's exercise habits.

But when more extended critical flights are attempted in this book, other more severe problems emerge. Kohfeldt has much to say about Synge's *Playboy of the Western World,* the Abbey production of which had so troubled a history both in Dublin and on tour. Her sense of the play seems to be somewhat blurred by unfavorable notions of "the Irish people." Thus she tells us that Synge's playboy, Christy Mahon, is "transformed into a hero and a lover by the admiration of the villagers who, in traditional Irish fashion, accept and glorify any act of lawlessness because the laws were made by England" (193). A reading of the *Playboy* that treats it in terms of the Irish conflict with England is certainly a unique one, but it may also be one that quite misses the essential ironies of the work. It is to the *Playboy* that Kohfeldt turns for comparison in her analysis of Lady Gregory's *Grania:* "When Christy's father comes back, Pegeen turns on him just as, when Finn returns, Diarmuid confesses that he loves Finn more than he ever loved Grania. Both lovers prove unworthy, and as a result, both Christy and Grania turn back to the authority from which they had attempted to escape" (216). This passage is a puzzling one in a number of ways. Syntactically, it tells us that Pegeen turns on Christy's father, when it must mean, if it is to make any sense, that Pegeen turns on Christy. It tells us that Christy turns back to authority, an utter misreading of the play's conclusion wherein Christy assumes authority over the father (who submits to the son) and repudiates Pegeen, who is unable to accept the heroic as a reality. Most puzzling of all, it misinterprets the conclusion of *Grania*, one of the most interesting and original of Lady Gregory's works, in which passion is at war with the heroic code of honor. At the conclusion of a play as bitterly ironic as Synge's, Grania submits to no authority at all—neither to Finn's nor to that of the dead Diarmuid. Her revenge on the warrior (who loved not Finn, but honor more than she) is to make a marriage without either love or honor.

One final illustration of the critical defects that beset this book should suffice. In *The Gaol Gate*, Lady Gregory came close to tragic intensity as she dramatized the discovery of the wife and mother of Denis Cahel that he had chosen to die rather than inform on his neighbors. Reflecting on this powerful one-acter, Kohfeldt does not ponder the ironies of a tragic choice but propounds a banal moralism neither implicit nor explicit in the play. She writes:

> The play goes deep into one of the central events of community life: the willing self-sacrifice of one individual for the good of the group. This was Augusta's idea of the ultimate in service. And though the person making the sacrifice is transformed into a hero, it also shows the great disadvantage of such service in that it allows one nothing of one's own, not even life, not even identity. The play also shows, though not intentionally, the perversion of the instinct for group loyalty by the long oppression of one people by another. The group becomes actually unable to evaluate what is actually for its own good. [189]

Certainly Mary Lou Kohfeldt is raising significant issues in this passage, but *The Gaol Gate* is being seen as a problem play that makes a criticism of "the Irish people" as Kohfeldt—not Gregory—conceives of them. Lady Gregory did not write a problem play or a text for moral deliberations. Hers was a more profound vision in which wife and mother recognize that the tragic hero makes choices compelled by the inescapable catastrophic circumstances of man's being. Tragedy has not to do with group evaluations; in this play it is an event in which a man in the isolation of his prison makes the choice he must make *as* an individual but *for* others. Tragically, dying for his neighbor, he dies for himself. (Denis Cahel is the Christ figure often in Lady Gregory's imagination.) To draw attention to Kohfeldt's handling of pronoun reference once again—in this passage the neuter third person refers back to the very remote antecedent "play," only to be followed by a second vague and ambiguous usage—would, under ordinary circumstances, be unnecessarily carping. But as one reads *Lady Gregory: The Woman behind the Irish Renaissance* inexplicably one is compelled to use a red pencil, for its modifiers often dangle, its pronoun references are frequently unclear, even paragraph coherence is sometimes lacking. For all that, this biography can not obscure one central truth: though Lady Gregory was not "behind" the Irish Renaissance, she was among those in its forefront.

Peter Kuch. *Yeats and A. E.: "The antagonism that unites dear friends"*
Gerrards Cross, Buckinghamshire: Colin Smythe; Totowa, New Jersey: Barnes and Noble, 1986.
Reviewed by *James F. Carens*

There is a passage of some four or so pages in Henry Summerfield's life of A. E. (*That Myriad Minded Man* [Totowa, New Jersey: Rowman and Littlefield, 1975], p. 112–16) in which the biographer gives an account of the relations of Yeats and A. E. from the composition of A. E.'s play *Deirdre* in 1901 to the time in 1905 when the friendship grew so strained that both men decided to avoid one another. To this same period in the lives of Yeats and A. E., Peter Kuch devotes the greater part of two chapters in his study of the love-hate relationship of the two poets. A critical observation so apparently quantitative is intended neither to disparage Summerfield's admirable, detailed, and comprehensive biography nor to suggest that Kuch's book makes too much of small matters. (Kuch's material is, in fact, very rich.) This quantitative contrast is apropros to the extent that it indicates the sharpness of Kuch's focus and the particularity with which he treats the association of two very complex beings. Peter Kuch describes his book as "a blend of literary history, biography and literary criticism" (xi); the blend of traditional modes is one that he handles adroitly for the most part. One of Kuch's central concerns throughout the study is Yeats's aesthetic; if it cannot be said that Kuch will alter views of a subject already extensively treated, it must be said that his combination of biography and literary history reveals in precise detail the extent to which Yeats's views gradually emerged from, and in response to, a particular context of personal association and literary events. For instance, Kuch describes how Yeats struggled from the time of his 1891 article on A. E. ("An Irish Visionary") to accommodate the too frequently didactic poetry of A. E. to his own more sophisticated view. Perhaps one could argue—in the jargon of New Haven—that Yeats's reading of A. E. was a misprision. More plausibly, Kuch demonstrates that Yeats was struggling to find ways of praising his friend and also attempting to reconcile his father's view of poetry as an expression of personality to A. E.'s notion of the "spiritual, oracular content of poetry" (148).

When, in 1884, Yeats encountered the Northern Irish George W. Russell (well before his pseudonymous dipthongization) at the Art Schools in Kildare Street, it was the junior Russell who appeared the more gifted. As a painter Russell could dazzle his fellow art students by the ease and facility with which he painted. Yeats himself was drawn to the subjects of A. E.'s paintings—ideal and transcendent and glimmering beings who appeared, A. E. insisted, in the visions of which he was the receptor. Kuch is careful to point out that most of what Yeats had to say about A. E.'s visions was written many years after the friendship had been established and shaken. Still, he credits Yeats's later claim that he detected early the influence of the romantic art of Gustave Moreau on A. E.'s drawings and paintings—pure transcriptions, A. E. wanted to believe, of the beings who peopled his visions. Thus, though the young Russell and Yeats were fast bound in an intense friendship and made common cause against Victorian materialism, there was from the start of their association evidence of a crucial divergence. A. E.'s attitude towards his visionary experience was passive and uncritical; indeed, he resented Yeats's inclination to probe the nature of his visions. Yeats's interest in visionary experience and the paranormal was analytical, tentative, and questioning, if not skeptical. An incidental benefit of Kuch's book is that it might demonstrate to those who continue to confuse with mysticism Yeats's interest in the occult and in a coherent symbolism derived from it how fundamentally different Yeats's sensibility was from that of an actual mystic like A. E.

Indeed, as Kuch follows Yeats and A. E. through the major events of their productive association until their growing alienation led, in 1907, to a prolonged break, he develops a series of illuminating contrasts between the two—antinomies Yeats could recognize but not enjoy. It was Yeats, Kuch points out, who saw the importance of Nationalism to the revival of Irish literature; by contrast, A. E., attracted by the vagueness of Oriental mysticism, had to lace his Nationalism with notions of universal ideality. Equally divergent were the unorthodox religious interests of Yeats and A. E. The latter, who was always the conventional Puritan moralist and who feared white magic as much as black, surrendered utterly to Theosophy. Indeed, A. E. was almost swallowed up by his life with "The Household," the Dublin Theosophist cooperative in which he resided for many years. Rejecting, as did A. E., the Protestantism of his forbears, Yeats, after an initial brief attraction to Madame Blavatsky and Theosophy, found the more important tradition of European Hermeticism a source of poetic symbolism. Before the turn of the century also, Yeats sensed that "Celticism" was inadequate to the new age. He abandoned the style of his early poetry, that of the Celtic Twilight he had created; but A. E., Kuch shows, never really moved beyond the *fin de siècle* Celticism. Even in 1925, A. E. (who never really forgot and consequently mourned the Yeats he had first known) could confide in the pages of *The Irish Statesman* that reading Yeats's earliest poetry he found "a boy living in me still, affected almost to tears" (5). Not surprisingly, as Yeats abandoned the "Celtic" for the "Irish" movement and as he rejected the poetic diction of the end of the century, A. E. refused to move with him, just as he refused to respond to what Lady Gregory and Synge were doing with Irish speech rhythms. Indeed, A. E. disliked Synge's powerful contribution to the dramatic movement and declined even to support Yeats in the critical days of the *Playboy* controversy and riots. It was a series of events in the development of the Irish theatre and of the Abbey that provided the occasion for the 1907 break between the two men. Kuch points out that throughout the early days of the theatrical movement, A. E. saw the emerging theatre as a democratic association of amateurs. Yeats, of course, sought to create a professional national theatre that could attract the attention of Europe and America. To A. E.'s credit, though he was always far more popular than Yeats and though he objected to Yeats's autocratic ways as strenuously as did any member of the company, he let himself be used by Yeats to reorganize the theatre society as a limited company, with Yeats, Synge, and Lady Gregory firmly in control. Thus, though in the process of breaking with Yeats, he ensured the survival of the Abbey.

One of the estimable qualities of Kuch's book is that he handles these innumerable contrasts between Yeats and A. E. and the record of their quarrels with one another in a genuinely objective way. Not to say that Kuch does not pass judgments and form conclusions. He does. But Kuch realizes that he writes of rivals who were also artists. He is no sentimentalist, nor is he a heavy-handed moralizer. One contrast he does not offer us is of a goody-good A. E. and a baddy-bad Yeats. His A. E. is a virtuous man, but one capable of pettiness, resentment, and self-deception. His Yeats is a great shaping imagination and a man capable of arrogance, egotism, and insensitivity to others less gifted than he. Still Kuch is tactful enough in his discriminations never to suggest that he is drawing up a moral scorecard; and he does not confuse ephemeral human imperfections with lasting accomplishments.

Doubtlessly Yeats really does come off best in what is one of the central issues of the book. One cannot read Kuch's account of how A. E., indifferent to stylistic considerations, refused to revise so banal and fatuous line as "How God was a big kind brother," (despite Yeats's understated suggestion that the line was inartistic [218], without recognizing that, in the matters that most concern posterity, Yeats was right. The A. E. who was always enough of a Puritan and a didact to distrust Yeats's aestheticism, who was always largely indifferent to matters of form, who regretted Yeats's constant revisions of his poetry, has suffered the consequences of his mysticism. There is something both ironic and sad in Peter Kuch's record of this literary-cultural alliance. A. E., Kuch persuades us, recognized that to preserve his identity and integrity, he must resist the compelling influence of Yeats. And yet, in doing so, A. E. chose for himself the rank of a lesser artist. Yeats (whose friendship in early manhood may have been the second major event of A. E.'s life), saw that his friend had—because of the choices A. E. made—surely not become the Irish poet Yeats hoped he would. Yeats thus could find no place for A. E., along with Synge and Lady Gregory, in his Nobel Prize acceptance speech. The sanity with which Kuch treats this sad truth encourages one to look forward to the companion volume he promises us in which he will deal with the later years of the two men and with their patronage of younger Irish poets.

Elizabeth Bergmann Loizeaux. *Yeats and the Visual Arts.*
New Brunswick: Rutgers University Press, 1986. 240 pp. Illus.
Reviewed by *Terence Diggory*

The publication of Elizabeth Loizeaux's impressive book is timely both for Yeats studies and for research in the broader field of the interrelationship between literature and the other arts. Yeats's own references to the visual arts are so abundant, yet so scattered and non-programmatic, that scholarly attention to those references has been not only inevitable, but, in its collective impression, inevitably chaotic. Loizeaux brings order to this chaos by thoroughly assimilating previous scholarship on the topic, and by organizing her study as a full chronological survey of Yeats's career. In the course of her survey, she usefully catalogues information on related topics, such as Yeats's own work in the visual arts, art books owned by Yeats, or artists who designed work for Yeats's volumes. Her publishers have cooperated by furnishing numerous reproductions, ten in color and fifty in black and white, of works that have been identified as sources for Yeats's work or for his ideas about art. But Loizeaux's book is much more than a compendium of past achievements. It abounds in suggestions for future research, and it clearly defines alternative methods by which such research might be pursued.

The method currently preferred in interartistic studies relies heavily on aesthetic theory as the realm in which the separate arts might be thought to have common roots. The potential disadvantages of this method are fairly obvious. It tends to accord only secondary status to the experience of individual works of art; moreover, it is ahistorical at best, at worst actually distorting in its view of historical development. Just as the individual work is discounted, so is the individual artist. Historical "movements" appear to create works as an inevitable unfolding of their aesthetic premises, and the artist, to the extent that he plays a role in such creation, appears to do so through reference to those premises, rather than through response to the works of predecessors, conversation with contemporaries, and engagement with the materials of his craft. In 1985, the interartistic ramifications of "modernism" were pursued through the theoretical method in books by Reed Way Dasenbrock, Michael North, and Alan Robinson, all of whom devote some attention to Yeats.

The alternative, historical methodology favored by Loizeaux is integral to the two principal arguments of her book: first, that Yeats's aesthetic remained essentially Pre-Raphaelite throughout his career; second, that sculpture eventually replaced painting as the visual art through which Yeats preferred to view his own practice in poetry. At first glance, the argument for Pre-Raphaelitism might seem to defeat any claims for historical development, much as happens in the case of Michael North's argument for the lasting influence on Yeats of fin de siècle aestheticism. (See my review of North's *The Final Sculpture* in the preceding number of this annual.) For Loizeaux, however, such terms undergo redefinition in successive historical periods. Thus, the aesthetes of the eighties and nineties, from whom Yeats took his first lessons in art, gave Pre-Raphaelitism an anti-materialist turn that would have seemed strange to the founders of the movement, as it does to art historians of our own day. Later, in the 1913 essay "Art and Ideas" (E&I 355), Yeats introduced his own redefinition, identifying as "our more profound Pre-Raphaelitism" a movement toward integrating not only the arts themselves, as the aesthetes had attempted, but the arts and the culture that produced them. As symbols of such integration, works of art are invoked throughout *A Vision* and repeatedly in Yeats's later poems. From the latter, Loizeaux selects for special attention "On a Picture of a Black Centaur by Edmund Dulac," "Lapis Lazuli," and "The Statues."

Vital to the integration that Yeats sought, in Loizeaux's analysis, is the relationship between the work of art and its audience, a relationship that is to some extent determined by the medium in which the work of art takes shape. I believe that Loizeaux overstates the extent of that determination, but that is a matter to be considered in relation to her second argument, regarding Yeats's shift in preference from painting to sculpture. With regard to her first argument, Yeats's connection to the Pre-Rahaelites, Loizeaux's attention to the differences among artistic media usefully exposes a shortcoming in previous studies, which have focussed on Pre-Raphaelite poetry. By examining the evidence for Yeats's knowledge of Pre-Raphaelite paintings, Loizeaux convincingly demonstrates that "for Yeats himself, the connection was as much, if not more, a matter of the visual arts" (6). Those arts being spatial by nature, they influenced Yeats's poetry most profoundly by way of a spatial concept, that of the poem as "a region into which one should wander from the cares of life," as Yeats expressed it in a letter to Katharine Tynan in 1889 (L 106).

Loizeaux devotes a chapter to an exploration of the analogies between three early poems by Yeats, "The Island of Statues," "The Wanderings of Oisin," and "The Song of Wandering Aengus," and three visual "regions" that are known to have attracted Yeats: Turner's *The Golden Bough,* William Morris's tapestries, and the symbolic landscapes of Samuel Palmer and Edward Calvert. Yeats's poems prove to differ from their visual analogues in the degree to which the poems insist on the absolute separateness of the ideal region they depict. Such insistence, Loizeaux surmises, may be partly a function of the difference in medium, since pictorial images, unlike those in poetry, necessarily take physical form, and hence will seem that much closer to the viewer's physical condition. Yet the limit to that closeness set by the two-dimensionality of painting permits the initial analogy between painting and Yeats's distancing art. "The viewer of a picture can never literally enter the pictorial world," Loizeaux explains. "Unlike a sculpture, which shares our three-dimensional space, a picture remains an arrangement of shapes on a two-dimensional surface" (52).

Accordingly, once Yeats had redirected his art to "a movement downwards upon life, not upwards out of life," as he announced in a 1906 letter to Florence Farr (L 469), we might expect that sculpture would replace painting in the analogies Yeats formed between the visual arts and poetry. The organization of Loizeaux's book would make it appear that this is, in fact, what happened. Yet if we read her closely, that appearance is belied; and we find, instead, that she pursues her second argument by a radically different methodology: one that is theoretical rather than historical. Whereas her argument about Yeats's connection to the Pre-Raphaelites is based on historical evidence, including the predominance of painting over sculpture in Yeats's early references to the visual arts (36–37), her argument about Yeats's shift toward sculpture is made in the absence of such evidence. In Yeats's later verse, Loizeaux acknowledges, "sculpture as source and reference occurs no more often than painting, and stone and metal are almost as frequent in the early as in the later poetry" (181). Nevertheless, she continues, "the images of the later poems are most often sculptural in a subtler way: they possess the qualities of sculpture without being linked directly to it." So indirect are the links Loizeaux allows that in her final chapter, entitled "Yeats's Sculptural Poetry," the two poems to which she devotes closest attention point to sources in painting: "News for the Delphic Oracle," to Poussin's *The Marriage of Peleus and Thetis* (now identified as *Acis and Galatea*); "Her Vision in the Wood," to an unidentified picture by Mantegna.

Because Loizeaux openly confronts the theoretical nature of her second argument only in her final chapter, that chapter is the least satisfactory within the framework of the book. Yet in some ways it is the most promising in the directions it points for future research. Noting the frequent casual allusions to sculpture in critical descriptions of Yeats's later work, Loizeaux proposes to uncover the substance underlying such allusions by asking, first, what qualities distinguish sculpture from painting, and, second, how those qualities can be said to operate in poetry. On both topics her speculations are provocative, but to grow beyond the status of speculation, they need more support from the scholarship on these topics, such as Loizeaux furnishes in her able handling of the scholarship on Yeats.

As I have already indicated, a crucial aspect of the experience of sculpture, as Loizeaux understands it, is the sharing of space by the art object and the viewer, made possible by sculpture's physical existence in three dimensions. Thus, an especially "sculptural" function in Yeats's poetry, for Loizeaux, is performed by those words that imply a shared situation between speaker and reader. This is primarily a matter of what linguists call "deixis." (See Beverly Olson Flanigan, "Nominal Groups in the Poetry of Yeats and Auden: Notes on the Function of Deixis in Literature," *Style* 18 [1984]: 98–105.) Yeats's style has supplied an important example of the function of deixis in literature ever since M. A. K. Halliday's analysis of "Leda and the Swan," a poem that, oddly, receives only a brief glance from Loizeaux. In Halliday's analysis, the word "the," for instance, in such phrases as "the great wings beating" or "the staggering girl" (P 214), acquires its meaning less from the noun that follows it than from its reference to a preexisting situation—in this case either an event or a work of art depicting the event—that is assumed to be present to both speaker and reader, as if the former were pointing out, "the girl you see over there." Reference to this tradition of linguistic analysis would not only lend technical rigor to Loizeaux's argument but also pose important challenges. Whereas Loizeaux sees Yeats as especially attracted to a dynamic quality in sculpture that she opposes to the traditional associations of "stillness," Halliday observes that the noun phrases that perform a crucial deictic function for Yeats also tend to assimilate, and hence detemporalize, verbal action. Note the participles "beating" and "staggering" in the phrases just quoted.

Loizeaux's distinction between sculpture and painting is based primarily on the phenomenological theory of sculpture elaborated by F. David Martin in *Sculpture and Enlivened Space* (Lexington: University Press of Kentucky, 1981). In addition to the notion of "enlivened space," shared between sculpture and its viewer, Martin proposes as a distinguishing feature of sculpture its appeal to the sense of touch even more than to the sense of sight, to which painting must confine its appeal. However, because Martin insists that the sense of touch is involved principally in the experience of space, rather than in contact with the material of the sculpture, the distinction with painting seems problematic, all the more so when Martin's theoretical generalization is tested by historical questions. In an argument that Martin merely dismisses out of hand (Martin, p. 253n29), Clement Greenberg has attempted to distinguish modernist sculpture by its increasing emphasis on "optical" qualities and a correspondingly decreasing emphasis on the tactile. (See "The New Sculpture," in Greenberg, *Art and Culture* [Boston: Beacon, 1961]: 139–45.) On the other hand, in an early manifesto of modernist painting, Albert Gleizes and Jean Metzinger describe an experience that sounds very much like that which Martin would reserve to sculpture:

> To establish pictorial space, we must have recourse to tactile and motor sensations, indeed to all our faculties. It is our whole personality which, contracting or dilating, transforms the plane of the picture. As in reacting this plane reflects the personality

upon the understanding of the spectator, pictorial space may be defined as a sensible passage between two subjective spaces. ["Cubism," rpt. in Herschel B. Chipp, ed., *Theories of Modern Art* (Berkeley: University of California Press, 1971): 212.]

For Loizeaux's purposes, of course, it is not necessary to decide which of these conflicting theories is finally "right," but which best accounts for Yeats's view of the visual arts, and which defines within the visual arts those criteria which are most helpful in an account of Yeats's poetry. From this perspective, the crucial issue appears to be not the role of touch in the experience of art, but the "presence" that a work of sculpture establishes in the space it shares with the viewer. Here Loizeaux's acuity as a reader of Yeats wins out over her theoretical predilections, and the theoretical framework supplied by Martin proves finally inadequate. For Martin, "the aesthetic experience of sculpture brings out our being with things physically in an exceptionally vivid way" (Martin, p. 52), but it can accomplish this revelation only because of the "thingness" of the work of sculpture itself, "because of its literal presence as an object in this world," as Loizeaux puts it (177). On the other hand, Loizeaux recognizes that, for Yeats, sculpture, and the "sculptural" image, always possess an "otherworldly" quality that Martin's sense of "presence" will not account for. While Martin's argument is, as Rudolf Arnheim has noted, "a frontal attack on 'aesthetic distance'" (*Journal of Aesthetics and Art Criticism* 40 [1982]: 435), the retention of aesthetic distance is the major tenet in Yeats's continuing allegiance to Pre-Raphaelitism, in Loizeaux's view. Thus she insists, "while he deploys devices for lessening aesthetic distance, for drawing the reader into the poetic world, for creating a sense of immediacy, he simultaneously asserts the artificial" (188).

In place of David Martin's theory, a view more congenial to Loizeaux's sense of the "sculptural" in Yeats is Michael Fried's concept of the "presentness" of the work of art. (See "Art and Objecthood," rpt. in Gregory Battcock, ed., *Minimal Art* [New York: Dutton, 1968]: 116–47; and *Absorption and Theatricality* [Berkeley: University of California Press, 1980].) Insisting that the work of art, whether painting or sculpture, is not an object, Fried coins the term "presentness" in explicit opposition to the minimalist or "literalist" notion of "presence" reflected in Martin's ideas. The latter notion suggests to Fried a kind of "stage presence," a "theatrical" positing of the object *as* an object over against the beholder, who is set at a distance, in a different place. Thus, Fried, too, like Loizeaux, seeks to explain art's overcoming of its distance from the beholder, but the movement is in the opposite direction from that which Martin would suggest. Rather than coming down into the space of the beholder, the artwork instead takes the beholder up into itself. In fact, there is a double movement: first the artwork withdraws from the beholder, and then it captures the beholder, "absorbing" him, as Fried likes to say, or "possessing" him, as Yeats might prefer to put it.

A correspondence between Fried's analysis and Yeats's account of his Noh plays helps to confirm Loizeaux's contention that Yeats's "sculptural" ideal first emerged through his experiments with the Noh, although that observation casts further doubt on the meaning both of Loizeaux's term "sculptural" and of Fried's term "theatrical." Loizeaux refers, for instance, to the following passage from "Certain Noble Plays of Japan" (1916), in which Yeats describes the Noh actor in terms that seem to anticipate Fried: "There, where no studied lighting, no stage-picture made an artificial world, he was able, as he rose from the floor, where he had been sitting cross-legged, or as he threw out an arm, to recede from us into some more powerful life. Because that separation was achieved by human means alone, he receded but to inhabit as it were the deeps of the mind" (E&I 224). Though it presents its own problems in this context, Fried's rejection of the "theatrical" aesthetic helps to correct a misleading implication of Loizeaux's argument: that Yeats's discovery was primarily a consequence of the physical conditions of theater, disposed, like those of sculpture, in three dimensions. Ultimately, the extent to which a particular medium limits artistic choice would appear to be minimal. Just as Fried's hero, Diderot, could imagine an alternative to "theater" that was nevertheless "dramatic," Yeats could imagine, within the theater, "the theatre's anti-self" (Ex 257). In both theater and sculpture, as in his poetry, what mattered to Yeats was neither the physical nor the imagined realm in isolation, but the joining of those realms; not the statue alone, but "the increased power that a God feels on getting into a statue" (quoted in Richard Ellmann, *The Identity of Yeats* [New York: Oxford University Press, 1968]: 240).

Because it offers a fresh perspective on so central a doctrine, we might accept Loizeaux's use of the term "sculptural" to designate that joining of realms, just as we accept Fried's use of the term "theatrical" to designate their separation. Unfortunately, we have no other terms for the formal qualities so designated, and we require some designation, because such formal qualities are fundamental to the experience of the individual work of art. But we must remember that such qualities are not essentially linked to the media from which their names derive. Yeats's development toward a "sculptural" poetry need not, and apparently did not, run parallel to an increasing concern for sculpture itself. The "sculptural," or "theatrical," or "painterly," or "literary" quality of a given work is determined by the individual artist, not by a particular art.

W. J. McCormack. *Ascendancy and Tradition in Anglo-Irish Literary History from 1789 to 1939.*
Oxford: Clarendon Press; New York: Oxford University Press, 1985. xi +423 pp.
Reviewed by *William H. O'Donnell*

This provocative, vigorous book pursues a course that W. J. McCormack had announced in his biographical study *Sheridan Le Fanu and Victorian Ireland*, published by the Clarendon Press in 1980. There he complained that literary scholars have paid too little attention to the importance of the Protestant middle class in the cultural history of nineteenth-century Ireland, and that Yeats's affectionate emphasis on Swift, Burke, and the Irish eighteenth century has led to an "unhistorical" view of the nineteenth-century Irish backgrounds from which Yeats and Synge emerged (*Le Fanu*, p. 6). Similarly, "political historians have quite rightly concentrated on the Famine, the Land War, and Fenianism as the major events of Irish history before Parnell, but these themes necessarily limit our attention to the victims of time. Perhaps," McCormack suggested, "we can now look at some of the survivors, who . . . spoke the language of Victorian success" (*Le Fanu*, p. 7). The "ascendancy"—expansively defined as "landowners, the established clergy, the genteel professions, [and] the Protestant commercial classes"—possessed "an important sense of common purpose" that is essential to an understanding of Irish culture (*Le Fanu*, p. 268).

Specifically, McCormack called for advancing the study of Anglo-Irish literature from beyond "what may be aptly called an infantile stage, obsessively concerned with certain prominent and important figures—Yeats, Joyce, Synge—but neglectful of the larger body of writing amongst which the masters must ultimately be placed. This uneven application of scholarship has particularly affected the Victorians, for their achievement (flawed and awkward though it was) was rejected as irrelevant by the exponents of cultural nationalism. To an extent which is too infrequently recognized, critics of Anglo-Irish literature have derived their techniques from Yeats, and so have entered into a conspiracy with that formidable reviser of history. . . . The need to apply techniques of the new school of literary historians to the study of Anglo-Irish literature is overwhelming" (*Le Fanu*, p. 266). The ardor with which McCormack pursues that program is the principal characteristic of *Ascendancy and Tradition in Anglo-Irish Literary History from 1789 to 1939*. This son of County Wicklow and Trinity College, Dublin will be our guide through a literature that, as he amusingly points out, has become "the locus of an advanced tourism" (2), but which without his native expertise would be as deceptive as the Irish landscape described in "A Blank Map," the opening poem in the first book of poems by McCormack (pseudonym Hugh Maxton):

> the countryside becomes
> suddenly impenetrable:
> the road inclines, but signposts lie;
>
> caught in a habit of imprecision
> they are half destroyed by rust
> or glimmer in heat double-miraged.
>
> The image cannot be trusted;
> no country has been so badly blessed.
> [*The Noise of the Fields: Poems 1970–1975*
> (Dublin: Dolmen Press, 1976), p. 9.]

McCormack usefully insists that a reading of Anglo-Irish literature must include the individual reader, the "effective text" (p. 363), and the epoch. Thus the reader needs to be aware that his own prejudices are engaged in a dramatic conversation with the text, and the reader should accept that significant absences in the text can contribute to meaning and that knowledge of the suppressed ideological history of the epoch in which the work was written can be valuable. In fact, a major purpose of the book is to show how Yeats is "the culmination of a mid- and late-Victorian rereading of the Irish eighteenth century" (364). Similarly, because of the importance of socio-economic factors in accurately understanding Irish cultural history, if Yeats, Synge, and Lady Gregory's idiosyncratic definition of "Protestant Ascendancy" wrongly pretended that "Ireland had no middle class" (9) and if, as McCormack further asserts, "Protestant Ascendancy" is "the central cultural assumption of Yeats's meditation on his own inheritance" (12), then the need for the book's detailed attention on the genesis of the term "Protestant Ascendancy" is clear. McCormack usefully challenges his readers to set a high value on literary history and thus not become fidgety at what might otherwise seem an overly thorough historical account of the term "Protestant Ascendancy."

The book applies that literary historical methodology to a diverse group of texts, beginning with Edmund Burke's *Reflections on the Revolution in France* (1790), although McCormack, seeking whenever possible to link Ireland with Europe, uses in his title "1789 to 1939"—the French Revolution to the death of Yeats (or, one wonders, the start of World War II). After Burke, McCormack moves to Maria Edgeworth's *Castle Rackrent* and *The Absentee*. Particularly in the chapter on *The Absentee*, readers will recognize McCormack's occasional willingness to support assertions for which he offers only weak evidence. For example, in attempting to show that Maria Edgeworth based a fictional villa,

Tusculum, on a County Wicklow villa, Bellevue, McCormack follows a pattern of first presenting minutely detailed information as evidence for the assertion, then withdrawing that evidence as having no direct connection with the assertion, but then closing by immediately advancing some indirect link (131–35). Briefer considerations are included on Sheridan Le Fanu, Charles Lever, political rhetoric, Celticism in Ernest Renan and Matthew Arnold, and Standish James O'Grady. A chapter on Joyce ranges from "Eveline" to a passage in *Finnegans Wake*. Yeats receives considerable attention, with extended demonstrations of McCormack's literary historicism on "Nineteen Hundred and Nineteen" and *Purgatory*. While readers certainly will take exception to some of the local applications of McCormack's generalizations, the book as a whole is lively and invigorating.

Steven Putzel. *Reconstructing Yeats:* The Secret Rose *and* The Wind Among the Reeds.
  Dublin: Gill and Macmillan, 1986. Totowa, New Jersey: Barnes & Noble, 1986. 242 pp.
  Reviewed by *Carolyn Holdsworth*

In *Reconstructing Yeats,* Steven Putzel advances a very apt metaphor for Yeats's creative process. Drawing from his own experience, he speaks of "the layering of Irish history" (64) and offers this example: "I have seen three buildings side-by-side: a tenth-century *clochar* or beehive cell, a seventeenth or eighteenth-century thatched or slated cottage, and a modern house. When the cottage was built, the *clochar* became a barn, and when the modern house was built, the cottage became a barn and the *clochar* was demoted to hen-house" (64–65). He summarizes this phenomenon as being "Nearly 1000 years of history at a glance" (65).

Putzel first uses this "layering" metaphor in discussing the story "Of Costello the Proud, of Oona the Daughter of Dermott and of the Bitter Tongue" from *The Secret Rose,* and he returns to it at the end of his study after likening Yeats's work to "a palimpsest" (217). The metaphor works on two levels to define Yeats's creative process. One level is that Yeats layered his early works (such as *The Secret Rose* and *The Wind Among the Reeds*) with fragments of history, myth, etc. drawn from his various interests. The second is that Yeats layered his later work with fragments of his early work. Putzel says, "His revisions, rejections, and recantations leave us with a *pentimento* poetic landscape resembling a countryside in which ninth-century *clochar* still exist in the shadow of eighteenth-century cottages, which in turn are adumbrated but not destroyed by twentieth-century homes" (217).

Putzel's metaphor, then, not only suggests a creative process but also, by extension, provides a justification for studying Yeats's early works in their first editions. Putzel's aim in *Reconstructing Yeats* is to show that in the first editions of *The Secret Rose* and *The Wind Among the Reeds* Yeats achieves an "effective yet psychologically dangerous and artistically limiting subjectivity by constructing an early symbolic system that unites his growing interest in alchemy, hermeticism, gnosticism, Neoplatonism, Irish mythology and folklore and the aesthetic principles gleaned from Blake, the Pre-Raphaelites, Walter Pater and the French *symbolistes*" (3). These extrinsic systems "provide models for approaching Yeats's work" (217).

As far as providing a rationale for the study of Yeats's early works in their early forms, Putzel's metaphor is sufficient to me, and apologetics seem unnecessary. Putzel, however, does defend such study. While he readily characterizes many of the stories of *The Secret Rose* as "stilted, overly formal and/or frustratingly simplistic" (19), he yet adds that "we must use a second set of criteria [i.e., non-aesthetic] to scrutinize the text fully and fairly" (19). This "second set" of criteria is hermeneutical, I guess, and is used to "read *The Secret Rose* as a seminal outline for a mystical system that would later be revised, refined and rethought to become *Per Amica Silentia Lunae*, 'The Phases of the Moon' and *A Vision*" (19).

I find Putzel's argument interesting. After all, Yeats said, "I am persuaded that our intellects at twenty contain all the truths we shall ever find" (Au 116), and we can easily see the "truths" of the early works reappearing in the later ones, the systems themselves more or less abandoned and the images boiled down to archetypes. Nevertheless, I think a necessary corollary of this argument is the admission that the early works are important primarily for what they show us of Yeats's progress towards the later works. In other words, most of the early works are historically interesting rather than intrinsically valuable. Perhaps Putzel agrees with this evaluation, but the problem to me is one of emphasis. For example, throughout *Reconstructing Yeats* Putzel undercuts biographical criticism, yet the very same reason exists for biographical criticism as exists for the study of sources and first editions: both kinds of criticism make richer the interpretation of Yeats's really great poems, written later in his life. Another example is Putzel's treatment of definitive editions, as when he places the word "definitive" in quotation marks. Putzel acknowledges as "correct," yet seems to question, "the standard editorial procedure of choosing an author's last revised version as a copy text" (13). Surely we can grant the importance of first editions (as we do of the manuscripts) without putting them into competition with the definitive texts, and surely we can grant the importance of reconstructive criticism without disparaging biographical criticism. I betray my own prejudices here.

Briefly, Putzel's thesis is this: the stories of the 1897 first edition of *The Secret Rose* "are arranged in historical order" for the purpose of presenting "a symbolic history of Ireland" (4), and, according to Yeats's introduction to the book, this symbolic history of Ireland has as its very basis "the war of spiritual with natural order" (13). Putzel is expanding the theory outlined by Augustine Martin in his essay "Apocalyptic Structure in Yeats's *The Secret Rose*," published in *Studies* 64 (1975), 24–33. Putzel says, "Martin shows that the stories were arranged in chronological, historical order, moving from pagan Ireland, to the monastic period, to the Middle Ages, to the seventeenth and eighteenth centuries, and finally to the *fin de siècle*" (15). Putzel shows how each story of the volume represents an era and how each era ends with an apocalyptic moment as a new era originates. He argues that Yeats presents "a world in which history is both linear and cyclic, and time is both diachronic and synchronic" (15). History is linear in that the stories move from pagan Ireland to the end of the nineteenth century. Time is diachronic for the same reason. History is cyclic in that each era repeats the mistakes and clashes of the previous era's pattern, and within each era, individuals reenact a dramatic encounter with the Ideal. In the cases of both eras and individuals, Yeats indicates mere process, not progress. Time is synchronic because the Rose, symbol of the ideal visionary wisdom, is a still point towards which mortals yearn and around which all else turns.

In addition to explicating the stories as they show encounters between era and era, and between individuals and the Rose, Putzel also glosses many details. He identifies source systems and shows how Yeats takes fragments of them to build his own symbolic system. Putzel further studies the tonal and thematic links between the stories, some expository and some imagaic. He pays particular attention to the dance motif.

To summarize Yeats's system in *The Secret Rose*, Putzel uses the illustration by Althea Gyles from the cover of the volume. He says:

> The serpent of wisdom winding around and up the straight trunk of the Tree of Life ... is Yeats's early map of history, recording both the linear and cyclical nature of time. Each coil of the serpent represents an age, each new turn represents both the end of the preceding age and the beginning of the next, and each story of *The Secret Rose* has its place on this 2000-year serpent of history. This is also the path of the individual who wanders through life waiting for the momentary lightning flashes of vision from above, but as Yeats tells us, the straight trunk of the tree is the direct path to "the heart of God" taken by "saint and sage." [130]

This illustration is indeed, as Putzel says, "a graphic way of summarizing the system of *The Secret Rose*" (130). Though the idea of the text and the idea of the cover surely coincide, so exact a correspondence between a text by Yeats and an illustration by Gyles should remind us of the flexibility of symbols.

Putzel's study of *The Secret Rose* is strongest in its explication of the stories. He also draws a valuable genetic connection between *The Secret Rose* and *A Vision*, and he provides good annotations of place names and other details in the stories.

My reservations about his study of *The Secret Rose* are two. First, in pointing out the tonal and thematic links between the stories, Putzel himself notes that many of them were added when the stories were collected to go into the volume (the stories were originally published separately in various journals). So, at least part of the unity of these stories was stamped on them after the fact of composition. Yeats went through a quite similar process in collecting the poems for *The Wind Among the Reeds*. But doesn't the fact that these links were not organic to the stories call into question Putzel's basic assumption that Yeats was intentionally constructing a system of symbolic history? Yeats is often obscure in his early works, but he is rarely so ingenious a writer as, say, Joyce. And while the stories do have an undoubtedly chronological sequence, Putzel's theory about the volume's structure would make *The Secret Rose* something of a literary precursor of the "Cyclops" episode in *Ulysses*.

Second, in detailing Yeats's sources for *The Secret Rose*, Putzel concentrates on the historical and the occult. He really neglects the Romantic tradition. He asserts that "Yeats takes his concept of historical eras and their captive individuals from this occult tradition and from nineteenth-century theories of Irish mythology and history even more than from the historical concepts of English writers such as Blake, Carlyle and Pater" (4). This assertion may be valid for Yeats's concept of historical eras, but I think it is not valid for his concept of the "captive individual." If one seeks a prototype of the individual who renounces the material world in his search for the Ideal (personified as a woman), one can scarcely avoid the protagonist of Shelley's poem "Alastor." Shelley's influence on Yeats was pervasive; as a young man, Yeats says, "I soon chose Alastor for my chief of men and longed to share his melancholy" (Au 39). I realize that Shelley's influence on Yeats has already been admirably dealt with in George Bornstein's *Yeats and Shelley* (Chicago and London: Chicago University Press, 1970), and I also realize that tracing the Romantic tradition is not Putzel's goal in his book. Nevertheless, Hanrahan and the other disappointed searchers in *The Secret Rose* are surely literary descendents of

Shelley, and the omission of this fact flaws Putzel's discussion of the "captive individual."

The second part of *Reconstructing Yeats* deals with *The Wind Among the Reeds*. In it, Putzel scrutinizes the poems of the volume by the light of the theory he developed for *The Secret Rose*. He says, "If *The Secret Rose* presents a symbolic system, a way of organising history and time and of explaining 'the war of spiritual with natural order', *The Wind Among the Reeds* speaks the language of that system" (136). He examines the poems as "symbolic action" (140), remarking that "Like *The Secret Rose*, this volume of poems is moulded around the themes of time, love and apocalypse. All but a few of the thirty-seven poems are concerned with the dialectic between time and eternity, between the imperfect world and the ideal world" (143). The quest for the Ideal "leads to apocalyptic visions of the synchronic moment when time will be burned away and the Ideal will be within reach" (143).

As a thematic summary, Putzel's statements are accurate, though they could just as well apply to almost all of Yeats's poems—life or art? Putzel then proceeds in this part of his study to look for an organizing system in the poems of *The Wind Among the Reeds* and to advance the connection between the poems and *The Secret Rose*. The system he finds in the poems is that "rhythmic patterning was at least part of the rational [sic] for the order or sequence of the poems" (142). He adds, "References to 'hiding hair', 'half-closed' visionary eyes and to the mystical nature of earth, air, fire and water bind the poems not only to each other but also to the stories of *The Secret Rose*" (143).

Putzel necessarily argues for "extra-poetic" concerns. He says, "If we read the poems after having read the first edition of *The Secret Rose*, many of the personae and virtually all of the themes and motifs are already familiar. Such a reading is extra-poetic in the same way that a reading of *The Tower* poems by the light of *A Vision* is extra-poetic; in each case the prose volume provides the theoretical basis and the philosophical and historical context for the poems" (213). This argument contains a false analogy, for *The Secret Rose* does not stand in relation to *The Wind Among the Reeds* as *A Vision* stands to *The Tower*. *The Secret Rose* may be prose, but it is prose fiction. It is a collection of stories with an implied philosophical basis, but it is not a philosophical outline, a credo, as is *A Vision*. *The Secret Rose* and *The Wind Among the Reeds* certainly share many affinities, but the latter is not derived from the former. This theory omits the emotion of the poems. The poems of *The Wind Among the Reeds* were not written as finger exercises to a system; rather, the system (occult, mythological, historical or whatever) was brought in to validate the emotion. I think that forcing the connection between *The Secret Rose* and *The Wind Among the Reeds* leads to the problems discussed below.

In chapter 7 of *Reconstructing Yeats*, Putzel presents a detailed and solid metrical discussion, one which shows that Yeats derived his peculiar chanting rhythms "suitable to his symbolic verse" (148) from variations of both English and Irish meters. Building upon this discussion, in chapter 8 he says, "In order to analyse the thematic and rhetorical patterns that bind these poems together while at the same time honouring the volume's sequential integrity and acknowledging the musical organisation, I have chosen to regard these alternations [the poems moving inward to subjective lyricism and then outward to objective ballad narration] as a structural motif" (167). Beginning at this point, I find Putzel's methodology faulty. He acknowledges that Yeats "creates a pattern or sequence, drawing on thematic and imagistic parallelism, opposition and repetition" and that Yeats "employs rhetorical schemes" in order to move "from poem to poem, not in a linear narrative but in the concentric circles of *The Secret Rose* system" (167), yet he chooses to "discuss the volume in five movements bounded by four ballads: 'The Host of the Air', 'The Fiddler of Dooney', 'The Cap and Bells' and 'The Blessed'" (167). He also chooses to find the poems "increasing in intensity, moving ever closer to the 'brink of revelation'" (167). If the pattern or sequence of *The Wind Among the Reeds* is based on themes, images, and rhetorical devices, why discuss the volume in the false categories of five movements defined by four ballads? If the volume moves in concentric circles, why propose a linear progression in intensity toward a visionary revelation? I think both of these confusions arise from the attempt to make *The Wind Among the Reeds* fit the pattern that Putzel outlined for *The Secret Rose*.

The first of the five movements that Putzel discusses is "The Entrance of the Wayfarer," where he says Yeats "introduces his major themes, creates a ritualistic mood, and begins the mystical seduction of his readers" (167–68). This section covers the poems beginning with "The Hosting of the Sidhe" and ending with the ballad "The Host of the Air."

The second movement is "The Voyage of Life," where Putzel says, "The five lyrics that lie between 'The Host of the Air' and the ballad, 'The Fiddler of Dooney', are no longer introductory; there is nothing tentative now about the opposition of the temporal and the timeless. The personae do not just hear the Sidhe or wish to sit apart on a green knoll, but instead are either caught up in the whirlwind and the flood of the initiatory process or they reject it entirely" (173). This is an elastic category! It's like a dichotomy in logic that divides the world into opals and non-opals—everything fits. Men, women, children, space, time, and mud pies are "non-opals." Because anything can fit an either/or category like this, it is hardly a useful classification. In this section, Putzel discusses "Breasal the Fisherman," "The Song of Wandering Aengus," and "Into the Twilight" as representing "involuntary initiation through images of nets and fishing" (173). Putzel does not connect "A Cradle Song" to the other poems in this movement; rather, he says it is "an intensified, more immediate and personal version of the warning in 'The Hosting of the Sidhe'" from movement one (178). The purpose in this movement of "The Song of the Old Mother," he says, is to be a "stark contrast" to the other poems (179), "a vivid demonstration of what happens when one cannot hear" the Sidhe (180). A very flexible classification.

Putzel also argues that the half-lyric/half-ballad poems and the lyric poems that make up these first two movements are used by Yeats "to lift readers into the mystical world of the volume," while the two ballads—"The Host of the Air" and "The Fiddler of Dooney"—function to "ease the reader back to earth" (180). However, "The Song of the Old Mother," with its catalogue of grievances about cooking and cleaning, hardly leaves the reader suspended in the rarefied atmosphere of the synchronic plane; thus the reader cannot be awaiting the bump of earth landing via "The Fiddler of Dooney" (which comes next in the first edition). Nor, thematically, does "The Host of the Air" return us to earth at the end of movement one. True, it is in the third person as opposed to the first, but so is the framework structure of "The Hosting of the Sidhe," and the whole subject of "The Host of the Air" is an encounter with the Sidhe. Thus, I cannot conclude with Putzel that each "sequence intensifies the visionary experience, then relaxes [with a ballad], creating an ebb and flow between the diachronic and the synchronic planes" (180). The poems repeat themes and images, but not in any readily discernible pattern and not at metrically marked intervals.

Putzel's third movement is "The Chase after the Ideal." In this category are eight lyrics involving a beloved woman and, incongruously, one lyric with a female persona. Putzel says "The Heart of the Woman" (the female persona poem) "leads toward the thematic and symbolic centre of *The Wind Among the Reeds*—the 'White woman'" (181), but he doesn't say how. This movement ends with "The Cap and Bells," and again we see that the ballad does not function to return us to the diachronic plane. Rather the reverse, for the poem leaves us in the synchronic plane—the queen's hair being a "folded" flower, her feet having the "quiet" of love in them, and the poor jester being dead.

Movement four is "The Passing through Darkness," and Putzel says its six lyrics "move deeper into dream, or, to use a Yeatsian formula, are influenced more than ever by the moon and the subjectivity it represents" (192). To give but one example, I compare "Hanrahan reproves the Curlew" in this movement with "The Everlasting Voices" from the first movement. The two poems very much resemble each other, the main difference being specificity. The "voice" has merely become a "curlew"; the narrator is clearer about his reasons for feeling depressed; and in both cases the narrator is clearly voicing a message of his own, which is "Leave me alone." This movement ends with "The Blessed," and Putzel says this ballad is "a fable that both illustrates the quest for wisdom in the preceding poems and introduces the theme of divine intoxication so important to the final lyrics of the volume" (198).

Movement five, "The Fiery Spear," is rather a catch-all category. "The Secret Rose," "Hanrahan laments because of his Wanderings" and "Hanrahan speaks to the Lovers of his Songs in Coming Days" are connected by Putzel because they "are associated with the eighteenth-century bard and had been included in *The Secret Rose*" (201). "The Travail of Passion" is explicated separately and compared to poems from the first, third and fourth movements and to "The Secret Rose" in this movement. "The Poet pleads with his Friend for Old Friends" is compared to a poem from the fourth movement. "Aedh pleads with the Elemental Powers" is more or less explicated separately with references to a poem from the fourth movement, to certain "Celtic Mystery" ceremonies, to *The Secret Rose*, to "The Second Coming" and so on. "Aedh wishes his Beloved were Dead" is discussed in terms of themes and imagery. Putzel compares "Aedh wishes for the Cloths of Heaven" to "Aedh tells of the Rose in his Heart" from movement one, and he says the later poem "seems to complete a circle, leading back" to the earlier poem (209). This is the reason I find his continued implication of linear initiatory progression so baffling, especially as he states that the volume "ends on a note of sexual and spiritual longing" and that "it ends as it began" (211). Yet he sees Mongan in "Mongan thinks of his Past Greatness" as a sort of summary of "the themes and motifs of the entire volume" and as "the quintessential visionary seeker and sufferer" (210). Are we deeper in the process or have we returned in a concentric circle to the beginning?

Putzel's treatment of *The Wind Among the Reeds* is far less successful than his treatment of *The Secret Rose* because he distorts the former to the system he developed for the latter. The linear thematic progression he implies in the poems, as discussed above, does not exist. He says it does not exist, but he treats the poems as though it does. The methodology he uses also does not work because the poems in each of his movements are not homogeneous enough to be classified as a unit, and the ballads between movements are not different enough (except technically, in form) to serve as a contrast. "The Host of the Air," "The Cap and Bells" and "The Blessed" are all one-way excursions to the "synchronic plane" rather than fail-safe mechanisms for returning to the material world. In fact, the only ballad that serves this function is "The Fiddler of Dooney." In this poem, one does indeed experience an ironic bump and a clearing of mists, which is probably why Yeats moved it to its position at the end of the volume in later editions.

Passim: Brief Notices

Mary FitzGerald

This section contains short reviews of books that consider the life and work of Yeats either in passing or rather more briefly than those accorded extended review in this volume.

English Literature and History.
 [Sotheby's sale catalog for 10–11 July 1986.]
 London: Sotheby Parke Bernet & Co., 1986.

The collection of James F. Gallagher (1912–79), a founder of the G. K. Chesterton Poetry Society and professor of literature at Fordham University and Long Island University, forms the basis for the Yeats offerings in this catalog of the July sales. The collection consists primarily of first editions, several of which are enhanced by their association with Yeats's friends. (There is, for example, Katharine Tynan's copy of the first edition of *The Countess Kathleen and Various Legends and Lyrics*.) But it also lists corrected galley proofs and autograph letters to various correspondents, most notably a series of letters written to John Drinkwater from 1909 to 1913.

In addition to the Gallagher collection, Sotheby's offered two letters to Gwen John, a fair copy of "The Lake Isle of Innisfree," and a proof copy of *The Ten Principal Upanishads*.

Modern Literature from the Library of James Gilvarry.
 [Christie's Sale Catalog for 7 February 1986.]
 New York: Christie's, 1986.

The Yeats portion of the treasure trove that was James Gilvarry's collection of books and manuscripts was included among the many items of modern literature offered for sale at Christie's, New York, slightly less than five months after Gilvarry's death on 16 September 1984. (A second, even larger sale of his books was held at the Swann Galleries on 27 March, but that sale did not include Yeats items.) Over two hundred pages of catalog description were needed to handle the Christie's portion of the sale, and Yeats was accorded over one hundred catalog entries, several of them for multiple items. First editions, working manuscripts, texts revised by Yeats and by Lady Gregory, and many unpublished letters dominated the Yeats offerings—and there are equally impressive collections of Joyce and Beckett documents, and a host of items relating to Yeats's literary friends.

Most Yeatsians will find this catalogue an invaluable source of information: some of what it contains has been "missing" for years.

Peter Balbert and Phillip L. Marcus, eds. *D. H. Lawrence: A Centenary Consideration.*
Ithaca and London: Cornell University Press, 1985. 261 pp.

One of the eleven essays in this collection deals with Yeats and Lawrence. Phillip L. Marcus's "Lawrence, Yeats, and 'the Resurrection of the Body'" explores the "surprising congruences as well as areas of divergence" (211) in both writers, especially as they are exhibited in Yeats's late play *Calvary* and Lawrence's late novella *The Escaped Cock*. As Marcus notes, he is not the first to compare the two moderns, and he makes no claim to exhaustive comparison of their work, but the narrow perspective that he chooses serves admirably to chart the parallel courses that they travelled, aware of each other's work but not greatly influenced by it. All the more interesting, then, is the degree to which they *seem* to have been mutually influenced and the degree to which they arrived at similar postulations and philosophies—rather like the way in which Yeats and Jung grew separately from the same cultural root, as James Olney has demonstrated in *The Rhizome and the Flower* (Berkeley: University of California Press, 1980).

At issue is the concept of death and afterlife, as treated in Yeats's play and Lawrence's novella, and Professor Marcus provides detailed analyses of these and their probable sources in contemporary thought.

Ronald Gene Rollins. *Divided Ireland: Bifocal Vision in Modern Irish Drama.*
Lanham, Maryland, and New York: University Press of America, 1985. 104 pp.

A series of signals warns the potential reader from this University Press of America offering. First is the strange ambiguity of the subtitle. (Does the author intend a treatise on corrective vision?) Second is the opening clause: "*As the title indicates* [emphasis mine] this book is a collage [sic]" (ix). Third is the assertion that the book handles "the abundance of configurations and crises, both personal and communal, in eleven plays by six different playwrights" (ix) in a volume that consists of 104 pages of photo-offset typescript. Lastly there is an explicit warning that the book is "deliberately disjointed" and a further, incredible directive to supply one's own connection if one is "annoyed by the absence of transitional bridges linking the chapters," because, after all, "if novelists like John Fowles can ask readers for assistance in completing their books, then so can critics" (x).

Anyone who foolishly persists beyond this point deserves what he or she gets, a pastiche ("collage"?) of plot summaries, snippets from an idiosyncratic selection of sixteen critics (including "Ruby *Coh*" on Beckett and "Carol *Klein*man" on O'Casey [104]—a 12.5% rate of error in authors' names alone), typographical errors (or is "tabula rasas" [83] an unfortunate plural?), and a decided paucity of fresh insight in what little analysis there is.

Professor Rollins quotes George Orwell's "Politics and the English Language" from the *Little Brown Reader* and two paragraphs from the justifiably fugitive program notes for the Canadian premiere of Brian Friel's *Translations* [102]. He uses "Ibid." 78 times in 131 notes. His Yeats chapter pairs *Purgatory* with Beckett's *Krapp's Last Tape* in a discussion of the decline of families and tradition that never rises above the level of a term paper, complete with misquotation of the poet (25); and the Yeats chapter is neither better nor worse than the rest of the book.

In short, *Divided Ireland: Bifocal Vision in Modern Irish Drama* gives eloquent testimony to the unwisdom of rapid "scholarly" publication at all costs. Readers of this annual are not likely to find it useful, except perhaps as an egregious example of pitfalls to be avoided.

Peter M. Sacks. *The English Elegy: Studies in the Genre from Spenser to Yeats.*
   Baltimore and London: The Johns Hopkins University Press, 1985. xv + 375.

"Man has created death," said Yeats (P 234). Peter M. Sacks's illuminating study would add the corollary that he has done so by creating the elegy. The central concern of the book is adumbrated in the title of its opening chapter, "Interpreting the Genre: The Elegy and the Work of Mourning." Here and in his discussions of poems by Spenser, Kyd, Shakespeare, Milton, Jonson, Dryden, Gray, Shelley, Swinburne, Tennyson, Hardy and Yeats, Professor Sacks contends that the conventions governing elegiac form spring from our common human need to comprehend and to cope with ultimate loss, and that—borrowing from Freud—the systematic pattern by which we do this is formed in infancy and carried through life. Successful elegies, then, merely accomplish verbally and with greater complexity the preverbal strategies that are among our earliest acquired responses.

The chapter on Yeats's Robert Gregory poems works two ways: the Gregory poems further refine and demonstrate Sacks's thesis, and the thesis—complemented by commendably thorough historical research—yields a learned, extended, and sensitive reading of "In Memory of Major Robert Gregory" (P 132). Sacks follows most Yeats critics in assuming that Yeats intends praise, but without actually embracing the minority view, he also accounts for Yeats's apparent holding back:

> It is not just that he, living, cannot resemble the distant dead. Rather, he can never simply resemble the man Gregory was when alive. For even while he admired the all-consuming flare of Gregory's life, Yeats saw its incompatibility with his own life and practice as a poet. The terms of this recognition are crucial to the elegy. . . . He himself would burn slowly in order to draft a poem whose end would simulate the sudden conflagration of Gregory's life and death. It is a brilliant and distinctly elegiac solution. [294–96]

Sacks seems to err on the side of generosity when suggesting that Yeats's comment, "To me he will always remain a great painter in the immaturity of his youth," deserves to be read with the emphasis on "great" rather than "immaturity." Those of Gregory's paintings that survive at University College, Galway, suggest that Yeats more probably intended his comment to be read with equal weight attaching to both phrases—if not with the natural rhetorical emphasis on the final phrase.

Sacks's handling of "Reprisals" (VP 791) finds it an ironic undoing of the consolation of the elegy, when some (myself included) see it as a more open revelation of Yeats's belief that for an "Irish airman" (or "perfect man") to have sacrificed his life and art and to have widowed his wife and orphaned his three children for nothing more than a "lonely impulse of delight" or, as Yeats quotes Gregory on the verso of the manuscript of "An Irish Airman Foresees His Death," out of comradeship with an England that had died long before, was to have thrown away both life and talent in an unfortunate—if not unworthy—exercise in egotistical self-deception. But this is a matter of some critical debate, and Sacks's discussion does note that in "Reprisals" the "elegiac contract between the living and the dead is cynically revised to a transaction between deceiver and deceived. Gregory has been disinterred only to be more devastatingly buried" (301).

"Under Ben Bulben" (P 325) and two of its responses, Ezra Pound's travesty (quoted in its pithy entirety) and W. H. Auden's "In Memory of W. B. Yeats," are accorded brief treatments in the epilogue on "The English Elegy after Yeats; a Note on the American Elegy."

On the whole, then, this is a book that Yeatsians should not miss, both for the excellence of its protracted discussion of the Gregory elegies and for the careful demonstration of its central theme.

Kieran Woodman. *Media Control in Ireland, 1923–1983.*
Carbondale and Edwardsville: Southern Illinois University Press, 1985. viii + 248 pp.

This excellent history and analysis of sixty years of religious and political censorship in Ireland and Northern Ireland was co-produced by its American publisher and the National University of Ireland, Galway. As Professor Woodman summarizes its content, it "examines the moral, political and intellectual climate in which occurred the changing conditions that [have] governed communications" since partition and the "statutory and societal measures" initiated "to control literary output and contemporary media performance" (vii). He gives the history of governmental intervention in the reporting of news and feature stories in the Republic and in Northern Ireland, especially "the problems of reporting terrorist activities . . . when government policy is at variance with the professional obligations of the journalist to provide for an informed electorate," and he weighs the history of contemporary literary censorship in the light of "the redefinition of individual responsibility for moral actions as a result of new directions in theology taken by the Catholic church" (vii).

Yeats figures *passim* in the discussion as an early and vigorous opponent of Irish censorship, as well as its occasional victim. His 1928 essay on "The Censorship and St. Thomas Aquinas" is quoted (105), as is the lamentably comic response of the *Catholic Bulletin* to his Nobel Prize. Noting that "Paganism in prose or in poetry has, it seems, its solid cash value," the *Bulletin* dismissed the award as "the Stockholm dole" (40).

R. A. York. *The Poem as Utterance.*
London and New York: Methuen, 1986. [viii] +214 pp.

This study of ten modern poets from the perspective of "the linguist's concern with pragmatic aspects of language" (11) opens with a pair of caveats that keep it grounded in reality: that "one should not too readily assume that any sensibility is prelinguistic: the spontaneous, unlearned, unformed experience evoked by such an idea belongs rather to a myth of innocence than to our actual consciousness, to which things always appear through words and have a sense bound up with that of the words that formulate them" and that "even if one were to accept the reality of a nonverbal intuitive knowledge at the root of literature, one could obviously not deny that words are the indispensable medium through which such knowledge is manifest" (1). Literature is worth discussing in pragmatic terms, he says, because "it creates a special harmony by making the conditions of utterance spectacularly appropriate to the utterance's total import, thus allowing language to justify itself" (11).

York allows equal time to Baudelaire, Mallarmé, Verlaine, Stefan George, Rilke, Eliot, Auden, Montale, Quasimodo, and Yeats, a fairly broad spectrum across which to trace his argument. The chapter on Yeats concentrates on "Leda and the Swan" [P 214], which York regards as central to Yeats's work and which he reads as being "about its own formulation, about the way the acts of the writer—narrating events, speculating, empathizing—by engendering a contemplative unity reproduce the sexual act of a god who engenders the unity of history" (113).

In addition to "Leda and the Swan," York considers bits and pieces of such other Yeats poems as demonstrate the various kinds of speech acts to which he wishes to draw our attention. In the process, he sheds new light on even familiar passages. Although most Yeatsians will not find anything startingly new in his readings, many will no doubt benefit from a fresh look at things from a new perspective and yet another demonstration of the master's mastery, as when, citing a catalog of typically Yeatsian rhetorical questions ("What matter, . . ." "Why should I blame her, . . . "Why should I be dismayed, . . ." and so on), York shows that Yeats denies significance to the secondary term in order to give primary importance to "the continuation of life, of passion and intense thought," a gesture "typical of Yeatsian affirmation" whereby the poet unites a knowledge of the world about him . . . with the pride that creates a life of dignity and vigour" (127).

13.00